The First Book of
GW-BASIC®

The First Book of
GW-BASIC®

Saul Aguiar

HOWARD W. SAMS & COMPANY
Macmillan Computer Publishing

© 1990 by Saul Aguiar

FIRST EDITION
FIRST PRINTING—1990

All rights reserved. No part of this book shall be reproduced, stored in a retrieval system, or transmitted by any means, electronic, mechanical, photocopying, recording, or otherwise, without written permission from the publisher. No patent liability is assumed with respect to the use of the information contained herein. Although every precaution has been taken in the preparation of this book, the publisher and author assume no responsibility for errors or omissions. Neither is any liability assumed for damages resulting from the use of the information contained herein. For information, address Howard W. Sams & Company, 11711 N. College Ave., Carmel, IN 46032.

International Standard Book Number: 0-672-27316-0
Library of Congress Catalog Card Number: 90-61475

Acquisitions Editor: *C. Herbert Feltner*
Development Editor: *Allen L. Wyatt*
Technical Editor: *Greg Guntle*
Production Editor: *Kathy Grider-Carlyle*
Production Coordinator: *Becky Imel*
Cover Art: *Held & Dietrich Design*
Illustrator: *Don Clemons*
Production Assistance: *Wm. D. Basham, Claudia Bell, Brad Chinn, Sally Copenhaver, T. R. Emrick, Tami Hughes, Bill Hurley, Chuck Hutchinson, Jodi Jensen, Jennifer Matthews, Joe Ramon, Dennis Sheehan, Bruce Steed, Mary Beth Wakefield, Nora Westlake*
Indexer: *Joelynn Gifford*

Printed in the United States of America

Contents

Introduction, *xi*

Who This Book Is For, *xi*
What You Will Need, *xii*
Book Conventions, *xiii*

1 Introduction to the PC Environment, *1*

What Is a PC?, *2*
Introduction to GW-BASIC, *5*
What Kinds of Programs Can I Write?, *6*
What Do I Need to Run GW-BASIC?, *7*
Summary, *8*
Quiz, *8*

2 PCs and Interpreters — The Details, *9*

How an Interpreter Works, *9*
Inside a PC, *12*
Summary, *22*
Quiz, *22*

3 Structure of a GW-BASIC Program, 23

Program Flow, *23*
Introduction of Fundamental Statements, *25*
Sample Program, *35*
Summary, *36*
Quiz, *37*

4 Editing GW-BASIC Programs, 39

The DOS Environment, *39*
Editor Basics, *43*
Exiting GW-BASIC, *44*
Getting a Program into the Interpreter, *44*
Saving a BASIC Program, *46*
Listing a Program, *48*
Editing a Specific Line, *49*
Erasing the Current Program, *50*
Other Features, *50*
Summary, *51*
Quiz, *51*

5 How to Run Your Program, 53

How to Start Execution in GW-BASIC, *53*
How to Stop GW-BASIC, *54*
Simple Debugging Using PRINT Statements, *56*
Debugging Using TRON/TROFF, *57*
Using the ON ERROR Statement, *59*
Summary, *60*
Quiz, *60*

6 *Variable Types,* 61

What Are Variables?, *61*
Naming Variables, *62*
Integers, *64*
Reals, *67*
Arrays, *70*
Strings, *74*
Declaring the Various Variable Types, *76*
Conversion Between Dissimilar Types, *78*
Sample Program, *80*
Summary, *82*
Quiz, *82*

7 *Controlling Program Flow,* 83

IF Statements, *83*
GOTO Statements, *86*
GOSUB and RETURN Statements, *87*
ON Statements, *90*
FOR and NEXT Statements, *91*
WHILE and WEND Statements, *95*
Sample Program, *96*
Reader Challenge, *99*
Summary, *100*
Quiz, *100*

8 *Communicating with the User,* 103

Various Ways to Read Data from the Keyboard, *104*
Character Output to the Screen, *115*
Retrieval of Screen Information, *120*
Formatting Output Data to Make It Readable, *122*
Interaction between Input and Output Commands, *127*

Character Output to the Printer, *130*
Summary, *131*
Quiz, *132*

9 *Disk Files,* *133*

Disk Operation: The Man behind the Curtain, *133*
Disk Operation: A GW-BASIC User's Perspective, *134*
How to Open and Close Disk Files, *135*
Simple File Output, *137*
The FIELD Statement, *140*
The GET and PUT Statements, *142*
The CVx and MKx$ Functions, *156*
Miscellaneous, *157*
Summary, *159*
Quiz, *159*

10 *Introduction to GW-BASIC Graphics,* *161*

Video Hardware, *161*
The CGA Display, *162*
The EGA and VGA Displays, *165*
The Line Command, *166*
The Circle Command, *168*
Summary, *169*
Quiz, *169*

11 *Sound from the Box,* *171*

The Tone Generator, *171*
The SOUND Statement, *172*
The PLAY Statement, *175*
The PLAY Function, *177*

Summary, *178*
Quiz, *178*

12 *Built-In Functions and Procedures,* 179

Trigonometric Functions, *179*
Mathematical Functions, *181*
Special String Functions, *184*
Miscellaneous, *186*
Summary, *193*
Quiz, *194*

13 *Programming with Style,* 195

Software Development Methods, *196*
Rapid Prototyping, *201*
Avoiding "Spaghetti Code", *203*
Comments, Comments, Comments!, *204*
The Human Interface, *204*
Summary, *205*
Quiz, *205*

14 *Where Do You Go from Here?,* 207

Directory Commands, *207*
Graphics Commands, *209*
Commands for Assembly Language Routines, *215*
Communications Commands, *219*
Miscellaneous Commands, *224*
Summary, *226*
Quiz, *227*

A *GW-BASIC Quick Reference Guide,* 229

B PC Character Set, *239*

Extended Codes, *241*

C GW-BASIC Error Code Quick Reference, *245*

Answers to Quizzes, *249*

Index, *255*

Introduction

Who This Book Is For

This book was written for people just becoming familiar with personal computers and how to program them. The first few chapters introduce you to the fundamentals of computers that are compatible with a standard initially devised by IBM in the early 1980s. These machines are by far the most prevalent computers used in homes and businesses in the United States today. This book explains what the GW-BASIC interpreter can do and the simple commands needed to create and run programs. After you have learned how to execute your own programs, you will be taught certain techniques that can help you find subtle errors. Later chapters teach you the details of sending information to the screen or printer and how to obtain information from the user via the keyboard. In the latter part of the book, you will learn how to read and write files to the disk, how to draw pictures on your screen (if your display hardware will allow it), and how to play tunes using the built-in tone generator. The last two chapters briefly touch on GW-BASIC's advanced features and discuss various programming philosophies that you may find useful.

This book gradually introduces material. It assumes the reader knows very little about personal computers (except how to turn them on and off and how to properly insert floppy disks in the drive). If you are familiar with PCs but don't know GW-BASIC, you may want to skim through the first few chapters until you find topics that are new to you.

What You Will Need

To successfully learn the material in this book, you will need:

- ▶ A personal computer running MS-DOS or IBM-DOS (the software that controls your computer)
- ▶ A copy of the GW-BASIC program

If you do not know whether your personal computer uses MS-DOS or IBM-DOS, check with the person who sold you the system.

There are other optional pieces of equipment that are desirable but are not absolutely necessary:

- ▶ A hard disk
- ▶ A printer
- ▶ A video display system capable of displaying graphics

A hard disk is a device that stores your programs and data inside your PC. If you don't have a printer connected to your PC, you will not be able to experiment with GW-BASIC commands that send output to one. If your video display system does not conform to CGA, EGA, or VGA standards, you may not be able to do the exercises in the chapter on graphics (check your owner's manual or ask the person that sold you your system to find out what type of display hardware you have). Do not be concerned if you do not have some of this optional equipment. You can still learn most of the features of GW-BASIC without them.

If you are not familiar with the fundamental operations of MS-DOS, you should read the introductory section of your MS-DOS manual because you will need to know enough to get to the area in your disk where GW-BASIC is stored. If you do not have an MS-DOS manual or find it difficult to read, you may want to pick up an introductory MS-DOS book from your local library or bookstore.

Book Conventions

Each chapter in the book covers a specific topic or theme. The chapters are subdivided into sections that discuss a specific detail or command. A summary at the end of each chapter reviews the information covered in that chapter. A small quiz at the end of the chapter helps test your understanding of the material. The answers to all of the questions are available at the back of the book.

At certain points in the book you will see "funny" symbols. The ⏎ represents a keypress of the Enter or carriage-return key (the large key to the right of the L on most keyboards). The <Ctrl> represents the Control key (which is usually located near the left shift key).

Another unusual convention is the use of square brackets to surround certain items. Items inside these square brackets are usually intended to be optional (which means that GW-BASIC will understand the command even if you do not provide this optional information). The square brackets are never intended to be present in a GW-BASIC program line. For example, the statement:

```
CLOSE [#][filenumber]
```

can be used as:

```
CLOSE
CLOSE 1
CLOSE #1
```

where the first form closes all files, and the other two forms only close file number 1.

It is now time for you to move on to the first chapter which introduces PCs and GW-BASIC.

Acknowledgments

Of the many helpful and talented people who have contributed directly or indirectly to this book, several deserve special recognition and thanks:

Keith Weiskamp for his encouragement and support.
G. C. for her love, patience, and proofreading.
R. Stark, H. Doyle, G. M. Campbell, N. Galloway, and G. Braun for laying the foundation upon which others have built.

Trademarks

All terms mentioned in this book that are known to be trademarks or service marks are listed below. In addition, terms suspected of being trademarks or service marks have been appropriately capitalized. Howard W. Sams & Company cannot attest to the accuracy of this information. Use of a term in this book should not be regarded as affecting the validity of any trademark or service mark.

MS-DOS, GW-BASIC, and Microsoft Word are registered trademarks of Microsoft Corporation.

IBM-PC, IBM-PC XT, IMB-PC AT, and IBM-DOS are registered trademarks of International Business Machines Corporation.

Intel 8086, 80186, 80286, and 80386 are registered trademarks of Intel Corporation.

The V-20 is a registered trademark of the NEC Corporation.

Wordstar is a registered trademark of MicroPro Corporation.

Chapter 1
Introduction to the PC Environment

In This Chapter

Welcome to the world of GW-BASIC! You are probably reading this book because you are curious about GW-BASIC and how it can help you perform a particular task. Perhaps you want to write a simple game or experiment with computer graphics. Maybe you are a business person who needs specialized job-related programs. GW-BASIC can handle this wide range of tasks while providing an environment in which working is easy. This chapter introduces GW-BASIC and explains some of the initial concepts required to use it. Some of this material may already be familiar to you if you have written programs in a computer language previously. If you are already familiar with personal computers (PCs) and computer languages, please skim over the material in this chapter before moving on. If you are not experienced with computers, relax. This chapter is designed to explain in a nontechnical and intuitive way how PCs work. Chapter 2 will explain more about GW-BASIC and explain in greater detail how the different parts of a computer work.

Chapter 1

What Is a PC?

This may seem to be a trivial question, but recent technological changes have made the distinction between different types of computers less pronounced. For the purposes of this book, a PC is defined as a computer that is compatible with the original International Business Machines Corporation (IBM) Personal Computer or IBM AT Personal Computer. These machines are manufactured by hundreds (perhaps thousands) of different companies, but they all have certain things in common:

- A *microprocessor* "brain" that is compatible with the instruction set of the Intel 8086 family. Such microprocessors can be (for example) 8088, 8086, 80286, 80386, 80486, and V-20.
- A *keyboard* that has the usual typewriter keys and special keys called *function keys* that allow the user to control computer actions more easily.
- A *monochrome* or *color display*. These displays are usually either cathode ray tubes (CRTs), which look like television sets, or flat panel displays, which are usually seen on laptop or portable computers.
- At least one *floppy disk drive* to hold the GW-BASIC program and the program files you will create. Many machines are also equipped with a *hard disk drive* that is permanently attached to the computer. Hard disks hold much more information than floppy disks, and hard drives can usually store and retrieve data faster than floppy drives.
- The computer uses a version of *PC DOS* or *MS-DOS*. DOS stands for disk operating system, which implies that the software that controls the machine usually is stored on a disk rather than in main memory. MS stands for Microsoft, the name of the company that also created GW-BASIC. PC DOS and MS-DOS are usually compatible if they are of approximately the same version.

Although there are apparently many different varieties of machines that can be called PCs, most of them are pretty much the same. The important items are DOS (some noncompatible manufacturers use their own operating software) and the microprocessor type (some competing manufacturers use different microprocessors that can't understand the instructions of the 8086 family of products).

The most obvious area of diversity is in display technology. The reason for this is very simple: the higher the capability of the display, the more it usually costs and weighs. Weight may seem to be a strange consideration for a computer, but it can be very important if you have a portable computer that you plan to carry on business trips. The simplest and least expensive displays are usually the *monochrome* (single-color) CRTs and *flat panel* displays. Frequently, these displays can deal only with *character* information (letters, numbers, punctuation marks, etc.) and are incapable of displaying pictures. A more sophisticated type of display is one that is CGA compatible. CGA stands for color graphics adapter and refers to a display architecture developed by IBM for the original PC. The CGA standard can display 25 lines of text (80 characters per line) in up to 16 separate colors or a maximum of 400 lines of 640 dots each in monochrome mode. This resolution is sufficient for simple drawings and low-quality pictures, but it is not as good as a standard television broadcast image. CGA equipment is very common (and affordable) and probably represents a large percentage of existing PC monitors. EGA (enhanced graphics adapter) and VGA (video graphics array) displays use a slightly different technology than the CGA equipment and can produce much more detailed graphics (some VGA pictures rival photographs in clarity). Unfortunately, increased capability comes with a price. A high-quality VGA display and graphics card set can cost as much as the PC itself! Fortunately, prices have continued to decline on these products, bringing them within reach of the ordinary person. As far as the GW-BASIC user is concerned, all of these technologies act more or less the same in *text mode* (when displaying only letters, numbers, etc.). In this book, the differences between the various displays will be indicated only when the reader is attempting to set colors (which is pointless on monochrome displays) or draw pictures on the screen.

Two other important PC-attributes are memory and disk storage. Memory generally comes in two types: read-only memory (ROM) and random-access memory (RAM). Memory (both RAM and ROM) is usually measured in kilobytes (K) or megabytes (M). A kilobyte has 1,024 memory locations; a megabyte has 1,048,576 memory locations. ROM chips are usually installed in the machine by the manufacturer and are rarely changed or updated. They usually contain information that tells the microprocessor where and how to communicate with devices such as the keyboard, the video display, and the disk drives. Because the original designers of the PC intended most of

Chapter 1

the "smart" software to reside on disks, the programs in ROM are usually very limited. Due to the technology involved, ROM chips can only be read from and not written to. If you attempt to write to a ROM, nothing will happen and the attempt is ignored. RAM, on the other hand, is designed for both read and write operations. If you write to a RAM location, the previous contents are lost and replaced by whatever value you have written. This is important because GW-BASIC provides the user with powerful tools that allow inspection and modification of locations anywhere within the computer's memory. (These instructions won't be covered until Chapter 14, and most users probably will never need to use them. They are included in this book for completeness and to support the more ambitious readers.)

Magnetic disk storage comes in two general categories: floppy and hard. Floppy disks are exactly what they sound like: circular pieces of flexible plastic coated with a magnetic material similar to that used in audio cassette tapes. In order to protect the magnetic material from dirt and fingerprints, these disks are usually covered in a protective sleeve or case. Floppy disks are available in 3 standard sizes: 8-inch, 5.25-inch, and 3.5-inch diameters. A large portion of PCs today use some form of 5.25-inch floppy disks. Many portables and the newer desktop PCs sometimes use 3.5-inch floppy disks. The 8-inch and 5.25-inch floppy disks have a flexible external sleeve. The 3.5-inch floppy disks are enclosed in a thin, rigid-plastic case that might remind you of an audio cassette. These floppies must be properly inserted into the appropriate slot in your floppy disk drive. (Consult the owner's manual that came with your machine to determine what type of drives were installed and the proper way to insert the floppies into these drives.) Floppy disk drives are similar to video cassette recorders (VCRs). They are capable of recording and playing back information, and the heads need to be cleaned occasionally. Some users are fortunate enough to have machines with two different drives installed and can use both 5.25- and 3.5-inch floppy disks on the same machine. Floppy disk size is important only when you purchase new software or new disks; you need to know which size disk media you want to purchase.

Hard disk drives are usually installed inside the computer so that they are not easily visible. They are completely sealed to keep out dust and moisture. Storage capacity for these drives is usually specified in megabytes. A hard disk typically holds at least ten times as much information as a floppy disk (some hard disks hold as much as 80 times what a floppy can hold). Because they hold so much data and eliminate the need to disk swap, they are very convenient to use. The main drawback to hard disks is that they are much more susceptible to damage from vibration or impact than floppy disks. This is a greater problem on portable PCs because they tend to get moved around more and may be exposed to adverse conditions such as cold, rain, and rough handling.

Chapter 2 discusses the attributes of these devices in much greater detail. Now let's return to the central topic of this book by answering the question: What is GW-BASIC anyway?

Introduction to GW-BASIC

GW-BASIC is a BASIC-language interpreter produced by Microsoft Corporation, the same people who created MS-DOS, the operating system that runs the majority of IBM-PC compatible personal computers today. In the early days of computers, BASIC and FORTRAN were two of the most prevalent general-purpose languages in existence (other languages such as COBOL and RPG tended to have narrower applications in areas such as accounting and business administration). BASIC has two major advantages over its rivals: BASIC is easy to learn and writing an interpreter for it is relatively easy. These factors made BASIC the language of choice for early microcomputer systems. In fact, most early machines based on the 6502 and Z-80 microprocessors came with BASIC built in as part of ROM. Even the original IBM PC came with a limited version of BASIC in ROM.

Of course, the original machines had little RAM and usually interfaced to either a "dumb" terminal or to a keyboard/television set combination. Storage often consisted of audio cassette tapes. In this environment, BASIC didn't need to be very sophisticated in order to flourish. As PCs became more sophisticated, the BASIC language had to expand or face extinction. The GW-BASIC versions released with MS-DOS versions 3.3 and 4.01 are as capable as the current versions of virtually every other language available for PCs.

Today's GW-BASIC can maneuver through DOS disk directories, read and write disk files, and generate elaborate color-graphics screens. It even has limited windowing capabilities which allow sophisticated interfaces so that independent actions appear on different parts of the display screen.

Of course, GW-BASIC still provides mathematical support and includes many built-in functions such as sine, tangent, square-root, and natural logarithm. It also provides powerful tracing capabilities that let the programmer step through a program to find why it is acting differently than expected.

What Kinds of Programs Can I Write?

As mentioned earlier, GW-BASIC is capable of running virtually any type of software application. The only real limitations have to do with the amount of memory available and the execution speed. Because GW-BASIC is an *interpreter*, it must reanalyze a line of code each time that line is executed. This makes execution slower than for a *compiled* language where everything is decoded once and cannot change without benefit of a recompile. Most users discover that interpreter speed becomes negligible if GW-BASIC is run on an AT-class machine. The other traditional problem with interpreters has to do with memory consumption. The original BASIC interpreters kept an exact copy of each line in memory for retrieval when the interpreter needed it. Newer versions of GW-BASIC perform a substantial amount of analysis when the line is entered. For example, if you enter the following line using the GW-BASIC built-in editor:

100 ×! = 0.00

and then display it again, you will see the following on your screen:

100 ×! = 0!

GW-BASIC analyzed the constant and eliminated the extra characters that weren't needed. Unfortunately, you do not yet know how to start GW-BASIC or use the built-in editor, so you will have to wait until later to verify that this really happens. GW-BASIC also uses other internal tricks to reduce the amount of memory required to store individual program lines. In any case, the availability of large amounts of memory in today's machines has eliminated most memory problems associated with earlier implementations of GW-BASIC.

What Do I Need to Run GW-BASIC?

GW-BASIC requires very few resources (memory, disk storage, etc.) from a PC. Although GW-BASIC can be used with a dual floppy disk drive system, it is usually best to run it from a hard disk if possible. For example, GW-BASIC version 3.23 (provided with MS-DOS 4.01) only requires 80K of disk storage for the program. Most modern PCs come equipped with 256K or more of RAM; therefore, memory limitations are usually not a problem today.

Displays are also usually not a problem because GW-BASIC uses the normal DOS standards for controlling the screen when operating in the built-in editor or when generating simple text output. If you have EGA/VGA display hardware and want to generate EGA-quality graphics, you must execute certain commands within the user program and specify the desired attributes of the screen. At all other times, GW-BASIC is intuitive and completely transparent. Those ambitious enough to want to generate high-resolution graphics will have to wait until Chapter 10 for a detailed discussion of the subject.

A printer (preferably a fast one such as a dot-matrix unit) is one optional piece of equipment that will become rather important for large programs. As programs get larger, displaying sections of a program over and over again becomes tedious. Paper listings (*hard copy*) can be quite valuable when debugging (isolating and correcting mistakes). Because GW-BASIC accepts as input and generates as output simple ASCII character files (such as those generated by the editor that came with MS-DOS) any printer capable of responding to a DOS TYPE command will work fine. ASCII character files are the standard method for representing letters, numbers, and other symbols in PCs. If you have a dot-matrix printer that can change print appearance from *letter-quality* to *draft* modes, select the fastest mode. Program listings must be readable, not pretty; you will probably write notes all over your listings, anyway!

If you work with a word processor, you will be happy to know that GW-BASIC can probably work with your files. Vir-

Chapter 1

tually every word processing program will accept GW-BASIC files because they are simple and don't contain any "strange" characters. Any problems usually occur when you try to have GW-BASIC read the output from the word processing program. Most word processors have an option that generates ASCII files. Microsoft WORD does this via the *Text-only* or *Formatted-No* options (depending on your version). Files for Wordstar must be edited in *non-document* mode. Check your word processor's manual for the commands required with your package.

Summary

This chapter briefly introduced GW-BASIC, which runs on personal computers that are compatible with the specifications of the IBM Personal Computer or the IBM AT Personal Computer. It requires either MS-DOS from Microsoft Corporation or PC DOS from IBM in order to operate properly. You were also exposed to computer terms, such as RAM and ROM, and received a brief explanation of the relative advantages and disadvantages of floppy disk and hard disk storage.

Now that you've had a quick look at the history and development of GW-BASIC, it is time to move on to a more in-depth explanation of how the GW-BASIC interpreter works and how it communicates with the different parts of a PC. These topics are covered in Chapter 2.

Quiz

1. What type of microprocessor is used in the machines identified in this book as PCs?
2. What are the two types of magnetic storage media typically found on PCs?
3. What is the name of the company that produces GW-BASIC?
4. What types of program files does GW-BASIC use?
5. Can GW-BASIC program files be edited by word processing programs?

Chapter 2
PCs and Interpreters —the Details

In This Chapter

The first chapter briefly introduced the GW-BASIC interpreter and its uses. This chapter begins with an explanation of how an interpreter works and then explains in greater detail what the different parts of a PC do. Even if you are familiar with personal computers, you may still want to review this material because a solid understanding of the operating principles will be necessary for some of the advanced topics which are covered in later chapters.

How an Interpreter Works

A language interpreter acts similarly to a human one. It takes information from one source and converts it to a form usable by another. Figure 2.1 illustrates the fundamental operations performed by GW-BASIC. As you can see from the figure, the entire program source (the words and numbers that represent the program) must reside in the computer's memory at one time. This is accomplished by *loading* the program (transferring it to main memory) from a storage device (usually a floppy or hard disk). When you tell the GW-BASIC interpreter to run the program, it

Chapter 2

finds the next line to be executed in order to analyze it. The order of lines is established by a *line number* which is a whole number in the range 1 to 65529. This number is always located at the very beginning (left side) of the line and is always followed by a space to separate the line number from the rest of the statement. GW-BASIC does not require that line numbers be consecutive, so there can be gaps in the numbering sequence (this can come in handy if you are planning to expand part of a program later). For example, the first line number can be 100, the second line number can be 327, and the one after that can be 12678. GW-BASIC will still execute the lowest line number first and then proceed to the next larger line number in memory. The interpreter analyzes each statement by separating the characters on the line into *keywords*, *variables*, *constants*, and *symbols*.

Keywords are specific groups of letters and other symbols (such as IF, NEW, PRINT, and SOUND) that are reserved for specific operations. GW-BASIC generally looks for these keywords first because they indicate very specific instructions to the interpreter.

Variables are the names of the memory locations that your program uses to temporarily store information. Think of them as storage bins with individual names like TOTALSALES or CUPSOFMILK (of course, you get to choose the names of these variables).

Constants are just that: things that don't change. They are usually groups of digits that represent some fixed quantity. *String constants* are groups of letters and/or numbers enclosed by a set of double-quotes. (Don't worry about strings for now, we will discuss them in detail in Chapter 3.) If you write a program to calculate the areas of circles, you may want to assign a variable to hold the value of pi:

2100 PI = 3.1415926535

which will come in handy because it is easier to type a two-letter variable name, such as PI, than it is to type all the digits that form the actual constant (3.1415926535).

Symbols are usually used to control the interaction of variables and constants. This category includes things like parentheses, equal signs, semicolons, etc. For example:

3010 TOTALSTATES = 48 + 2

instructs GW-BASIC to take the constant 48, add the constant 2 to it, and save the result in the variable TOTALSTATES. The plus sign and the equal sign are both symbols that tell GW-BASIC to take some known action.

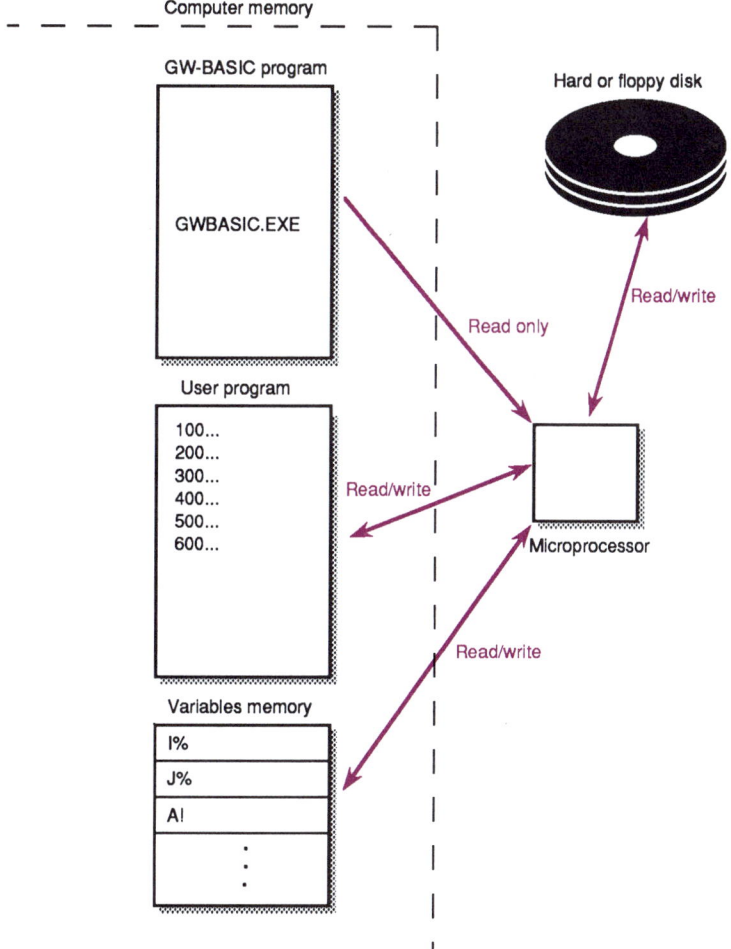

Figure 2.1 *The fundamental operations of GW-BASIC*

If the interpreter finds a group of letters and/or other symbols that doesn't fall into a recognizable category, it immediately gives the user an error message and indicates on which line the error occurred. The big advantage of an interpreter over a compiler is that with an interpreter the user can call up the line with the error, correct it, and immediately re-execute the program to

Chapter 2

see if the change eliminated the problem. Language compilers often compel you to go into the editor, make the change, save the file, exit the editor, and re-compile the program. As you can see, the interpreter is much simpler to use when attempting to correct problems.

In order to successfully use all of the features of GW-BASIC, you must understand how BASIC interacts with your machine. Therefore, we will now discuss the fundamental building blocks of PCs and how programs can use them to best advantage.

Inside a PC

All PCs that run GW-BASIC have certain common characteristics. They all use microprocessors compatible with the Intel 8086 family. Their memory is organized so that ROM is located at the top and RAM is located at the very bottom of memory. Also, they communicate with *peripherals* (such as keyboard, video displays, etc.) that adhere to certain communication protocols.

These requirements make the software extremely portable. The software that you run on one system should work identically in a system of similar capability made by a different manufacturer. This may seem an obvious way to do things, but for many years computer manufacturers jealously guarded the internal details of their machines. This resulted in a variety of large computers (costing millions of dollars) that were both hardware and software incompatible with each other. Because of these incompatibility quirks, even programs written for "standard" languages usually required modification when moved from one manufacturer's machine to another's. For the most part, PC popularity has forced manufacturers to go in the other direction and be more open. If a manufacturer produces a machine that isn't extremely compatible with existing equipment, people won't buy it and the manufacturer can go out of business. One way a manufacturer can provide special features (and obtain a marketing advantage in a highly competitive marketplace) is to add *enhancements* that do not conflict with the "standard" design. Consumers are always interested in new features, as long as all of their old software still runs on the new machine. Fortunately for everyone, there is a second way of providing enhancements.

When the PC was first invented, its designers wanted to provide a way to add new hardware features to the system in the future without completely replacing the "brains" of the machine. Their solution was to design equipment connections called *expansion slots*. These slots permit the addition of special purpose electronics to the basic machine. For example, some companies sell music boards that let the user capture music on a PC by converting sounds to numbers. The user can manipulate the numbers, via a program, and play back the modified sounds on the special hardware. Another specialized electronics board that can be connected to a PC is a *modem*. A modem connects the PC, via a normal telephone line, to other computers that can be located in other cities or even other countries. You can even send electronic mail to other computer users with your modem through an *electronic bulletin board* service. Entire industries have developed around services provided to PC owners with modems.

Another advantage to PC consistency and compatibility is that it allows for the mass marketing of products such as GW-BASIC. Standardization allows companies, like Microsoft, to sell tens or hundreds of thousands of copies of the same program. The large potential sales volume inspires competition, which helps keep down prices. Also, expensive software development costs can be spread out over the large number of copies to be sold. (A professional quality program that costs a few hundred dollars for a PC can cost tens of thousands of dollars when purchased for a large computer because there is little competition and very low sales volume.)

Memory Organization

Figure 2.2 illustrates, in general terms, the memory map of a PC designed to run MS-DOS. As you can see, there are reserved areas used by the *microprocessor* (the brains of your PC) located at the bottom of memory. These areas usually contain information that tell the microprocessor where to find the specialized programs that interpret information from the various peripherals. The next area contains the *resident* portion of the operating system. This software is read from either a floppy or hard disk when the computer is first turned on. Special programs (such as device drivers which are used to talk to special equipment and terminate-and-stay-resident [TSR] programs, which often provide features like pop-up calculators, notepads, and recall of previous DOS commands issued to the system) can re-

Chapter 2

side in the next area. Programs like GW-BASIC will be loaded in the area above this.

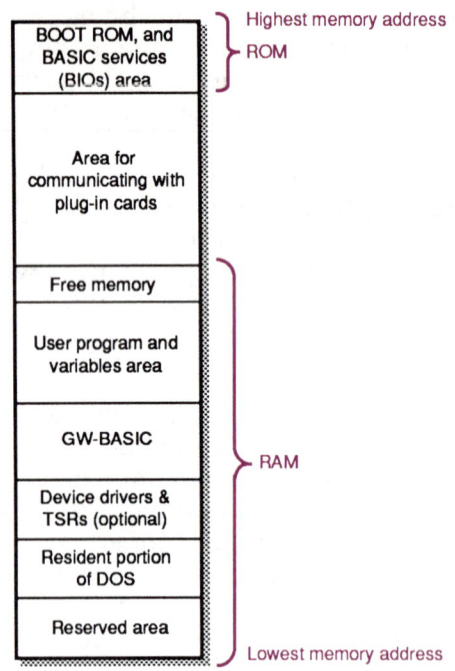

Figure 2.2 *General memory map for PCs*

GW-BASIC requires additional memory areas to store the user's program that is to be executed. The remaining RAM above where the applications program resides is called *free memory*. GW-BASIC may use some or all of this memory for special purposes.

The area above RAM is reserved for access to plug-in cards, such as those that drive the video monitor or control the disk drives. Finally, the top area of memory holds read-only memory (ROM) that tells the microprocessor how to get started when power is first applied.

In later chapters, we will provide more specific information about some of these special areas and show you how to access them for your own purposes.

Keyboard Input

Most PC keyboards have a large group of switches (one under each key) which is connected to a special controller. This controller circuit determines which keys are being pressed and sends this information to the PC, where an interrupt is generated. This interrupt forces the microprocessor to stop what it is doing and respond to the message from the keyboard. The message from the keyboard is then processed by a special program, and the information is placed in a reserved-memory area called a *buffer*. The codes for the individual key presses can then be read by other programs, such as GW-BASIC. Appendix B shows the codes associated with the different keys.

As shown at the end of the table in Appendix B, special keys, such as function keys, require two numbers. The first number is always zero and the second number identifies the key. This numbering scheme was established because the original definition of character codes known as ASCII (American Standard Code for Information Interchange) was made long before the invention of the PC. The engineers who originally designed the PC needed to represent the newly designed key functions without violating the definitions in the ASCII standard. This numbering trick allows them to do just that.

Display Output

PC video displays come in two general varieties: those compatible with monochrome display adapters and those compatible with color/graphics adapters (CGA). With the exception of machines that have built-in displays (such as portable PCs), the electronics associated with a display are located in two separate places. An electronic circuit card (called a display adapter) inside the PC receives codes from the microprocessor and stores them in a special memory area (see Figure 2.3). Another circuit on this card then reads this memory many times per second and uses the information to build electrical signals which are then sent out of the PC to the video display terminal (VDT). Additional electronics in the VDT convert the signals to voltages that can be used to display the desired characters or graphics on the screen. VDTs only understand dot intensity (from black to very bright) and color (if the VDT is capable of displaying colors at all).

Chapter 2

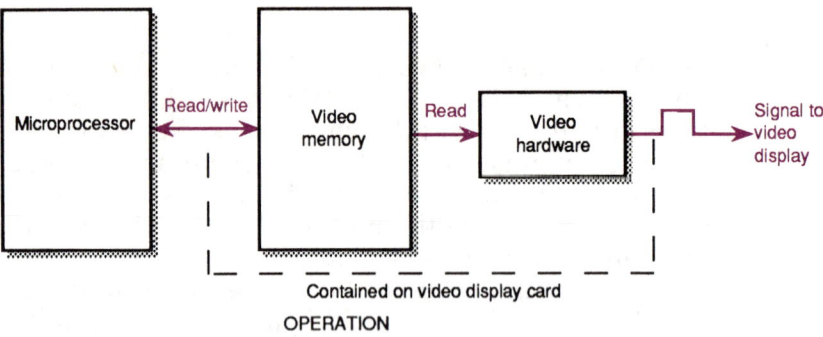

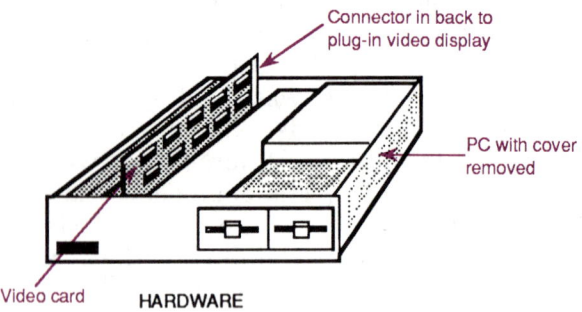

Figure 2.3 Display adapter card

In the case of monochrome display adapters, the microprocessor sends the standard ASCII codes mentioned in the previous section. The adapter can also produce certain "funny" characters which can be used to make displays more appealing. These cards were originally developed to provide an excellent quality text display for users who spend their entire day looking at the PC screen. However, monochrome display adapter cards are not very prevalent today. Thanks to continued improvements in display technology, many color display adapters can now provide quality similar to the monochrome adapters and also let the user display true pictures (graphics).

Color display adapters are almost universal today, and they are available with varying capabilities from many different manufacturers. The three most prevalent types of graphics displays are CGA, EGA, and VGA (with several more standards either just entering the market or under development).

The Color Graphics Adapter (CGA)

As mentioned in the previous chapter, CGA is the color graphics adapter standard that first appeared in the early 1980s. CGA is usually capable of displaying 25 rows by 80 columns of text in up to fifteen different colors. The CGA display is also capable of displaying limited graphics using a 320 by 200 dot grid in four different colors. This is adequate for simple drawings and charts but isn't very good for more sophisticated applications. The CGA adapter card can also display monochrome graphics in a 640 by 400 dot grid. This is sufficiently detailed to create modest quality pictures (for example, the Microsoft Flight Simulator program creates a reasonable picture in monochrome CGA mode). The biggest problem with the CGA graphics modes is that there is no way to control the *intensity* of the dots. For a given color, the dot can either be turned on or off. This makes the contrast in CGA graphics too high to be pleasing to the eye. Also, the combinations of 4 colors that can be used at one time in graphics mode are defined by the hardware, with no substitutions! The main advantage of CGA is cost: it is quite affordable in comparison to the higher-capability standards. Additionally, it has been out for so many years that there is a huge installed base of CGA displays, so most programs available for PCs support this standard. The only programs that do not work with CGA are those that require high-resolution graphics (such as computerized drafting packages).

The EGA and VGA Graphics Adapters

The EGA and VGA standards are newer than CGA and they have several advantages over it. First, they are capable of displaying much finer grids of dots in color (standard VGA mode can go as high as 640 by 400 dots in color and some special VGA cards are capable of extending this to 800 by 600 dots in color). Additionally, these standards allow the *definition* of 16 or more colors to be seen on the screen at the same time. This is important because the CGA color combinations in graphics mode were defined by the hardware and tended to be restrictive. In EGA and VGA cards, the individual colors are defined by the user software (there are also default combinations available). These newer standards also allow the user to control the *intensity* of the individual dots. This permits television-quality pictures to be displayed on the computer screen.

Although EGA and VGA displays are quickly becoming the technology of choice in the PC world, market penetration has been delayed for some time by the relatively high cost of these products. In addition, new graphics standards are now entering the market that may displace VGA from the top spot. Because all three adapter technologies still allow for the basic 25 by 80 text mode, we will usually use this mode in our examples of screen text.

Disk Storage (Floppy and Hard Disks)

Disk storage is important to the user for several reasons. First, these devices hold the DOS and other programs (such as GW-BASIC) which our PCs need in order to be useful. These devices also enable us to quickly and reliably store and retrieve important data files. In the early days of microprocessors, many people stored their files on audio cassette tapes. This method was excruciatingly slow and prone to errors. The original IBM PC (introduced in 1981, well after the days of vacuum tubes) had a jack in the back for communicating and controlling a cassette deck! The extraordinary market that developed for PCs possibly helped accelerate the development of both floppy and hard disk technologies.

Today we have it relatively easy. Both types of disk storage (floppy disk and hard disk) are affordable and extremely reliable. Both systems consist of a circular magnetic medium that is spun by a small motor at a constant speed. Small magnetic read/write heads similar to those in audio recording equipment are mounted on high-precision motion control systems. These motion systems allow precise and repeatable positioning of the read/write heads so information can be reliably stored and retrieved.

In the case of floppy disks, the magnetic medium is made of flexible plastic and is coated on both sides with a magnetic material, such as iron oxide. When the drive is selected, the red LED light comes on, and the read/write heads are brought into direct contact with the magnetic material. When the read or write operation is completed, the heads are separated from the floppy to prevent premature wear of the disk (remember, the heads are touching the magnetic material and will eventually rub it off).

Hard disks, on the other hand, are made by coating a disk of rigid material (such as metal) with a magnetic material. Due to the tight tolerances used in the manufacture of hard disks, the heads are designed to "fly" over the magnetic material without actually touching it. This is why hard disks generally last longer than floppy disks; there's no rubbing to wear down the magnetic material or damage the heads. This is also why PCs with hard disks should never be moved when powered-up. A sudden bump could force the head to rub against the disk, causing irreparable damage.

Both types of disks are organized into *tracks* and *cylinders* (see Figure 2.4). The tracks nearest the rim usually are reserved for the operating system and contain a special structure called a *directory*. Disk directories are similar to directories in tall buildings or shopping centers. They let you quickly find the location of something without having to search sequentially from one end of a structure to the other. Disk directories can be connected together as subdirectories of another directory. This allows for easy separation of software by type or by application. If you are not familiar with how to use subdirectories, you may want to read the explanation in a book on DOS (your computer may have come with one or more books explaining DOS and how to use it).

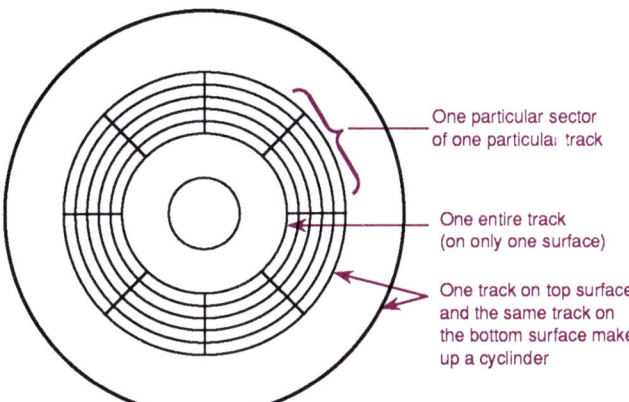

Figure 2.4 *Disk tracks and cylinders*

I/O Ports (Serial and Parallel)

PCs have one other standard way to transfer information to and from the machine: the input/output (I/O) *ports*. In your home,

Chapter 2

you probably have at least one telephone line and possibly even a cable TV line. Conceptually, these lines are I/O ports to your home. They let you access information available from sources outside of the physical structure you call home. Think of PC I/O ports as communications lines connecting your PC to other equipment. These PC ports also use wires and electrical signals to move information into or out of the box. If you think about it, there are several major differences between your telephone and your cable TV service. The telephone allows you to send information (talk) or receive information (listen) and the information comes in at a slow rate (human speech). Cable TV systems allow you to receive large amounts of information (many different TV channels) but few systems allow you to send information out of your home to another place. These parallels also apply to PC I/O ports. *Serial* ports let you send and receive data at the same time, but usually at modest rates. *Parallel* ports can send information at faster rates, but are generally used only to send data in one direction (such as to printers).

Today, most PCs come equipped with at least one parallel and one serial port. Many machines can handle up to four ports (if you are willing to purchase the additional hardware and you have an available expansion card slot in which to plug it). A serial port consists of an input line, an output line, grounding lines, and various control lines (each line is a metal wire that carries signals in the form of voltages or currents). Information is sent over the input or output line one bit at a time, conforming to a hardware specification known as RS-232 (a *bit* is a 1 or 0 which is easily represented by the presence or absence of a voltage or current). Each serial port can be operated at one of several standard rates: 300, 1200, or 9600 bits per second (BPS). Because there are eight bits in a *byte*, a 1200 BPS line can transfer at most 150 bytes per second (1200 divided by 8). This rate is somewhat analogous to a posted speed limit on an expressway at rush hour. In heavy traffic, you usually can't travel very fast. The actual data transfer rate, however, will usually be within 20% of the theoretical value, so these numbers still give a reasonable indication of how long it will take to transfer a file from one machine to another. For example, if you have a 30,000-byte file and you plan to send it from one PC to another at 1200 BPS, the elapsed time will be (approximately):

30,000 Bytes / 150 Bytes per second = 200 seconds

which isn't really very long. On the other hand, the same file sent at 300 BPS would take four times as long (800 seconds), which would probably be enough time to eat a sandwich. As you can see, using the fastest reliable transfer rate available prevents user boredom and frees equipment for more productive uses.

Because serial ports use separate lines for input and output, it is possible to send information to another machine while simultaneously receiving information. This is what happens when you use a *modem* to call another computer. The modem converts the bits from your computer to tones that can be sent to the other machine. The other computer simultaneously sends you data on a different set of tones, which your modem detects, converts to RS-232 signals, and sends to your input serial port. The DOS in your machine already provides programs to control the serial ports, but GW-BASIC can control these signals directly.

A parallel port usually consists of at least eight (usually 12) bi-directional data lines. This device is often also called a *line printer port* since it is usually used to send information to printers. When your PC transmits a character, it will place the data on eight specific lines (it sends one bit per line). It also sets a voltage on another wire to inform the device receiving the information that the data is ready. This is analogous to placing mail in a rural mailbox and then flipping up the red flag to inform the postman that you have some mail for him to pick up. After a short period of time, this signal wire (sometimes called a *data clocking line*) is returned to the inactive state. The cycle then repeats for the next byte to be sent. The computer can also read these lines to obtain information from the other device. This is how your computer knows when the printer runs out of paper or is taken off-line by the operator; the information is received from the printer through the parallel port.

If we assume that the electronics used for the serial port are also used for the parallel port, then a parallel port can theoretically carry eight times as much data as a single serial line. For example, if each data wire in a parallel port can move 1200 bits per second, then the entire parallel port can move a total of:

```
1200 BPS * 8 lines = 9600 BPS total
```

Thus, a parallel port is a relatively easy way to increase the effective BPS rate between computers.

You may wonder why someone wouldn't simply increase the BPS on a serial port rather than having to deal with all of those extra wires in a parallel port. Frequently, the maximum rate at which electrical signals can be reliably sent by a port is influenced by three factors: the distance between computers, the amount of electrical interference around the wires, and the electrical characteristics of the wire itself. In many cases, the first two problems are beyond the control of the computer user. The third constraint may be overshadowed by economic factors (it may actually be cheaper to install eight inexpensive lines than one super line). The disadvantage of the parallel port is that it can only be used in one direction at a time. It can either send or receive information, but it can't do both at exactly the same time. This is why it is typically used in applications where most of the traffic is in one direction (such as with a high-speed printer that needs a high data rate to keep busy and rarely needs to send information back to the PC).

Summary

This chapter briefly reviewed the various parts of a PC and how they work. This basic level of understanding is necessary to use some of the more advanced features of GW-BASIC; however, a detailed understanding is not necessary for someone who wants to program simple applications using only the keyboard and the screen. Now, we will move on to an overview of the structure of a GW-BASIC program.

Quiz

1. True or False: An interpreter analyzes the entire program before beginning execution.
2. What technique does GW-BASIC use to keep program lines in order?
3. What are the four fundamental components of a GW-BASIC statement?
4. If GW-BASIC detects an error, what does it typically do?
5. What are the two components of most PC displays?
6. What are the three major color display technologies?
7. What are common methods for transferring information between PCs?

Chapter 3
Structure of a GW-BASIC Program

In This Chapter

In the previous two chapters, you were provided a brief introduction to what GW-BASIC is, how a language interpreter works, and the fundamental blocks that make up a PC. This chapter begins with a brief discussion of the art of programming and then explores simple BASIC statements. The chapter concludes with a simple, example program which you will be encouraged to modify.

Program Flow

Computers are really very simple-minded machines that meticulously follow our commands. For years, science fiction movies have been filled with instances of "computer error." The truth is that today it is highly unlikely that a computer will make a mistake due to a hardware malfunction. The most likely causes of error are bad input data or faulty programming (which are usually caused by humans)!

If you analyze the operation of virtually any computer program, it can be simplified into three parts. Figure 3.1 diagrams these parts as data retrieval or input, information processing,

Chapter 3

and storage of results or display of output. GW-BASIC can receive input from the keyboard, from a disk file, and from I/O ports.

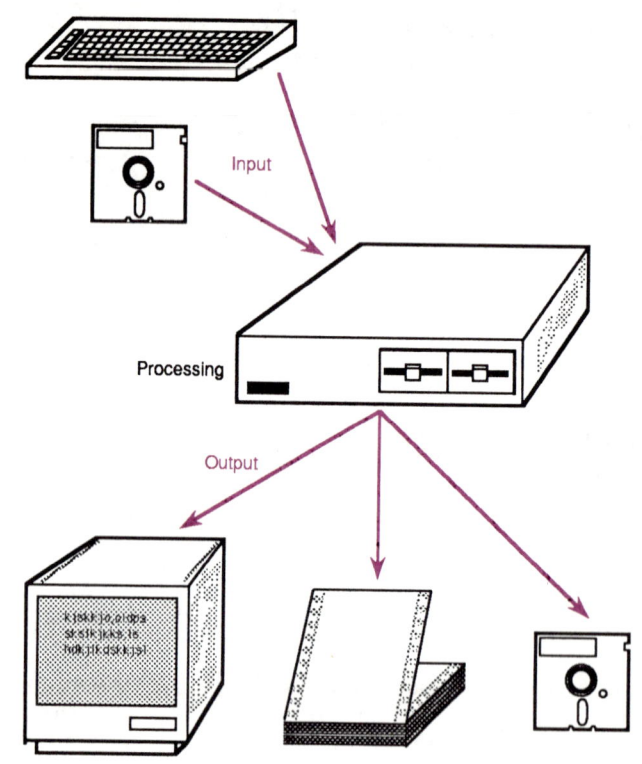

Figure 3.1 Operational parts of a typical computer program

When all of the needed information is obtained by the program, processing begins. Processing can be as simple as searching a disk data file for specific information in order to display a person's name and address on the screen. It can also be as complex as calculating the trajectory of a spacecraft on its way to the outer planets. Sometimes processing doesn't even change the information. For example, a program that copies the contents of one file to another had better not modify anything!

Finally, output can consist of information or graphics displayed on a screen, data saved in some easily retrievable form such as a disk file, paper output from devices such as printers and plotters, or as the change of some physical setting such as the motion of a robot arm (yes, there are companies that sell robotics products that can be connected to PCs).

When the BASIC language was originally created, it was intended to be easy to understand and use. The statements and keywords were intended to make sense to people who speak English. For example, if you want to send information to the screen, a PRINT command can be used. To send the same information to the printer, an LPRINT (which stands for Line PRINTer) command is used. Now, let's take a look at some simple GW-BASIC statements.

Introduction of Fundamental Statements

BASIC statements fall into one of various categories:

- ▶ Arithmetic assignment
- ▶ Input/Output
- ▶ String processing
- ▶ Flow control
- ▶ Special operations

In the remainder of this chapter, you will be briefly introduced to input/output statements and arithmetic operations. Then you will inspect a short program that illustrates how these statements can work together to produce a useful tool. This will provide you with a simple example of a working program so that you can get a feel for what the language looks like.

What Does a GW-BASIC Statement Look Like?

As mentioned in Chapter 2, a useful GW-BASIC statement is usually made up of three parts: a line number, a space, and a statement body:

```
1200 A = 5
```

Valid statement numbers are in the range 1 to 65529. Some BASIC interpreters consider the space between the statement number and the statement body optional, but it is usually regarded as bad programming practice to leave it out because doing so makes reading the program very difficult. The statement body usually contains arithmetic statements (as shown above) or keywords that instruct GW-BASIC to perform some specific operation. The following sections provide examples of the various types of GW-BASIC statements.

Assignment Statements

As with most computer languages, GW-BASIC uses *variables* to temporarily store data within a program. As you may recall from Chapter 2, variables are memory locations to which you have assigned names. These locations can then be used to temporarily store data. The simplest assignment statement is of the form:

```
COUNT = 3
```

This tells the GW-BASIC interpreter that a numerical value of 3 should be stored in the memory location associated with the variable COUNT. Figure 3.2 illustrates how GW-BASIC performs this. GW-BASIC can represent the number three in various ways depending on the attributes of the variable COUNT. For example, if COUNT is an *integer*, two bytes of memory will be used to hold the value and no fractional part will exist because integers are, by definition, whole numbers. GW-BASIC lets you define integers in several ways. The most obvious way is to specify the variable name immediately followed by a % symbol. If you want to define COUNT as an integer, name it **COUNT%**. To prevent confusion, this convention will be used in the next few chapters.

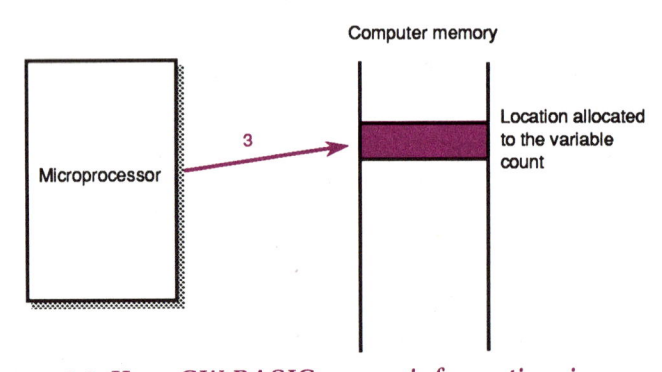

Figure 3.2 How GW-BASIC saves information in a variable

If COUNT were defined as a *single-precision* variable, it would require four bytes of memory and would represent the numbers differently than an integer because single-precision variables belong to a class called *floating-point numbers*. Floating-point numbers always have an implied decimal part which can be zero if representing a whole number. The GW-BASIC naming convention for single-precision variables is to follow the name with an exclamation point (!). To define COUNT as single-precision, the variable name COUNT! would be used in the sample statement.

Chapter 6 discusses in detail the various types of variables made available by GW-BASIC, so further discussion of numerical variable types will be deferred until then. All you need to remember about assignment statements is that the variable receiving a value goes on the left of the equal sign and that the variables, constants, and mathematical operators used to calculate the value go on the right side of the equal sign.

The fundamental arithmetic operators supported by GW-BASIC are:

+	Addition
−	Subtraction (or in some cases negation)
*	Multiplication
/	Floating-point division
\	Integer division
^	Exponentiation
MOD	Modulo arithmetic

Addition, subtraction, multiplication, and floating-point division are the same as the math you learned in school. The result of a floating-point division operation is always a floating-point number. If you multiply two integers together, the result will be an integer. If you multiply two floating-point numbers together, the result will be a floating-point number. If you multiply a floating-point number by an integer, the result will also be a floating-point value because GW-BASIC always attempts to perform mathematical operations with the highest precision variable type used in an expression. In the case of mixed operations with integers and floating-point numbers, floating-point numbers are regarded as more precise. The characteristics of the different variable types will be discussed more thoroughly in Chapter 6.

Chapter 3

Negation (making a positive number negative or a negative number positive) is a second use of the minus sign, It tells GW-BASIC that you want to change the sign of a quantity, but not its magnitude. For example:

```
3500 I% = 5
3510 J% = -I%
```

The negation operation in the second line takes the value of I% (5), negates it (-5), and assigns that value to the variable J. After line 3510 is executed, I% still contains the number 5. The negation operation does not affect variables on the right side of the equal sign. Another way to change the contents of I% would be the following:

```
4720 I% = -I%
```

In this example, GW-BASIC fetches a copy of the contents of I%, changes the sign of the number, and then stores this new value in the variable I% (replacing the old value). In the following example:

```
3600 I% = -5
3647 J% = -I%
```

the value of J% ends up being a positive 5 because it negated a value that was already negative (again, I% would still contain a negative 5 after this code is executed).

The exponentiation symbol (caret) indicates that you want to raise the number on the left of the symbol to the power at the right of the symbol. Another way to view this is that the number to the left of the caret will be multiplied times itself several times (the exact number of multiplications is determined by taking the number to the right of the caret and subtracting one from it). Exponentiation is often used in scientific and business calculations. For example:

```
8300 I% = 2^3
8400 x! = 4.5^0.5
8500 PRINT I%,x!
```

requests that the integer I% be assigned the value for 2 to the 3rd power and that single-precision variable X! be assigned the value of 4.5 to the 0.5 power (which means to take the square root of 4.5). If executed, this outputs the following line on the screen:

```
8                   2.12132
```

where 8 is the value for 2^3 (which is the same as 2*2*2) and 2.12132 is the square root of 4.5 (if you get out your calculator and multiply 2.12132 by itself you get something like 4.499998).

Integer division and modulo arithmetic are closely related. For example, if GW-BASIC executes the following:

```
100 I% = 7 \ 3
```

the answer saved in the variable I% would be **2**. This happens because you told the interpreter to take an integer (whole number) **7** and perform an integer division operation (indicated by the backslash symbol) on it using the integer **3**. Because 3 goes into 7 twice plus a remainder, the computer returns a result of **2** and forgets about any fractional part. This makes sense if you assume that the result of an integer division will usually be saved as an integer. If you multiply the result of an integer division by the divisor you will often get a number that is less than the number to the left of the backslash. The only time the numbers will be equal is when the number on the left of the backslash is an exact multiple of the number on the right so that there is no remainder.

The MOD operation also performs an integer division operation but it returns only the residue or remainder. Thus, the line:

```
100 J% = 7 MOD 3
```

yields an answer of **1** because 3 goes into 7 twice and leaves a remainder of **1**. This can be useful if you are writing, for example, a section of program that determines whether one number is a multiple of another. If the result of the MOD operation is zero, you know that it is an exact multiple. Notice that the integer division and MOD operations complement each other. If GW-BASIC executes the following lines:

```
7200 I% = 7 \ 3
7300 J% = 7 MOD 3
7400 K% = (I% * 3) + J%
```

what would you expect K to contain? The answer is **7** again! I%
holds the number of times that the divisor (3 in this example)
goes into 7. Because J% holds the remainder of the same integer
division, multiplying the value of I% by the divisor gives us a
number close to the original dividend. The result of the MOD
operation fills in whatever accuracy was lost as part of the integer division operation by providing the remainder.

Notice that a new language feature was demonstrated in the
last example. Parentheses were placed around the first part of
the calculation to tell GW-BASIC that the operations inside the
parentheses are to be performed before the rest of the calculations on that line. In the previous example, GW-BASIC multiplied the contents of I% by the constant **3** to get a value of **6** for
everything inside the parentheses. The program then took the **6**
and added the contents of J% (1 in this case) to get a final value
of **7**. If you had written the last line of the previous example as:

```
7400 K% = I% * (3 + J%)
```

what would you expect the answer to be? In this case, K%
would hold a value of **8**. GW-BASIC would first take the value of
J% (which was **1** in the previous example) and add it to **3** to get a
result of **4** for the operations within the parentheses. When it
multiplies **4** by the value contained in I% (**2**) it comes out with
an answer of **8** rather than **7**! It is amazing how frequently people get the wrong answer because of such details. What usually
happens is that the programmer knows exactly the order in
which a calculation should be performed, but he writes the
equation in an ambiguous manner. Fortunately, the creators of
GW-BASIC saw this problem coming and they built into the language default rules to be followed. This will be discussed next.

Operator Precedence

In order to make programming predictable, GW-BASIC follows
certain default rules of precedence. These rules can almost
always be overruled by the intelligent use of parentheses. Think
of these default rules as a safety net: They are there so that both
you and GW-BASIC can predict how a calculation is to be made
when there are no parentheses present to force the sequence of
evaluation. The first rule is that GW-BASIC scans a line from left
to right. This means that it will begin calculations at the part

nearest the equal sign and will work its way to the right until it reaches the end of the line. Next, it gives priority to certain arithmetic operations over others. The order of precedence from highest to lowest is:

^	Exponentiation
−	Unary minus or negation
*,/	Multiplication and floating-point division
\	Integer division
MOD	Modulo arithmetic operator
+,−	Addition and subtraction

Given this information on precedence, can you predict the answer to the following line?

```
5000 ANSWER% = 2 + 26 / 3 * 4
```

Let's go through the operations one step at a time. When scanning from left to right, you first discover that there are no parentheses so you must follow the precedence rules. Again, while scanning from left to right, you notice that the highest priority operations are the division and the multiplication. Therefore, begin by dividing the number 26 by the number 3 to get a result of **8.666667** (remember, you performed a floating-point division operation even though both numbers appear to be integers, so you wind up with a floating-point result for now). This result will then be multiplied by 4 to obtain **34.66667**. Finally, add the number 2 and then round the resulting 36.66667 to save the answer **37** in the integer ANSWER%. As mentioned earlier in this chapter, when GW-BASIC deals with an arithmetic operation that includes an integer and a floating-point number, it will convert the integer to a floating-point before performing the arithmetic operation, and it will keep the result as a floating-point number.

The result of the line can be dramatically affected by changing the floating-point divide to an integer division symbol:

```
5000 ANSWER% = 2 + 26 \ 3 * 4
```

Because of the precedence rules, this simple change has profound effects. When GW-BASIC scans the line, it will determine that the multiply symbol has the highest precedence (the previous table indicates that multiplication is of higher precedence than integer division). Thus 3 will be multiplied by 4 to obtain an integer result of **12** (because both numbers being multiplied were integers, the result was also an integer). The next higher precedence operation is the integer division, so 26 will be divided by 12 to yield an integer **2** (remember, integer division does not keep the fractional part). To this you finally add an integer 2 for a result of **4**!

Therefore, changing one symbol from a floating-point divide to an integer divide changed the final answer from **37** to **4**. This is a contrived example for illustration purposes. People don't usually mix integer and floating-point operations. But, as the television ad says, "It can happen to you." There are two rules that will keep you out of trouble most of the time: use floating-point operations as much as possible, and when in doubt, use parentheses to specify the order of evaluation. Floating-point operations tend to be a bit slower than integer operations and are subject to rounding errors, but they tend to provide results that are closer to your expectations.

This section provided a brief overview of integer and single-precision variables. The intent is to provide enough material so that simple programs will make sense to you. Chapter 6 is dedicated entirely to explaining the differences and limitations of the different variable types and how to convert data from one variable type to another. Now let's take a brief look at one way of getting information into a program.

Simple Input

The simplest way to obtain data for a program is to ask the user to enter it from the keyboard. The INPUT command in GW-BASIC performs this simple operation. For example, the line:

    100 INPUT COUNT

displays a question mark on the screen and waits for the user to type a value and press the Enter (or Return) key. If the entered value is valid for COUNT, the program will assign that value to the memory location reserved for the variable and continue executing the program. GW-BASIC has rules regarding data input to variables. For example, if COUNT were defined as an integer and the user entered a number including a decimal point, GW-BASIC would stop execution and display an error message stating that a floating-point number was entered for an integer variable. Another validity check concerns the size of the number. GW-BASIC limits integers to values no larger than 32767 (we'll explain why in Chapter 6), so an attempt to enter the total federal budget as input to an integer would "confuse" GW-BASIC (not to mention many adults). Fortunately, GW-BASIC does not require that input for floating-point variables have decimal points, so the examples in the next few chapters will avoid the problem by responding to most input requests with whole numbers.

A question mark on the screen probably isn't very useful if you are using the program for the first time or if you are otherwise confused about what is expected. Therefore, GW-BASIC supports a variant of the INPUT statement that instructs the program to provide a comment (prompt) that informs the user what is desired. For example:

```
INPUT "Please enter a count between 1 and 10";COUNT
```

displays the following on the screen:

```
Please enter a count between 1 and 10?
```

As you can see, the comments contained between the set of double quotes are displayed on the screen followed by a question mark. This provides useful information about what is expected from the person running the program. Chapter 8 will provide extensive discussion of the various ways to receive input from the user.

Simple Output

A pocket calculator with a display that can't be read won't be used much, and a computer program that generates results that can't be read isn't very useful either. So this section will now discuss how to get the information back out of the PC after GW-BASIC has done the processing! First, let's review the characteristics of displays. As mentioned in Chapter 2, most PC screens hold 25 lines of 80 characters each. Some portable PC displays hold fewer lines and columns, some high-performance

Chapter 3

displays can show as many as 43 lines and 132 columns. For the purpose of our discussion, assume that you are using the industry standard 25-by-80 character display. As shown in Figure 3.3, the address of the character position in the top left corner is (1,1) and that of the bottom right corner is (25,80).

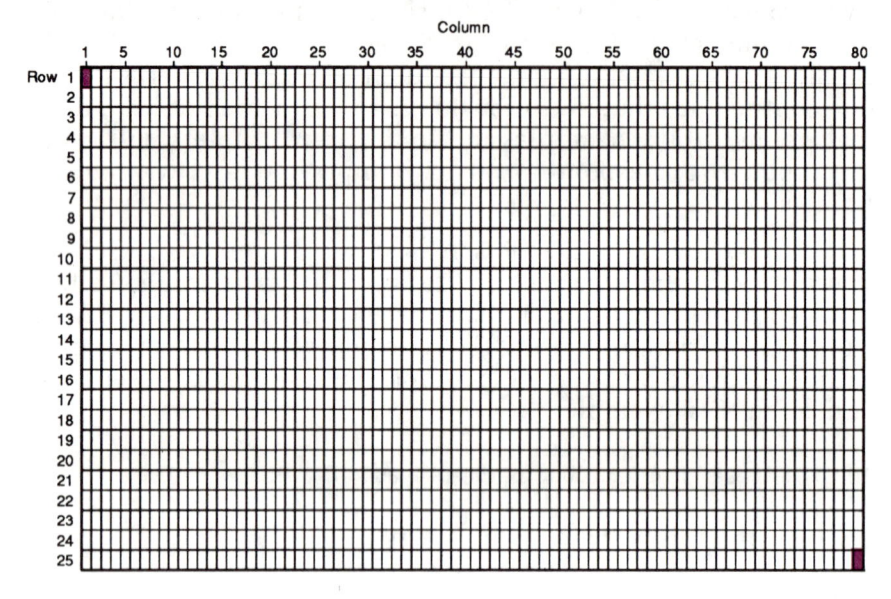

Figure 3.3 Typical screen organization

    The fundamental output statement in GW-BASIC is PRINT. In its simplest form, PRINT will send the contents of any variable type to the screen and display the contents starting at the current cursor position. The cursor is usually a blinking or solid box or an underline on the screen. It performs the same function as the v-shaped piece of metal or plastic near the middle of a typewriter and indicates where the next character will appear on the screen. The PRINT statement is capable of printing several variables on the same line and will automatically space them so that all the digits in a particular number will be visible and that at least one space will separate one number from another. GW-BASIC accomplishes this by dividing the screen into fields that are 14 characters wide. GW-BASIC then adds a space after each field so that the numbers won't run into each other. This is why in the previous example on exponentiation the second number started so far to the right of the first number; the previous 15 locations were allocated to the integer. Chapter 8 will discuss output in greater detail and will show how to better control the size and placement of number fields on the screen.

Sample Program

This section will tie together the various topics covered in this chapter by introducing a small program that requests an interest rate as input and generates a table on the screen that shows how money compounds over a five-year period. Because program flow control has not been discussed yet, these calculations were performed using a brute-force method. The first few lines (100, 110, and 120) are nonexecutable *comment lines* that tell the person looking at the program what will happen next. Comment lines can be inserted virtually anywhere in a program. They are easily recognized because they start with a single quote. Notice that you do not need another single quote at the end of each comment. GW-BASIC assumes that the comment ends when it reaches the end of each line.

```
100 'This is a simple program to calculate the
110 'growth of $ 1.00 at a specified interest rate
120 'for a five year period.
150 CLS
160 PRINT "Please enter a number for the desired"
170 PRINT "interest rate (i.e., 6.5 for six and"
180 PRINT "one-half percent interest)."
190 PRINT
200 INPUT "Interest rate";RATE!
210 FACTOR! = 1! + (RATE!/100!)
220 VALUE!=FACTOR!
225 PRINT
230 PRINT "Year            Factor"
240 I%=1:PRINT I%,VALUE!
250 VALUE!=VALUE!*FACTOR!:I%=I%+1:PRINT I%,VALUE!
260 VALUE!=VALUE!*FACTOR!:I%=I%+1:PRINT I%,VALUE!
270 VALUE!=VALUE!*FACTOR!:I%=I%+1:PRINT I%,VALUE!
280 VALUE!=VALUE!*FACTOR!:I%=I%+1:PRINT I%,VALUE!
290 END
```

Line 150 invokes a GW-BASIC function (CLS) that clears the entire screen and locates the cursor at the top left corner of the screen. The next four lines print a greeting message to the user and tell what the program does and what it expects for input. Line 200 prompts the user for an interest rate to use in the calculations. Lines 210 and 220 *initialize* variables to be used in the calculation. Line 225 creates a blank line on the screen after the previous input line. Line 230 prints a header so that the user will understand what the numbers on the screen represent. The remaining lines calculate the new growth value and print out the answer. Notice that the last few lines were made very compact by hooking together three separate statements on one line with colons (:) used as separators. This is a useful feature of GW-BASIC. However, the main disadvantage to this technique is that, if overused, it can make the program difficult to read. In this particular case, it actually makes the program more visually pleasing because the repetitiveness of lines 250 through 280 is obvious. Chapter 7 explains how to avoid program repetition by using flow control statements to force certain lines to be executed more than once.

If this program were entered and run with an interest rate of 5.0 percent, the following would appear on the screen:

Year	Factor
1	1.05
2	1.1025
3	1.157625
4	1.215506
5	1.276281

If you are getting anxious to enter some of these sample programs, relax. The next chapter will teach you how to enter, run, and debug programs. The programs in this chapter were provided only as examples. The following chapters provide much more interesting material with which you can experiment.

Summary

Several topics were introduced in this chapter. First, there was a brief discussion of the typical phases of a program (input, processing, and output). Then there were examples of typical GW-BASIC statements, definitions of integers and single-precision variables, and a discussion of precedence rules and parentheses and how they affect the evaluation of simple assignment statements. Next there was a brief explanation of INPUT and OUTPUT statements, and you were shown a short program that used the statements discussed in this chapter. The only problem is that you still don't know how to start up GW-BASIC. Now that you know enough to write small programs yourself, you are probably getting impatient to turn on your PC and start using GW-BASIC. This will be the topic of the next chapter.

Quiz

1. What are the three major parts of most programs?
2. What are the four parts of a typical GW-BASIC assignment statement?
3. What do you call a number that represents both a whole number part and a fractional part?
4. Which operator has higher precedence—a multiplication symbol (*) or an addition symbol (+)?
5. What simple GW-BASIC statement would you use to send the contents of a variable to the screen?

Chapter 4
Editing GW-BASIC Programs

In This Chapter

As you may recall from Chapter 1, there are two different ways to create and maintain GW-BASIC files: using the built-in editor or using a compatible word processing program. This chapter explains how to use the built-in editor to create, save, and load BASIC source files. It also briefly explains what your favorite word processor must provide to be compatible with GW-BASIC. Before you get into editing, though, you will need a brief review of the DOS environment.

The DOS Environment

GW-BASIC was designed to operate in an MS-DOS environment. Therefore, you need to know how to work with a disk and how to specify subdirectories. If you already know how to do these things, please skip to the next section, *Editor Basics*. If you are unfamiliar with MS-DOS, read on as we take you through a tour of a DOS disk.

Imagine that you have a roomful of empty four-drawer filing cabinets and you are given the task of storing several crates of papers in a systematic method of your own choosing. One way to organize them is to write a letter of the alphabet on the outside of each file drawer and place the papers in files in alphabetical order based on folder title.

Another way to organize the paper files is to first separate the files by general topics (accounting, personnel, and marketing) and allocate groups of filing cabinets for each topic. The files can then be alphabetized within each topic so that the "A" files for accounting are in the top drawer of the accounting cabinets, the "A" files for personnel are in the top drawer of the personnel cabinets, and the "A" files for marketing are in the top drawer of the marketing cabinets.

A third way to organize the files is based on who needs to use the information. For example, one group of filing cabinets can be allocated to the marketing representative responsible for the eastern half of the United States and another set can be allocated to the individual responsible for the western half of the country. The advantage of this method is that it is now possible to move all of the marketing filing cabinets to one corner of the large room and designate it the marketing area. Another part of the room can be designated the accounting area and their filing cabinets can be moved there. This way, it is possible for each group to have completely separate file organizations in their respective areas without disturbing the others.

The last organizational system is rather analogous to what MS-DOS lets a user do with disk storage. A brand-new disk is like the large room filled with empty storage areas: it has no real organization or data yet. When you create a subdirectory on the disk (using the MKDIR DOS command), it is analogous to placing a "this cabinet will be used for accounting records" sign on top of an empty filing cabinet. The cabinet contains no data yet, you are reserving a storage area for a particular purpose. Once you create a subdirectory, you can move files into it, you can move files out of it, you can create new files within the directory, or you can delete a file completely off the disk. Figure 4.1 illustrates a typical directory.

As can be seen in the figure, every disk created by MS-DOS has a *root directory*. From this directory, it is possible to slowly move down the *tree diagram* (which is what the picture in Figure 4.1 is called because it looks a bit like an upside-down tree) using the *change directory* command (usually abbreviated *cd*). For example, if you are in the root directory for drive C (which is usually a hard-disk drive on PCs) and you want to move down to the DOS directory, use the following command:

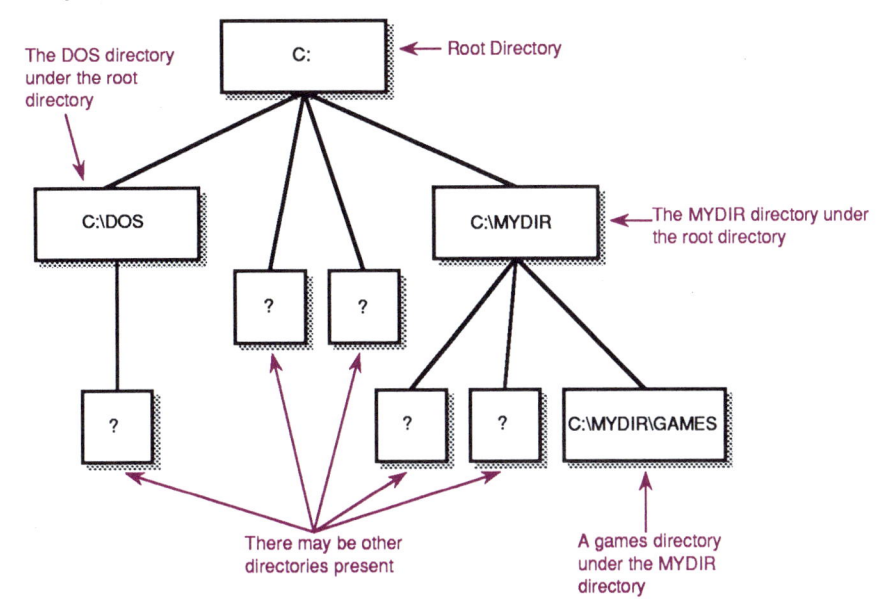

Figure 4.1 A typical tree directory structure on an MS-DOS disk

```
C>CD C:\DOS
```

In this example, the first two characters on the line are provided automatically by MS-DOS and are called the *system prompt*. The system prompt tells you which disk drive you are currently accessing (in this case, drive C). The CD command instructs MS-DOS to set the DOS directory under the root directory as the *default directory*. In the filing cabinet analogy, the default directory is equivalent to the filing cabinet immediately in front of you. It is the one in which MS-DOS will first look for the information. If you want to know the complete names of all files in the current default directory, enter:

```
C>DIR
```

The problem with this command is that, if there are more than 25 files in the default directory, the file names will scroll off the top of the screen so quickly that you can't read them. One way to avoid this problem is to issue the

```
C>DIR/W
```

Chapter 4

command, which tells MS-DOS to list the files in several columns on the screen. This allows many more files to be displayed than is possible with the simple DIR command; however, the size and date information is omitted with the /W version. The important thing to remember is that it is possible to move from any disk and/or directory to any other disk and/or directory by using the long form of the CD command shown above.

Another important MS-DOS concept is the operation of the PATH statement. First, find the root directory of the disk used by your PC on power-up. There you will probably find a file called AUTOEXEC.BAT which provides default information for DOS. The AUTOEXEC.BAT file is a set of commands that DOS executes whenever it begins execution for the first time (such as at initial power-up or after you have pressed the computer reset button). This normal ASCII character file can be viewed by commanding DOS to send it to the screen using:

```
C>TYPE AUTOEXEC.BAT
```

Within the AUTOEXEC.BAT file, there is usually a command that looks like:

```
PATH C:\DOS;C:\MYDIR
```

This line specifies the directories for DOS to search to locate a file that can't be found in the current directory. The PATH command begins with the word PATH, followed by full subdirectory specifications that are separated by semicolons. In the filing cabinet analogy, the PATH command tells MS-DOS in what other cabinets it should look for a file that can't be found in the default cabinet. DOS uses the directory list from left to right when searching for a file. This means that in the previous example MS-DOS first searches in the C:\DOS directory if the file does not exist in the default directory. If the file isn't in the C:\DOS directory either, DOS will look in the C:\MYDIR directory. Because we only specified two places for it to look, MS-DOS will give up if it doesn't find the desired file in C:\MYDIR either.

The PATH statement is valuable because it allows you to keep one copy of a program (such as GW-BASIC) in a specific subdirectory and lets you invoke the program from anywhere on that disk. If you have a PATH statement pointing to the DOS subdirectory (as in the previous example) you can place your GWBASIC.EXE file there and it will be accessible from any directory on that disk. This means you can create several directories to hold your BASIC programs but you do not need to copy GWBASIC.EXE into every one of those directories.

Entire books are written about how to use DOS, and it is impossible for these topics to be covered in depth here. This book simply provides sufficient background information for an intelligent discussion of GW-BASIC's capability to store and retrieve files. If you are not familiar with these topics, you should consult the MS-DOS manual that came with your machine.

Editor Basics

The GW-BASIC editor is an integral part of the GW-BASIC interpreter. To invoke it, simply type in **GWBASIC** at the system prompt. As mentioned earlier, the system prompt is usually an A> or a C>. It can also contain path information delimited by backslashes. If you set up GW-BASIC so that it can be reached from any directory, GW-BASIC will appear to be an integral part of your machine.

If you invoke GW-BASIC without specifying a file name, you will usually get a clear screen with a message at the top specifying the version of the program and the amount of free memory available. Ten groups of letters that identify the default actions of function keys F1 through F10 will appear on the bottom line of the screen. These one-key commands can save keystrokes, so you may want to get accustomed to using them.

You should note one other item on the screen: the word Ok. When you see this in columns 1 and 2 of the screen, GW-BASIC is waiting for you to give it a command. It is the equivalent of the A> prompt in DOS. When GW-BASIC displays the Ok prompt, it is in *direct mode*, which is a command processing mode. GW-BASIC can be in one of two states: in *direct mode* when waiting for user commands or in *indirect mode* when program lines are being entered. Direct mode is also known as "immediate-execution" mode because GW-BASIC will act on commands immediately. The indirect mode is also known as "computer-controlled execution" mode because the computer decides when it will perform an operation (based on program logic flow).

Chapter 4

Exiting GW-BASIC

A corollary to Murphy's Law states, "As soon as you invoke a software program, you will be overcome by an overpowering desire to exit back to DOS." Normally, it would take you ten minutes to find the obscure command that lets you out of GW-BASIC. Because you have purchased this book, you have been saved a great deal of consternation. If you are in direct mode (at the Ok prompt), you can exit to DOS by typing in the word **SYSTEM**↵. *Please* note that exiting to DOS will cause you to lose whatever code was in the interpreter at the time you exited. If you want to save your work first, read about the SAVE command later in this chapter.

Getting a Program into the Interpreter

At this point, you have several options. Because you do not have a program in memory (you didn't tell GW-BASIC which one), you can tell it to load one from the current directory by pressing the **F3** key. The word

```
LOAD"
```

will appear on the next available line on the screen. The cursor is located immediately after the double quote, so you can immediately type in the name of a file and the closing quote, such as:

```
LOAD"MYPROG.BAS"↵
```

GW-BASIC program file names must consist of one to eight characters, followed by a period and the three letters BAS (the file extension). If the desired program has the *file extension* .BAS, you don't have to type the extension. GW-BASIC also treats the double quote after the file name as optional. Thus, the previous LOAD command can be simplified to:

```
LOAD"MYPROG↵
```

GW-BASIC automatically assumes that you want to load a BASIC file. Remember, the symbol ↵ is used in this book to identify the carriage return or enter key on your keyboard. (It is usually a bit to the right of the L key.) If GW-BASIC finds the file, it displays another Ok after the LOAD command. If it can't find the file, it displays the message:

```
File not found
Ok
```

If you are at the original display screen after invoking GW-BASIC but don't have a program to load, you can begin to write one using the editor. To easily create a program, first decide what line number you want as your first line and what increment to use to separate each line of code. Then the AUTO command automatically creates lines for you. For example, the command:

```
AUTO 100↵
```

tells GW-BASIC that you want to start writing code starting at line 100. Because an increment was not specified, the program will assume a value of 10. When this AUTO command is entered, GW-BASIC responds with

```
100 _
```

so you can type in your first line of code. When you press the carriage return, GW-BASIC will return with the next line number. For example:

```
100 DEFINT I-N↵
110 _
```

This process will continue indefinitely until you simultaneously press the <ctrl> and <break> keys. Note that the line in which <ctrl><break> is pressed will not be saved, so always press ↵ first to create a new line number and then <ctrl><break> to quit auto numbering. Upon exiting AUTO, GW-BASIC will display Ok and return to direct mode. If you enter only the word AUTO, then numbering will start with line 10 and will increment by 10. If a line number is specified and followed by a comma but no increment value, GW-BASIC will use whatever increment was used previously. If the AUTO command generates a line number that already exists, it will display an asterisk next to the number to warn you:

```
100 ...
```

Chapter 4

```
200 ...
300*_
```

If you press the carriage return immediately after the asterisk, GW-BASIC will skip the present line and move on to the next line as determined by the selected increment value. If the user types in data and presses the carriage return, the old contents of the line are lost and replaced by the newly entered information.

In direct mode, you can also type in a statement directly. If you simply want to add a statement that adds B to C and saves the result in A, you really don't want to invoke AUTO for only one line. So simply type:

```
350 A=B+C↵
```

Now, GW-BASIC will capture the information and make it a part of the program.

Saving a BASIC Program

Once a file exists in the editor/interpreter, you will probably want to save it to disk storage before a power outage wipes out an entire night's work. When F4 is pressed, the keyword

```
SAVE"_
```

appears on the next available line on the screen. All you need to do is type in a valid MS-DOS file name (one to eight characters in length and with no unusual symbols), a period, and an optional extension (make your life easy and use .BAS). If you enter the command

```
SAVE"MYPROG.BAS↵
```

GW-BASIC will save the file in a special way called *tokenized format*. Unfortunately, this format is incompatible with most word processors and may, therefore, not be desirable. As with the LOAD statement, GW-BASIC treats the double quote after the filename as optional. If you simply provide:

```
SAVE"MYPROG↵
```

GW-BASIC automatically assumes that the file is a .BAS file and saves it in the tokenized format. If you want to save the file in a more flexible form, use:

```
SAVE"MYPROG.BAS",A↵
```

where the ,A (comma A) appendage after the double quote tells GW-BASIC to save the information as an ASCII character file that even EDLIN can read. (EDLIN is a low-level line editor provided with your MS-DOS software that lets you create simple things like the AUTOEXEC batch file.) Virtually every word processor program created for the PC can read ASCII character files. After mastering GW-BASIC, you will even be able to write a BASIC program that can read and edit ASCII character files. If you want to save your program as an ASCII file, you must supply a double quote between the filename and the comma (it is not optional in this case). Additionally, there should be no spaces in this statement.

To safeguard your sensitive programs, the *protection option* is also available in the SAVE command. The program is saved as a .BAS file, but the data in the file is encoded in a binary format that cannot be *listed* when loaded into GW-BASIC again. This protection option is invoked by:

```
SAVE"MYPROG.BAS",P↵
```

Again, the second double quote, comma, and capital letter P must be present for this statement to work properly. The algorithm used to save the file in protected mode may be breakable, so the protection option is not an ironclad way to ensure the confidentiality of your program. However, using it will keep most users from being able to inspect your code. The protected mode will help prevent casual users from modifying your program (which can be a problem if your PC is used by several individuals). This mode should be selected when you plan to distribute a program but do not want the users to see how the program works. If you really want security, you may need to use a BASIC *compiler*. The output of a compiler is virtually impossible to decipher because the variable names and attributes are not present in the executable program file.

Chapter 4

Listing a Program

After you have loaded a program or have typed in some lines, you may want to view a group of lines together to check program flow and consistency. To invoke the LIST command, press the **F1** key in direct mode. The following line will appear on your screen:

LIST _

If you simply press the carriage return, GW-BASIC will list all the lines currently in memory. If there are more than 24 lines in memory, the first lines will scroll off the top and out of view very quickly. If the command

LIST 200

is entered, GW-BASIC will display only the contents of line 200. If a range of lines is desired,

LIST 100-900

will display all program lines between lines 100 and 900 (inclusive). GW-BASIC doesn't care if lines 100 and/or 900 don't actually exist. It will look for all lines in that range. By the way, GW-BASIC recognizes only line numbers in the range 1 to 65529, so don't specify a greater line number in a LIST command. This command has a couple of other convenient options. For example:

LIST -600

tells GW-BASIC to display all lines between 1 and 600. The command

LIST 2300-

tells GW-BASIC to display the program starting at line 2300 and ending when it runs out of lines. Another option lets you send the list to a file rather than the screen. Thus:

LIST 500-7000,"ANOTHER.BAS"

writes lines 500 through 7000 to a file called ANOTHER.BAS and saves the data as an ASCII character file.

Editing a Specific Line

When you list your program, you may find a typographical error. For example, you may have the line:

400 DEFINT I-8P

and you really wanted it to be I-P. There are two ways to correct the error. The first is to simply retype the entire line (including the line number). In this case, the screen might look like this after the line is listed and then reentered:

```
Ok
LIST 400
400 DEFINT I-8P
Ok
400 DEFINT I-P
_
```

When a line is entered in GW-BASIC that has the same line number as one already in memory, the new line replaces the old line. You can also correct the error by using the arrow keys and other specialty keys to move the cursor to the spot where the error is. In this example, you can use the arrow keys to move the cursor to where the 8 is and press the <delete> key to remove it. Another way to accomplish the same thing is to locate the cursor under the P and then press the <backspace> key (which is usually located above the carriage return key in the main part of the keyboard). To save the change, press the carriage return before moving off that line. If you do not, GW-BASIC will assume that you changed your mind and will not update the line in memory!

Now imagine that your line of code is:

400 DEFNT I-P

The letter *I* is missing in the word DEFINT. To correct this, move the cursor to the letter N on the screen, press the <insert> key, enter an uppercase **I**, and press the carriage return to save the change. You should spend a few minutes experimenting with the editor until these commands feel natural to you.

Erasing the Current Program

As with most editing programs, GW-BASIC lets you clear out memory without first having to exit. When **NEW** is entered in direct mode, all existing program lines are discarded and the editor gets ready to receive new program instructions.

Other Features

One other operation can be performed in direct mode. You can command GW-BASIC to immediately execute program instructions. For example, you can ask GW-BASIC to calculate a value for you:

```
PRINT 27+12
39
Ok
```

Any command that is valid in a GW-BASIC statement can be executed directly. Notice that no line number is associated with the PRINT command in this example. The absence of a line number tells GW-BASIC to execute the command immediately. Chapter 12 briefly lists all of the keywords recognized by GW-BASIC. Any of those commands can be executed in direct mode. By the way, the formula in the PRINT statement above could have been quite elaborate, as in the following:

```
PRINT SIN(3.14159/6.0)
.4999997
Ok
```

The immediate execution feature becomes extremely important when you are debugging a program because it lets you interactively display the value of a variable after a break in execution has occurred. The direct command:

```
PRINT I,X
```

makes GW-BASIC print the current value for these variables on the screen after locating them in memory. The next chapter discusses this topic in greater detail when it teaches you how to run and debug a program.

Summary

In this chapter, you learned how to invoke GW-BASIC and how to load, edit, and save program files. The difference between direct and indirect modes in GW-BASIC was explained. You learned that GW-BASIC can execute virtually any command in direct mode that it can execute when running the program, allowing the user to access the current value of program variables when execution is interrupted.

Now that you know how to edit files, you need to learn how to determine where a problem is when something goes wrong during execution. The next chapter will teach you how to run and debug a program, so you can find a problem and fix it.

Quiz

1. What is the name of the structure used to organize MS-DOS directories?
2. What special symbol is usually present in the system prompt provided by MS-DOS?
3. What command tells DOS to display all of the files in the current directory?
4. What command tells GW-BASIC to fetch the file TEST.BAS from the disk into the editor?
5. What command tells GW-BASIC to save the current contents of the editor into a disk file called TESTA.BAS as a simple ASCII file?
6. What command would you use to have GW-BASIC discard everything currently in the editor?

Chapter 5
How to Run Your Program

In This Chapter

So far, you have learned the fundamentals of GW-BASIC operation and the details of the editing process, but you have not yet learned how to execute and debug your program. Debugging techniques are very important to programmers who typically spend a great deal of time testing their programs and correcting design errors. The faster you can determine what is wrong, the sooner you will be done with the testing/validation phase of your effort.

This chapter discusses the various methods available for understanding what the program is doing. Some techniques date back to the days of punchcard decks and some are modern built-in features of GW-BASIC.

How to Start Execution in GW-BASIC

If you start up GW-BASIC without specifying a program to be run, the screen displays a set of characters along the bottom line of the page. These characters identify the GW-BASIC commands that are directly available by pressing the function keys. Function key F2 is

Chapter 5

the RUN command; pressing it will begin the execution of whatever program is in memory beginning with the lowest-numbered statement. If this function key has been disabled for some reason, you can still type in the word **RUN** and press the Enter key (sometimes called the carriage return) to start program execution. When you're driving a car, it's nice to know where the brake pedal is before you start to roll. Likewise, it's nice to know how to apply the brakes when running a program. The next section discusses how to stop program execution,

How to Stop GW-BASIC

When GW-BASIC is executing, it will continue to execute until one of several things happens:

- ▶ The program completes successfully
- ▶ The program encounters some type of error
- ▶ The interpreter encounters a STOP or END statement
- ▶ The user presses <Ctrl> <Break>
- ▶ Power to the computer is cut off or RESET is pressed

The most common reason for a halt to execution is that an error condition exists. When GW-BASIC encounters an error, it immediately stops execution and displays a message on the screen that indicates the type of error and the line number where the error is first detected. It is, however, possible that the cause of the error may be on a previously executed line, but the effect of the problem was not detected until the line identified by GW-BASIC was executed.

Another important way to stop execution is to use the <Ctrl> <Break> keys. If your program goes into an *infinite loop* (it appears to be stuck performing the same operation over and over or it appears to be doing nothing at all), then control can usually be regained by simultaneously pressing the control and break keys. GW-BASIC looks for this particular key sequence every time it begins a new line of BASIC. Of course, if you do something truly awful (such as calling a nonexistent assembly language routine), then you may have to press the RESET button on your computer (if you have one). If you use the RESET button, you will lose whatever modifications you may have made to your program and to data files that you had been manipulating. Fortunately, you should not have to reset very often. Of course, if electrical power to your PC is lost, any changes to the program and open data files will also be lost. The best way to minimize loss in these scenarios is to save your programs occasionally, especially before you begin an execution. In order to prevent damage to your real or permanent files, save temporary or intermediate versions of your program in a file with a dummy name, such as DUMMY.BAS (see Chapter 4 if you have forgotten how to save files from GW-BASIC). You will be able to recover your most recent version later if a catastrophe strikes.

The normal way to stop a program is to use a STOP or END statement. STOP statements let the programmer investigate the current state of variables in the area where an error is suspected. After a STOP is executed, GW-BASIC returns the message:

Break in 1234

where the number shown is the line number where the STOP was encountered. This can be useful because you can insert STOP statements at various points in the program and then see if you encounter them in the expected order. After the STOP is executed, GW-BASIC returns to direct mode. Then you can type in statements such as:

PRINT A,S,J

The contents of the variables A, S, and J (as of the moment that the STOP was encountered) will be displayed on the screen. The variable contents will not be affected unless you enter an assignment statement, such as:

A=27

After you perform the necessary investigation, you can instruct GW-BASIC to continue executing the next instruction immediately after the STOP statement by typing in:

CONT

Such actions may introduce errors that would normally not exist. Of course, execution of the END statement tells GW-BASIC that the program has successfully completed and closes all open files before returning to the command level.

Simple Debugging Using PRINT Statements

Debugging with PRINT statements dates back to the early days of computers. Frequently, a programmer has a fairly good idea where a problem in a program lies and what variables are probably involved. As you will recall from Chapter 4, it is very easy to insert temporary lines in GW-BASIC if the line numbers have been spaced at intervals of 10 or greater. You can insert PRINT statements at suspected locations so that intermediate values of calculations can be seen on the screen. This can be a very powerful debugging tool if only one calculation is behaving differently than expected, and that one miscalculation affects other calculations. A typical debug PRINT statement might look like:

```
1451 PRINT "Line 1451 ",A,M1,J
```

Notice that the line number of the PRINT statement is identified. This can be valuable if you have many PRINT statements in several parts of your program. It may be the only way to keep track of the debugging information on the screen. You will learn how to create more elaborate PRINT statements capable of identifying the different variables being printed. The main disadvantage of PRINT statements is that they can ruin an attractive screen. Fortunately for us, most programs use either the screen intensively or the printer intensively, but not both. If the screen is used extensively, you may want to send the debugging data to the printer by using a statement like:

```
1451 LPRINT "Line 1451 ",A,M1,J
```

If your program uses both the screen and the printer, you may consider sending the data to a disk file that you can inspect at a later date. Sending data to a disk file is complicated and is generally used only when both devices are heavily used. Data can be sent to a disk file with a PRINT # statement. Doing so can be a bit complicated because you first must learn how to OPEN and CLOSE disk files while running GW-BASIC. This topic is covered in great detail in Chapter 9, so please read that chapter carefully before attempting to send data to a disk file. The point is that you can replace the PRINT or LPRINT debugging statements with the PRINT # statements and send your debugging information to a permanent disk data file.

Occasionally, GW-BASIC will flag a program line with an error message and you won't be able to figure out what the problem is. If you have compound statement (where several program statements are located on one line using colons as terminators), split it into separate lines and then rerun the program. GW-BASIC will flag the specific program line containing the error so you can quickly isolate the problem to one statement. When you have corrected the problem, put them back together into one compound line again. For debugging flexibility, all programs in this book are illustrated with lines spaced at intervals of 100. Numbering lines in large increments makes it easier to modify and enhance a program and also makes it easier to include temporary print statements.

Debugging Using TRON/TROFF

So far, the programs in this book have executed in a simple fashion (GW-BASIC executed lines in ascending order without skipping or repeating lines). This type of coding makes boring programs! Chapter 7 will explain in detail how to repeat certain sections of code and skip others. This process, however, brings up an additional form of confusion: do you really know which statements were executed and in which order? Coding can be very tricky and sometimes it is difficult to tell how execution flow is progressing. Under such circumstances, it is often useful to use GW-BASIC's built-in trace capability, known as TRON and TROFF (for TRace ON and TRace OFF). When you type **TRON** in direct mode, each program statement executed after that point is identified on the screen as a line number enclosed in square brackets. The results of any PRINT statements executed while TRON is in effect will be mingled with the trace output. *Tracing* stops when the user enters **TROFF** in direct mode. If you type in the following simple program and then turn on TRON with the F7 key, the screen will look like this:

Chapter 5

```
1000 I% = 3
1100 J% = 4
1200 K% = I% + J%
TRON
Ok
RUN
[1000][1100][1200]
Ok
```

The numbers in the square brackets show the order in which the program lines were executed. (Obviously, if you have many program statements, these trace images can fill the entire screen.) Normally, trace statements are used in conjunction with STOP statements and temporary PRINT statements to provide fairly thorough coverage of the actions taken by the program in one specific area. This can be accomplished by inserting the TRON and TROFF commands into the GW-BASIC program itself. For example, see what happens if the following short program is executed:

```
1000 I% = 3
1100 J% = 4
1200 TRON
1300 K% = 5
1400 L% = I% + J%
1500 TROFF
1600 M% = J% + K%
1700 END
RUN
[1300][1400][1500]
Ok
```

In this case, tracing does not begin until GW-BASIC encounters the TRON command in line 1200. Tracing then continues until the TROFF command is encountered (line 1500 in this example). Notice that line 1500 is listed in the trace list because tracing was still enabled when GW-BASIC interpreted it, but line 1600 was not shown in the list because TROFF was executed before line 1600 was encountered. In order to familiarize yourself with TRON and TROFF, you may want to pause here and enter these simple programs using GW-BASIC.

Using the ON ERROR Statement

The ON ERROR statement is another unique way to deal with errors in GW-BASIC programs. The general form is:

ON ERROR GOTO linenumber

where *linenumber* is the beginning of a specialized error handling program. Normally, the ON ERROR statement is placed at the beginning of the program to provide immediate coverage, but it can appear anywhere in the program. If any kind of error is encountered, program execution will transfer to the line number identified by the GOTO. When the error handler begins to execute, it can interrogate two variables that contain the error code (ERR) and line number (ERL). Appendix C contains a list of the GW-BASIC error codes. Armed with this information, the error handler routine can print selected information and/or abort program execution. If you want the program to continue execution with the statement following the one that caused the error, insert a RESUME NEXT statement in the appropriate spot in the error handler to instruct GW-BASIC to continue. ERR and ERL can also be used with GW-BASIC program control flow commands such as IF or ON/GOTO statements.

If the error is unrecoverable or if you wish to cancel the use of the error handler, execute a statement:

12340 ON ERROR GOTO 0

to return *error trapping* to the usual GW-BASIC methods. ON ERROR statements are useful when an unexpected problem occurs in a program that performs disk input/output (I/O) because unexpected program interruptions can mess up the files and leave them in a disorderly state. For this reason, simple error handling in a program might look like this:

```
100 ON ERROR GOTO 40000
    .
    .
    .
40000 CLOSE
40100 PRINT "Error in line ",ERR," error number ",ERL
40200 END
```

The CLOSE statement in line 40000 terminates GW-BASIC's control of disk files, printers, and I/O ports. Line 40100 gives the user fundamental information about what went wrong so that the program can be corrected. Line 40200 simply terminates the program so that GW-BASIC will be happy. Of course, error routines can get very complicated and beyond the scope of an introductory text.

Summary

In this chapter, you learned the typical approaches used to debug a program. These methods include the use of PRINT, STOP, and TRON/TROFF statements. ON ERROR GOTO statements, which can be used to invoke error recovery routines, were also discussed.

With the material covered in the first five chapters, you have enough knowledge to create, edit, and debug simple GW-BASIC programs. You may want to stop reading here and experiment a bit, or you may not yet feel comfortable enough to attempt new programs. In either case, there is still a great deal to learn about GW-BASIC. How do you process non-numeric information like names and addresses? Does GW-BASIC let you draw pictures on the screen? These topics will be covered in subsequent chapters. But first, you need to understand more about the different variable types that GW-BASIC supports, as discussed in Chapter 6.

Quiz

1. What fundamental GW-BASIC command executes the program currently in the editor?
2. What key combination stops a GW-BASIC program?
3. What command sends information to your lineprinter?
4. What commands enable and disable GW-BASIC's built-in tracing capability?
5. What is the function of the ON ERROR statement?

Chapter 6

Variable Types

In This Chapter

The previous chapters introduced you to the GW-BASIC interpreter and taught you how to enter, edit, execute, and debug a simple program. A great deal of important material was skipped in order to get things rolling. The next few chapters will cover some important topics in detail and answer many of the questions raised in the introductory chapters. In this chapter, you will learn the characteristics and limitations of the different variable types. Virtually all computer languages place limitations on the size and accuracy of numbers that can be represented. The material in this chapter will help you better understand what the limitations are and how to work with them.

What Are Variables?

As briefly explained in Chapter 3, variables are memory locations that the computer uses to store information. When GW-BASIC encounters a variable in a BASIC statement, it searches a special list called a *symbol table* to see if it has previously created that variable. A symbol table is usually composed of individual entries that contain at least three pieces of data: the name of each variable,

Chapter 6

the beginning address (in the computer's memory) of the variable, and the variable type. Usually, the symbol table also contains additional information such as whether the variable is a single element or an *array* (an array is a group of variables of the same type that are referred to by one name and an index number). Figure 6.1 illustrates what a symbol table may look like in memory.

	Variable name (40 bytes)	Address	Type	Length
Entry 01	|||||• • •|||||||			
Entry 02	|||||• • •|||||||			
Entry 03	|||||• • •|||||||			
Entry 04	|||||• • •|||||||			
Entry 05	|||||• • •|||||||			
Entry 06	|||||• • •|||||||			
Entry 07	|||||• • •|||||||			

Figure 6.1 Sample symbol table

If GW-BASIC finds the variable name in the symbol table, it retrieves the information necessary to execute the program statement. If it doesn't find the variable name in the table, it assumes that you want to create a new variable. To create a new entry in the table, GW-BASIC first uses certain "grammar" rules to determine what type of variable you are defining. When it knows the type, it searches upper memory for a free location that it can assign to the new variable. All of this information is supplied to a new entry in the symbol table. The ability to create variables on demand is one of the characteristics of GW-BASIC that makes it so powerful and easy to use. If you need additional statements that use new variables, you can create them with the editor and begin execution from some point other than the very beginning of the program. With virtually all other languages, the user must begin execution from the very beginning of the program every time the program is changed. Of course, there are always certain risks when you start a program in the middle; variables may not be initialized to values that you take for granted.

Naming Variables

The rules for naming variables in GW-BASIC are very straightforward. A variable name:

▶ Can be from 1 to 40 characters long
▶ Must consist of characters and numbers
▶ Must always start with a letter

As with most rules in life, there are a few exceptions, but if you keep these three simple rules in mind you will avoid most problems.

The rule about always starting with a letter makes sense because it makes it easier to identify variables and distinguish them from other elements. Imagine analyzing a typical line of BASIC by hand. First, you need to know that GW-BASIC uses a space or blank as a *delimiter* (a character that marks the beginning or end of a unit of data) to separate language elements. If you see a number after a space or operator (such as plus sign, etc.) you can immediately guess that a numerical constant is about to be supplied. If you see a character after a delimiter, you can speculate that the next group of characters represents either a variable or some type of reserved word (such as a function call).

The rule that variable names can only be composed of letters and numbers can be very useful when you try to assign meaningful names to variables (such as using SALES1990 to represent sales in a particular year). Actually, GW-BASIC allows one other character in variable names, the period. Because it can be hard to read (therefore easy to miss), programmers tend to avoid periods in names except as legal spacers for variables such as WEEKS.IN.YEAR, etc. Some older BASIC interpreters may not accept the period as a valid character within a name, thus introducing a portability problem if the program is ever moved to a different machine. Therefore, it may be a good idea to avoid periods in variables names.

When it begins to process a variable name, GW-BASIC assumes that everything up to a delimiter or other special character is part of the name. This leads up to the third rule.

If you look again at Figure 6.1, you will note that one of the entries in the symbol table is the variable name. To simplify and accelerate the search for a variable name, make the length of the data associated with each variable the same size. Therefore, if the data for each entry takes 50 bytes, GW-BASIC will be able to skip quickly from entry to entry by simply adding 50 to the address of the current entry to find the start of the next entry. In order to achieve these types of efficiencies, the creators of GW-BASIC placed an upper limit of 40 characters for each unique name.

One last observation must be made regarding variable names and *reserved words*. Reserved words are names that GW-BASIC has reserved for itself. They are usually either GW-BASIC commands or function names. Appendix A contains a list of GW-BASIC reserved words with a brief explanation of each. If you attempt to use a reserved word as a variable or if you create a variable that begins with a reserved word, GW-BASIC will generate an error message. The interpreter looks at a list of reserved words before it looks at the symbol table. If the variable is a reserved word, GW-BASIC tries to implement the operation indicated by the reserved word. You can avoid any problems by placing a dummy letter in front of the offending name. For example, SIN is a reserved word used to invoke the trigonometric sine function. If you want to create a variable to hold a special sine value, call the variable ZSIN, or MYSIN, or THESIN. When the interpreter looks for a match in the reserved word list, it looks for ZS, MY, or TH (rather than SI) and, therefore, does not find a match.

Now that you've learned the rules of variable naming, it is time to move on and explain the different types of variables and how they are used.

Integers

The simplest numerical variable type is the *integer* which consists of two bytes of memory for a total of 16 bits of storage capacity. Each bit is a location that can be set to one of two states: 0 or 1. By using 1 to denote when the position is *active* (holds data), it is possible to organize 16 bits to represent whole numbers in the range −32768 to +32767. This is all you need to know about integers in order to program in GW-BASIC. The remainder of this section is included for readers who are curious about the way computers represent integers. If you are not interested or find this material confusing, please skip ahead to the next section on reals.

Figure 6.2 illustrates the typical organization of an integer, and Figure 6.3 illustrates patterns of bits that can be used to represent some of these different positive and negative numbers.

Variable Types

	Numerical Weighting	
	Upper Byte	Lower Byte

S I G N	1 6 3 8 4	8 1 9 2	4 0 9 6	2 0 4 8	1 0 2 4	5 1 2	2 5 6	1 2 8	6 4	3 2	1 6	8	4	2	1

Bit position 15 14 13 12 11 10 9 8 7 6 5 4 3 2 1 0

Figure 6.2   Typical organization of an integer

Decimal Number	Binary Number
32767	0111 1111 1111 1111
32766	0111 1111 1111 1110
16	0000 0000 0001 0000
15	0000 0000 0000 1111
14	0000 0000 0000 1110
13	0000 0000 0000 1101
12	0000 0000 0000 1100
11	0000 0000 0000 1011
10	0000 0000 0000 1010
9	0000 0000 0000 1001
8	0000 0000 0000 1000
7	0000 0000 0000 0111
6	0000 0000 0000 0110
5	0000 0000 0000 0101
4	0000 0000 0000 0100
3	0000 0000 0000 0011
2	0000 0000 0000 0010
1	0000 0000 0000 0001
0	0000 0000 0000 0000
−1	1111 1111 1111 1111
−2	1111 1111 1111 1110
−3	1111 1111 1111 1101
−4	1111 1111 1111 1100
−5	1111 1111 1111 1011
−6	1111 1111 1111 1010
−7	1111 1111 1111 1001
−8	1111 1111 1111 1000
−9	1111 1111 1111 0111
−10	1111 1111 1111 0110
−11	1111 1111 1111 0101
−12	1111 1111 1111 0100
−13	1111 1111 1111 0011

Figure 6.3   Typical integer bit patterns

Chapter 6

```
   -14              1111 1111 1111 0010
   -15              1111 1111 1111 0001
   -16              1111 1111 1111 0000
-32767              1000 0000 0000 0001
-32768              1000 0000 0000 0000
```

Figure 6.3 *Typical integer bit patterns (continued)*

As you can see from the two figures, the leftmost bit is reserved to hold the *sign* of the number. When this bit is on, the number is negative. To get the proper bit pattern for a negative number, use Figure 6.2 to evaluate the bits for a positive value and rewrite the pattern so that all of the 1s are changed to 0s and all the 0s to 1s. Finally, add one to the "mirrored" value (remember that 1 plus 1 yields 0 with a carry of 1 to the next bit to the left). Figure 6.4 illustrates how this works for several negative numbers.

```
Decimal 14  ───▶  0000 0000 0000 1110  ┐ Binary complement
                  1111 1111 1111 0001  ┘ operation
                                  +1
                  ─────────────────────
                  1111 1111 1111 0010  ◀── This is -14
                                            in binary

Decimal 32767 ──▶ 0111 1111 1111 1111  ┐ Binary complement
                  1000 0000 0000 0000  ┘ operation
                                  +1
                  ─────────────────────
                  1000 0000 0000 0001  ◀── This is -32767
                                            in binary

Decimal -32768 ─▶ 1000 0000 0000 0000  ┐ Binary complement
                  0111 1111 1111 1111  ┘ operation
                                  +1
                  ─────────────────────
Oops! An overflow forced ─▶ 1000 0000 0000 0000
the value back to -32768!
```

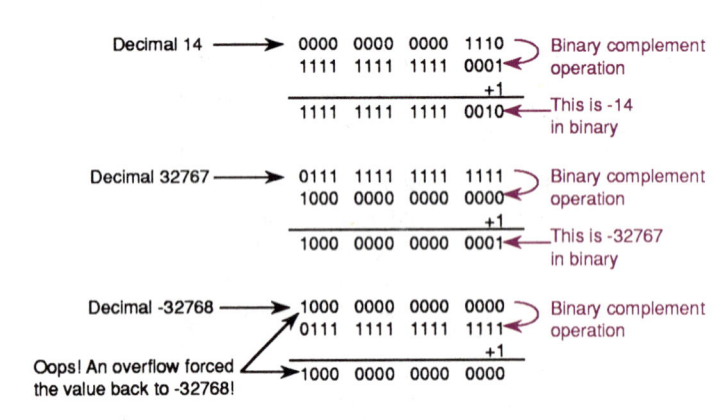

Figure 6.4 *Two's Complement numbers*

At first the tricky representation of negative numbers, known as Two's Complement Arithmetic, may seem like a waste of time and effort. The beauty of Two's Complement is that any two numbers can be added together directly to get the proper result without having to worry about whether either of them are negative! This property of Two's Complement Arithmetic also leads to an unusual effect known as *wraparound*. Wraparound occurs when a positive number is continuously added to another positive number, eventually leading to a numeric overflow which causes the result to transition from positive to negative. Figure 6.3 illustrates the circular pattern followed by positive and negative integers. When you keep adding positive numbers, you eventually reach 32767 which is the largest positive number that can be represented by a 16-bit integer. If you add 1 to the bit pattern for 32767 (0111 1111 1111 1111), a carry bit will propagate along the entire number and end up in the bit farthest to the left, which is the sign bit! As you can see from Figure 6.3 and the preceding discussion, the bit pattern 1000 0000 0000 0000 (which is located at the bottom of the page) is associated with the largest *negative* number, which is −32768. If you keep adding a positive number to this value, the negative number continues to decrease and eventually gets to zero again. Visualize adding a positive number by going up the columns in Figure 6.3, and visualize subtracting a number (or adding a negative number) as going down the figure. Figure 6.5 is a short GW-BASIC program that illustrates the principle of wraparound. If GW-BASIC detects a wraparound condition, it will stop execution with a wraparound error.

```
100 CLS:I%=32765
200 PRINT I%
300 I%=I%+1
400 PRINT I%
500 I%=I%+1
600 PRINT I%
700 I%=I%+1
800 PRINT I%
900 I%=I%+1
1000 PRINT I%
1100 I%=I%+1
1200 PRINT I%
2500 END
```

Figure 6.5 Wraparound program

Because of the properties of Two's Complement Arithmetic, the same overflow effect occurs if you subtract a number from a large negative number. As an experiment, you may want to modify the program in Figure 6.5 to start at −32765 and then repeatedly subtract 1 from it to see how it works in the other direction.

Reals

Chapter 3 described another numeric type called *reals* or *floating-point* numbers. Unlike integers, these numbers can store fractional

Chapter 6

parts and are routinely used for financial and scientific calculations. GW-BASIC defines two distinct types of floating-point numbers called *single-precision* and *double-precision*. Single-precision variables use four bytes of memory storage and can represent numbers in the range from 10 to the −44 power to 10 to the +37 power, with approximately seven digits of precision. A brief lesson in scientific notation is probably now in order.

To avoid writing clumsy expressions such as "10 to the −44 power," mathematicians and scientists devised a shorthand notation that represents that number as E-44. As you can see from Figure 6.6, this notation lets you write very large or very small numbers compactly.

Normal Representation	Scientific Notation
123.4	1.234E2
56.78	5.678E1
1.07	1.07E0
0.100	1.0E-1
0.05	5.0E-2
0.009735	9.735E-3

Figure 6.6 Illustration of scientific notation

As shown in the figure, the number after the capital E represents how many places to the left or right the decimal point must be shifted to represent the actual number. This number can also be viewed as the power of 10 by which the number preceding the E must be multiplied to yield the actual number. In the first example, the number 1.234 must be multiplied by 10 to the second power (which is 100) in order to get the actual value. The negative numbers after the E indicate that the number must by *divided* by that particular power of 10 in order to represent the actual number. Therefore, the last example (9.735) must be divided by 10 to the third power (1000) to obtain the actual value of 0.009735 shown in the left column. By definition, 10 to the zero power means multiplication by 1, so a number taken to the power of zero is not changed at all.

Returning to our discussion of single-precision variables, note that this type of variable can represent numbers in the range of E-44 to E+37 (which means that a single-precision variable can represent numbers as small as one digit preceded by 43 zeros and a decimal point). In the same four bytes, you can also store a number consisting of a digit followed by 37 zeros and a decimal point (which is appreciably larger than our national debt). The problem is that the single-precision variable can only represent seven digits of accuracy. The accuracy limitation is due to the way the numbers are stored using Two's Complement Arithmetic, and the explanation is well beyond the scope of this book (if you are interested in learning more about this, find a book on digital mathematics at your local library or bookstore). There is, however, a very practical aspect to this limitation. Imagine that you have an accounting program for a multinational corporation and you can afford to ignore fractions of a dollar. Because it is a large business, your company also has large sales numbers. Let's imagine that someone has written an accounting program (using single-precision variables) to add the monthly sales, as shown in Figure 6.7:

Month	Monthly Sales	Year-to-Date Sales
January	$ 500,000	$ 500,000
February	$ 1,500,050	$ 2,000,050
March	$ 3,300,027	$ 5,300,077
April	$ 4,960,000	$10,260,070
May		

Figure 6.7   Partial sales figures for Engulf & Devour

Notice that something funny happens to the year-to-date sales when the total exceeds ten-million dollars. Somehow you lose seven dollars in the calculation! As a number exceeds the number of digits that can be saved, GW-BASIC is forced to throw away something, so it keeps the numbers on the left (obviously, millions are more important than single dollars) and discards the digit to the right. The example in Figure 6.7 is only for illustration. In a real single-precision calculation, the error will depend on the specific values being added. The important thing to keep in mind is that if you perform calculations close to the precision limits of a variable type, certain inaccuracies can creep in.

Let's consider again the problem of summing the sales of Engulf & Devour. If single-precision variables won't work, is there something else that you can use? Fortunately, the answer is yes: double-precision. Double-precision numbers use twice as much memory as single-precision (eight bytes instead of four), but double-precision numbers are capable of representing up to 16 digits of precision (which is enough to calculate even the federal budget).

You might ask yourself why one would bother with single-precision when double-precision seems to handle all cases without error. As always, there is no free lunch. Double-precision use can have some serious drawbacks. The first drawback is memory storage. Double-precision requires twice as much memory as single-precision. This isn't much of a drawback if you are writing a personal checkbook program that handles less than 100 entries per month. But, if the program needs to handle tens or hundreds of thousands of entries, you could run out of memory fast. The second drawback is speed. If you do not have a special piece of hardware called a *floating-point co-processor* on your system, it could easily take four times as long to perform a double-precision calculation as a single-precision one. If you are performing tens of thousands of calculations, the double-precision routine could take a great deal longer to finish.

What it really comes down to is balancing requirements. If you need more than six or seven digits of precision, you *must* select double-precision. If you don't need great precision and have many calculations to perform, use single-precision. If you only have a few variables or calculations to make, splurge and use double-precision; at some point or other it will pay off in avoided headaches.

Arrays

Imagine that you are approached by the owner of a rabbit farm and asked to write a simple program to keep track of unit production on a weekly basis (where, in this case, unit production translates into number of rabbits born that week). One way to attack this problem would be to create 52 separate variables, such as:

```
UP01 = 10
UP02 = 20
UP03 = 42
       .
       .
       .
```

Needless to say, such an approach would be tedious to set up and would be extremely clumsy to use. Fortunately, GW-BASIC lets the user take a more intelligent approach through the use of a variable *array*. An array is recognized as a variable name followed by a set of parentheses which contains numbers or other variable names separated by commas. The variables or constants within the parentheses are the *indices* used to select the particular *array element*. Returning to our rabbit farm example, you can define a unit production array of 52 elements where the single index represents the week within the year. In this case, you could now save the weekly data as:

UP(1) = 10
UP(2) = 20
UP(3) = 42
.
.
.

At first glance, this may not seem like much of an improvement because you've simply replaced similar but unique variable names with a single name followed by a number. In actuality, you've taken a major step forward that lets you read, store, and process these related numbers as one unit. By replacing the constant inside the parentheses with an integer variable, you can now use software loops (to be covered in Chapter 7) to search for the largest element, the smallest element, etc. in the array. The index value must be an integer because it doesn't make much sense to talk about fractional elements. (You either want the contents of element 2 or the contents of element 3. The contents of element 2.7 has no meaning).

Although the index defining a specific array element must be an integer constant or a variable, the element itself can be an integer, single-precision, double-precision, or string type (you'll learn about character strings a bit later in this chapter). An array element can be used anywhere a variable of the same type is allowed. One interesting limitation is that because an array index must be an integer, and only positive index values are allowed, then the maximum allowed index value is 32767. Another important point is that arrays start with the element (0) rather than (1). Programmers frequently ignore the 0th element because using it makes index calculations clumsy. For example, the program to count monthly rabbit unit production started with element UP(1) rather than UP(0). This is perfectly legitimate and makes sense to the programmer because most people associate the first week in the year with the number 1 rather than the number 0. All that happens is that the memory location associated with UP(0) is never read from nor written to. You only need to remember the zero element when printing the values of the array. Because GW-BASIC doesn't know that you are ignoring this element, it will attempt to print it out. One easy way to avoid headaches is to use the *OPTION BASE* command to define the lowest subscript value. This statement is one of two forms:

OPTION BASE 0

or

OPTION BASE 1

In the first case, *all* arrays will start with the 0th element. In the second case, *all* arrays start with a subscript of 1. Therefore, if you never use element 0 in arrays, the command OPTION BASE 1 tells GW-BASIC not to create them in the first place. Unfortunately, GW-BASIC does not let you specify only some arrays for the OPTION BASE 1. If you *do* need a 0 element for some of your arrays, you will have to deal with unwanted 0 elements in the other arrays.

So far, we've discussed what are called single-dimensional arrays. These arrays only have one index value. Imagine that the rabbit farm has been in operation for several years and you need to access the weekly unit production information for several years. You can define unique arrays for each year, or you can add a second index that correlates to the year. The easiest way to visualize a two-dimensional array is as a plastic ice-cube tray (see Figure 6.8). In the case of the unit production array, you would now have:

```
UP(1,1) = 10
UP(1,2) = 20
UP(1,3) = 42
      .
      .
      .
UP(1,12)= 89
```

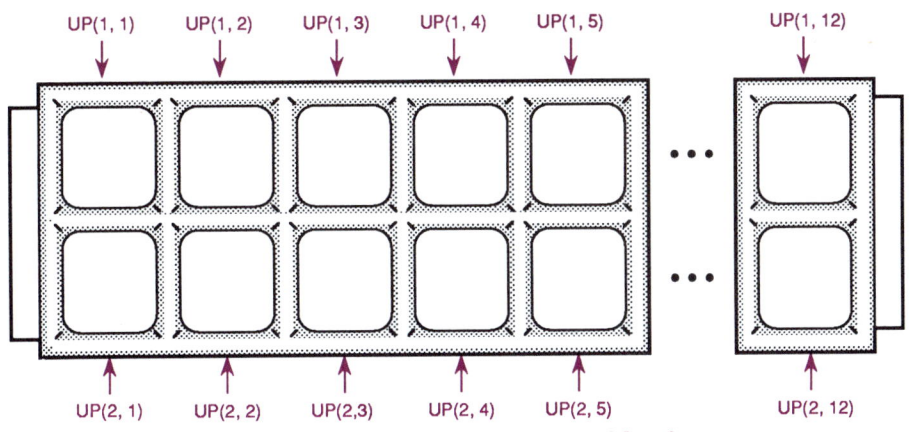

Figure 6.8   Two-dimensional array for rabbit farm

for the first year, and:

UP(2,1) = 100
UP(2,2) = 125
UP(2,3) = 153
    .
    .
    .
UP(2,12)= 349

for the second year. Because each dimension is an integer, each can go up to 32767, so you can store the weekly rabbit production for more years than recorded history (the Greek Bronze Age described in Homer's works apparently occurred less than 3500 years ago).

As you can see, arrays make it very easy to manipulate large amounts of data. This can also be a trap! Even though GW-BASIC allows arrays to have up to 255 separate dimensions (255 separate indices separated by commas), it is usually a good idea to avoid arrays that have more than three or four index variables. Keeping track of the meaning of many individual index parameters can get very confusing. In addition, the more index variables you have, the longer GW-BASIC takes to calculate the position of the specific array element.

Strings

So far, you have been exposed to several different ways to represent and store numeric information. What about letters and words? GW-BASIC lets you store this information in structures known as *strings*. Strings can be thought of as variable length single-dimensional arrays. Generally, they are assigned values enclosed between sets of double quotes ("). For example, let's assume that you have defined variables with any letter between F and P to be strings with the following statement:

```
DEFSTR F-P
```

The following statement tells GW-BASIC to make NAMEFIELD of length zero:

```
NAMEFIELD = ""
```

Notice that there are no spaces between the sets of double quotes. This forces NAMEFIELD to be an *empty* string and the string length is zero. Now let's look at a slight variation from the previous example:

```
NAMEFIELD = " "
```

This time, there is a space between the set of double quotes, so the length of the string becomes 1 because it contains one blank. Now a more typical string application:

```
NAMEFIELD = "Joe Hacker"
```

In this case, the string is of length 10 (nine letters plus one blank) and contains both uppercase and lowercase letters. GW-BASIC strings can contain all of the normal typewriter characters and even certain special ones known as control characters. The only real constraint is that the entire string cannot exceed 255 characters in length. This limitation is important because GW-BASIC allows one operation on strings; this is called *concatenation* (joining together). The following lines of code illustrate concatenation:

```
FIRSTNAME = "Joe"
LASTNAME = "Hacker"
FULLNAME = FIRSTNAME + LASTNAME
```

If three variables FIRSTNAME, LASTNAME, and FULLNAME have been defined as strings, the contents of FULLNAME would be "JoeHacker" which consists of the contents of LASTNAME tacked directly to the back of the contents of FIRSTNAME. Notice that no space was inserted between the two names (as humans would automatically do). GW-BASIC did *exactly* what you told it to do and no more. If you want to create a string that contains a space between the names, modify the third line to:

```
FULLNAME = FIRSTNAME + " " + LASTNAME
```

A string constant consisting of a single blank was inserted to make the contents of FULLNAME into "Joe Hacker" as desired. If the program is supposed to create the full name as *lastname*, a comma, and the *firstname*. This can be done with:

```
FULLNAME = LASTNAME + ", " + FIRSTNAME
```

Note that the string constant consists of a comma and a blank in order to put a space between the first name and the comma.

You can define a string array the same way you can define a numeric array. Each string is accessed as a name followed by a set of parentheses containing the index values. It is interesting that elements within a string array can be different lengths. For example, if you declare a string array of four elements called PHRASES, the following is perfectly legal in GW-BASIC:

```
PHRASES(1) = "This is a long string"
PHRASES(2) = "Hello"
PHRASES(3) = ""
PHRASES(4) = "1237"
```

In this example, the first array element is a string of length 21, the second of length 5, the third of length 0, and the fourth of length 4. The fourth string is interesting because it appears to represent a numeric quantity. As far as GW-BASIC is concerned, it is simply another string of characters which just happen to be numbers. GW-BASIC does not know how to add or subtract such strings. Chapter 12 discusses built-in functions (such as VAL and STR$) which can convert a number to a string and vice-versa. The VAL function can be used to convert the contents of PHRASES(4) into an integer which can be manipulated as a normal number.

Declaring the Various Variable Types

You are probably wondering how variables are defined to be of a particular type. The simplest way is to use the *type declaration character*. This is a special character that always trails the variable name. Figure 6.9 illustrates the various type declaration characters recognized by GW-BASIC.

```
$       String
%       Integer
!       Single-precision
#       Double-precision
```

Figure 6.9 Type declaration characters

The following are examples of various variable names and their types:

```
A$, FIRSTNAME$, ADDRESS$            Strings
I%, DAYSINYEAR%, PLAYERSONTEAM%     Integers
F!, TOTALSALES!, FEETPERMETER!      Single-precision
Z#, GALAXYDIAMETER#, FEDBUDGET#     Double-precision
```

GW-BASIC always gives precedence to type declaration characters over other forms of declaration. The main drawback to type declaration characters is that typing the character after every use of the name can become tedious (especially if a complex program performs a great deal of computation).

Another drawback is that the original BASIC language allowed variables with the same name but different type declaration characters to exist at the same time. This was because the original BASICs only allowed two-character names (therefore, limiting programmer options). In such cases, the variables A$, A%, and A! were treated as separate variables and all existed at the same time containing totally different information! Needless to say, some of these old programs could be very confusing.

A third drawback to using type definition characters is that if you forget the type declaration character, GW-BASIC automatically declares the untyped variable to be single-precision. This may not necessarily be what you want.

Fortunately for us, GW-BASIC provides an alternate way to declare variable types via the commands DEFINT, DEFSNG, DEFDBL, and DEFSTR. The format for these commands is as follows:

```
DEFtype I-K,M,N-Q
```

where type stands for either INT, SNG, DBL, or STR (INTeger, SiNGle-precision, DouBLe-precision, and STRing, respectively). The letters following the DEF keyword are the beginning letters or range of letters that will be automatically assigned to that variable type. For example, if type is INT, then all variables starting with the letters I,J,K,M,N,O,P, and Q will automatically be defined as integers unless the variable has a type definition character (which overrides the default definition). The dash separating two letters tells GW-BASIC that you want to define a range of letters that will be of that type. The same thing can be done for automatically defined single-precision, double-precision, and string variables. Care should be taken when defining ranges to avoid overlapping. For example:

```
DEFINT A-D
DEFSNG C,E-G
```

has a conflict because variables beginning with the letter C are already covered by the range A-D. Even though your particular GW-BASIC program may handle this conflict gracefully, this type of conflict should be avoided because there is no guarantee that future versions of the language will act in the same way.

The main disadvantage of the DEFtype statements is that they can force unusual (cryptic) names that may be a problem later on. Of course, both techniques can be used in the same program to provide maximum flexibility.

Conversion Between Dissimilar Types

One final topic that should be covered here is conversion between numeric types. As explained earlier in this chapter, the integer and floating-point types of variables use different amounts of storage and can hold numbers of varying precision. This can sometimes get programmers into trouble, so you need to understand how GW-BASIC will treat these conflicts.

If a number of one type is assigned to a variable of a different type, the precision kept will be that of the *target* variable (the one to the left of the equal sign). For example:

```
I% = 6.25
```

will result in the integer being assigned a value of 6. The fractional part (.25) is discarded because an integer can't represent it. The same sort of thing happens when double-precision numbers are assigned to single-precision variables. Therefore,

```
SPVAL! = 123.45678901#
```

will result in a value of 123.4568 in the variable SPVAL! because single-precision numbers are only accurate to approximately 7 places. Notice that something else happened when converting from double-precision to single-precision. The last digit in SPVAL! became an 8 rather than a 7 because GW-BASIC always rounds up when converting from a lower precision to a higher one.

Another conversion rule is that no improvement in precision occurs when converting from a lower precision to a higher one. For example:

```
A# = 123.456789#
B! = A#
C# = B!
```

assigns a double-precision constant to the double-precision variable A# and then assigns the double-precision variable to a single-precision one. This forces the contents of B! to round to 123.4568 (as explained earlier). The third line assigns the contents of the single-precision variable B! to another double-precision variable (C#). When this code is executed, C# will end up with the value 123.4568000 because that is as accurate as the number was received from B!

It is important to note that the conversion rules previously described apply any time that numerical values are evaluated. Therefore, conversion errors can occur in simple assignment statements and as a result of evaluating a numerical expression (addition, multiplication, etc.).

Another rule that was briefly mentioned is that GW-BASIC always converts numbers of different types to the higher precision *before* evaluating the expression. The following line multiplies an integer by a double-precision number and stores the result in a single-precision variable:

```
SPVAL! = IVAL% * DPVAL#
```

In this case, GW-BASIC first converts the value in the integer up to a double-precision form. Next, a normal multiplication is performed between two double-precision values, yielding a double-precision result. Because the answer is supposed to be stored in a single-precision variable, GW-BASIC performs the appropriate rounding and stores the result in A! as instructed. If the multiplication had been between a single-precision value and a double-precision one, the single-precision value would have been converted to a double-precision one and everything else would have occurred as in the example with the integer.

One last caution about conversions. Imagine that you have a single-precision variable called FPVAL and an integer called IVAL. What do you expect to be the result of the following short program?

```
100 FPVAL! = 78525.0
200 IVAL% = FPVAL!
300 PRINT FPVAL!,IVAL%
400 END
```

Are you surprised to get an error message instead of a numeric value? As previously discussed, the largest positive number that can be represented by an integer is 32767, which is appreciably smaller than the number in FPVAL. Newer versions of GW-BASIC will stop execution and display the message:

```
Overflow on line 200
```

Chapter 6

to indicate where the problem occurred. Older versions of GW-BASIC (or even current versions of other BASIC interpreters) may not be as helpful or may not even detect the error. Therefore, it is always a good idea to keep overflow in mind as a potential problem.

Sample Program

This chapter introduced the characteristics and limitations of the different variable types. It also explained what arrays are and how they can be used. The following sample program illustrates the material covered in this chapter. It asks for the name, price, and inventory number for three different items and saves the information into appropriate variables. After all of the information has been stored, it clears the screen and displays the information again, including a total for the value of the three items. Admittedly, this is not very useful in its current form, but in later chapters you will expand it to make it more powerful and useful.

```
100 'This is an extremely simple personal inventory program
200 'intended to illustrate the use of simple variables and
300 'arrays. Because you haven't yet learned about program flow
400 'control, the program is designed without the benefit
500 'of loops.
600 DEFINT I-M
700 DEFDBL A-H,O-Z
800 DEFSTR N
900 DIM NEWNAME(3),ITEMNUMBER(3),PRICE(3)
1000 CLS
1100 PRINT "Welcome to the Very Limited Home Inventory"
1200 PRINT "Program. This program can only keep three items"
1300 PRINT "in memory. Please enter the name, value, and"
1400 PRINT "item number of each item when requested to do"
1500 PRINT "so. The item number must be in the range -32768"
1600 PRINT "to +32767 and will be used for inventory."
1700 PRINT "Please provide the first item name as a string"
1800 INPUT NEWNAME(1)
1900 PRINT "Please provide the item price (i.e., 753.27 )"
2000 INPUT PRICE(1)
2100 PRINT "Please provide inventory number as a whole number"
2200 INPUT ITEMNUMBER(1)
```

```
2300 CLS
2400 PRINT "Please provide name of second item"
2500 INPUT NEWNAME(2)
2600 PRINT "Please provide price of second item"
2700 INPUT PRICE(2)
2800 PRINT "Please provide inventory number for second item"
2900 INPUT ITEMNUMBER(2)
3000 CLS
3100 PRINT "Please provide name of third item"
3200 INPUT NEWNAME(3)
3300 PRINT "Please provide price of third item"
3400 INPUT PRICE(3)
3500 PRINT "Please provide inventory number of third item"
3600 INPUT ITEMNUMBER(3)
3700 CLS
3800 PRINT "The following items are entered in the file:"
3900 PRINT:PRINT
4000 PRINT NEWNAME(1)
4100 PRINT "$",PRICE(1),"ID # ",ITEMNUMBER(1)
4200 PRINT
4300 PRINT NEWNAME(2)
4400 PRINT "$",PRICE(2),"ID # ",ITEMNUMBER(2)
4500 PRINT
4600 PRINT NEWNAME(3)
4700 PRINT "$",PRICE(3),"ID # ",ITEMNUMBER(3)
4800 PRINT:PRINT "* * * * * * * * * * * * * * * * *"
4900 NETWORTH# = PRICE(1)+PRICE(2)+PRICE(3)
5000 PRINT "Your total net worth is $";NETWORTH#
5100 END
```

The first five lines (which begin with a single quote) are purely comments and are not executed by GW-BASIC. Lines 600 through 900 define the beginning letters for various variable types and *dimensions* the three arrays that you want to create. Please note that line 800 defines the letter *N* for the beginning of string variables. Therefore, when you dimension NEWNAME(3) in line 900, you are defining a *string array* that can go from NEWNAME(0) to NEWNAME(3). Line 1000 is a GW-BASIC built-in function that clears the entire screen and repositions the cursor at the top left corner. Lines 1100 through 1600 are a greeting message to the user. Lines 1700 through 2200 request the information associated with the first item. The section starting at line 3700 clears the screen and displays the contents of the array elements. Finally, line 4900 computes the user's net worth by adding the value of all three prices.

Summary

In this chapter, you learned the characteristics and limitations of the four GW-BASIC variable types (integers, single-precision, double-precision, and strings). You also learned how to define the different types of variables using both the type declaration characters (%, !, #, $) and the starting letter method (using DEFINT, DEFSNG, DEFDBL and DEFSTR). The concept of arrays was explained, as well as GW-BASIC's rules for converting information from one numeric variable type to that of another. Finally, a sample program illustrated the proper use of the different variable types and arrays.

You now know enough about GW-BASIC to write programs that can execute a precise series of operations without variation. What would you do if you needed to change the sequence of operations based on the result of a comparison of two quantities? Such situations are handled by a class of GW-BASIC statements called *program flow control*. These statements are the subjects of Chapter 7.

Quiz

1. How many characters does GW-BASIC look at when attempting to recognize a variable?
2. All GW-BASIC variable names must start with a what?
3. What range of numbers can be represented by an integer?
4. Approximately how many digits of precision can be held by a single-precision number? A double-precision number?
5. What GW-BASIC statement would you employ to start all arrays with element 1 rather than element 0?

Chapter 7
Controlling Program Flow

In This Chapter

It is virtually impossible to write a program of any complexity without needing to vary program execution based on some criteria. For example, you may want to take a different action if the contents of a variable are negative rather than positive. If you write a program to search an array for a particular value, how will you know when you have found a match? These are the types of actions supported by program control statements. In this chapter, you will learn the various ways to control program execution and the circumstances under which each should be used.

IF Statements

One of the simplest ways to affect program flow is through the use of the IF-THEN-ELSE statement. This statement is of the general form:

IF *expression* GOTO *line-number* [ELSE *clause*]

where the square brackets ([]) indicate that the ELSE term is optional. Thus, an example of the simplest form of IF statement is:

```
IF I%>0 GOTO 1000
```

which indicates that if the integer I% contains a positive number greater than 0, program execution should jump to line 1000; otherwise, execution will continue with the next line number. The expression in the IF statement can be anything that can be evaluated to a TRUE or FALSE condition. If a complex expression is to be evaluated, it can be contained within parentheses for clarity and can contain other parentheses to control the order of evaluation. For example:

```
IF (((A!-7.5)/2.0)>4.0) GOTO 800
```

tells GW-BASIC that it should transfer execution to line 800 if the evaluation of the numeric expression yields a TRUE result. In this particular example, execution jumps to line 800 when the value in the single-precision variable A! is greater than approximately 15.5, thus satisfying the condition. (Note that the value is approximately 15.5 because the evaluation of floating-point expressions is subject to a certain amount of rounding error.) The outermost set of parentheses in the previous example makes the line more readable for humans, but this set of parentheses is not needed by GW-BASIC. Thus, they can be deleted to yield:

```
IF ((A!-7.5)/2.0)>4.0 GOTO 800
```

Expressions in IF statements can also contain calls to functions. Functions are a form of built-in programs that perform specific tasks. The statement

```
IF (1.0-SIN(ALPHA))> 0.5 GOTO 2010
```

is an example of how a built-in function (in this case for the trigonometric sine of an angle in radians) can be used as part of the IF expression. GW-BASIC's built-in functions are discussed individually in Chapter 12.

As mentioned earlier, the longer form of a GOTO-type IF statement can have an ELSE part followed by an expression. This provides for an alternative action if the expression is not TRUE. The previous example could be modified to:

```
IF (1.0-SIN(ALPHA))>0.5 GOTO 2010 ELSE J%=1
```

where the second statement J%=1 is executed only if the result of the computation turned out less than or equal to 0.5 so that the GOTO was not implemented. The next statement after the IF statement then is executed on completion of the ELSE clause.

One other form of the IF statement exists:

IF *expression* THEN *clause* [ELSE *clause*]

In this case, program execution always continues with the program line following the IF statement; the difference is that one of two program clauses is executed as a result of this statement. A clause can be any valid GW-BASIC statement (such as the assignment statement J%=1) or it can consist of a group of statements separated by colons. Imagine that you want to set an integer variable J% to 1 if the result of a mathematical expression is TRUE and set J% to 0 otherwise. The following statement would implement this:

```
IF (A! * B!)> 0.727 THEN J%=1 ELSE J%=0
```

In this case, if the result of the multiplication of the single-precision variables A! and B! is positive and greater than 0.727 in magnitude, J% is assigned the value 1. If the result of the multiplication is a negative number or a positive number smaller than 0.727, J% is set to 0.

Because any valid GW-BASIC statement is legal for the clauses of the IF statement, it is also possible to invoke functions from these statements. For example:

```
IF BLANKIT% = 1 THEN CLS ELSE BEEP
```

Here, GW-BASIC is told to call the built-in function CLS (which clears the display screen and relocates the cursor at the top left corner) if the integer BLANKIT% contains a value of 1. If the integer variable contains a value other than 1, GW-BASIC calls a totally different built-in function that causes a short duration beep to play through the computer speaker.

One restriction should be mentioned here: all parts of an IF statement (including the THEN clause and ELSE clause) must be part of *one* statement line. Each clause can consist of several instructions separated by colons, but the entire IF structure must be on one line. For example:

```
2010 IF (A%=3) OR (A%=5) THEN X#=3.5:J%=0 ELSE X#=0.0:J%=12
```

is perfectly legal because the entire statement uses only one line number and the various parts of each clause are separated by colons. On the other hand:

```
2010 IF ((A%=3) OR (A%=5)) THEN J%=0
2020 ELSE J%=12
```

is illegal because the ELSE part is on a separate line with a different line number. In these examples, there was yet another twist: a compound expression was evaluated that is TRUE if either A% is 3 or 5. This is accomplished through the use of the *OR* keyword (which is a Boolean operator). You could have also used other Boolean operators in the expression. Thus:

```
2010 IF (((J%=1) AND (C$="JOE")) OR (D#=0.0)) GOTO 3000
```

is a statement that requires that either D# be 0.0 or that both J% be 1 and the string C$ contain "JOE" (note how the parentheses accomplish this grouping).

GOTO Statements

You have already seen the GOTO statement as part of an IF statement, but GOTOs can also exist as independent statements. They are used whenever a section of code is terminated. Consider a case where you want to execute one group of lines if an integer I% is positive or zero, and a different set of lines if the integer contains a negative number:

```
2000 IF I%<0GOTO 3000
2100             'Here begins the code for I% positive
2200
2300
2400
2500
2600 GOTO 3300   'Jump to next section of common code
```

```
3000               'Here begins the code for I% negative
3100
3200
3300               'Here begins the common code
```

Line 2000 acts as a two-way branch. If I% contains a value that is greater than or equal to 0, program execution continues with line 2100. When GW-BASIC reaches line 2600, the GOTO statement forces an unconditional branch to line number 3300 and resumes execution there. If, on the other hand, I% were negative, execution would jump from line 2000 to line 3000 and eventually also arrive at line 3300. GW-BASIC does not require that both branches of the IF return to a common statement, but human beings tend to think in terms of action "frames" where one of two actions is taken to solve a problem before moving on to another task. If you were to insert a line:

```
3295 GOTO 40
```

then execution of the "negative" branch results in the program performing an unconditional jump to line 40 when the end of the I% negative program section is reached. This simple example illustrates the danger of reckless use of GOTO statements: you can quickly end up with programs that seem to hop around all over the place and are extremely difficult to understand and debug. Even some software professionals vehemently insist that GOTOs should never be used. Often beginning programmers overuse GOTO statements to the point that their programs almost become unusable. If you carefully plan what your program is supposed to do and in what order, you find that your program has a minimal number of GOTOs and that most of them are justified. As with most things in life, moderation is best.

GOSUB and RETURN Statements

Another useful command for controlling program flow is the GOSUB statement. As you probably observed during the previous discussion, GOTO statements work in one direction. When a

GOTO is executed, GW-BASIC makes no attempt to keep track of where program execution came from. Using GOTOs is like jumping out of an airplane with a parachute; once you let go of the aircraft, there is no easy way to get back! The GOSUB statement is similar to a GOTO except in one important respect: it keeps track of the exact line from which it came and returns to the next executable statement after the GOSUB when a RETURN statement is encountered. Using GOSUB is analogous to using a rope to lower yourself into a cave; once you are done exploring, you have every intention of using the rope to get back to the spot from which you started. For example:

```
2000
2100 GOSUB 9000
2200
2300
  .
  .
  .
9000            'Beginning of a subroutine
9100
9200
9300
9400 RETURN     'End of the subroutine
```

Imagine that GW-BASIC encountered line 2100 while executing a program. It first stores information about the location of the GOSUB statement on a *stack* before performing a GOTO to line 9000 (a stack is a sort of scratch pad area that stores things in order). Execution then resumes at line 9000 and continues until the end of the subroutine is reached. Each subroutine should be written to guarantee that all possible branches within it eventually lead to a RETURN statement. This is important because the RETURN statement is what instructs GW-BASIC to resume execution at the next statement after the GOSUB statement. In the previous example, execution resumes at line 2200 after the RETURN at line 9400 is processed. Care should be taken to prevent program execution from unintentionally falling into a subroutine, because unpredictable things can happen if a return statement is encountered where there is no address on the stack to return to!

A brief discussion of the concept of a stack is probably in order. Stacks generally operate on the concept of Last-In/First-

Out (LIFO). This means that if you first write a 10 to the stack, then a 400, and then a 60 to it, a stack-read operation at this point will return a value of 60. A subsequent stack-read will return a 400, because this is the second most recent item (see Figure 7.1). Because stacks are intended to hold many numbers in the order in which they were received, GW-BASIC can handle any combination of GOSUBs and RETURNs as long as the stack is big enough. GW-BASIC uses free memory for this stack, so the more free memory available, the deeper the routines can be nested. This also implies that the maximum number of GOSUBs in a row can also be affected by increases in memory use due to additions to the program or enlargement of arrays.

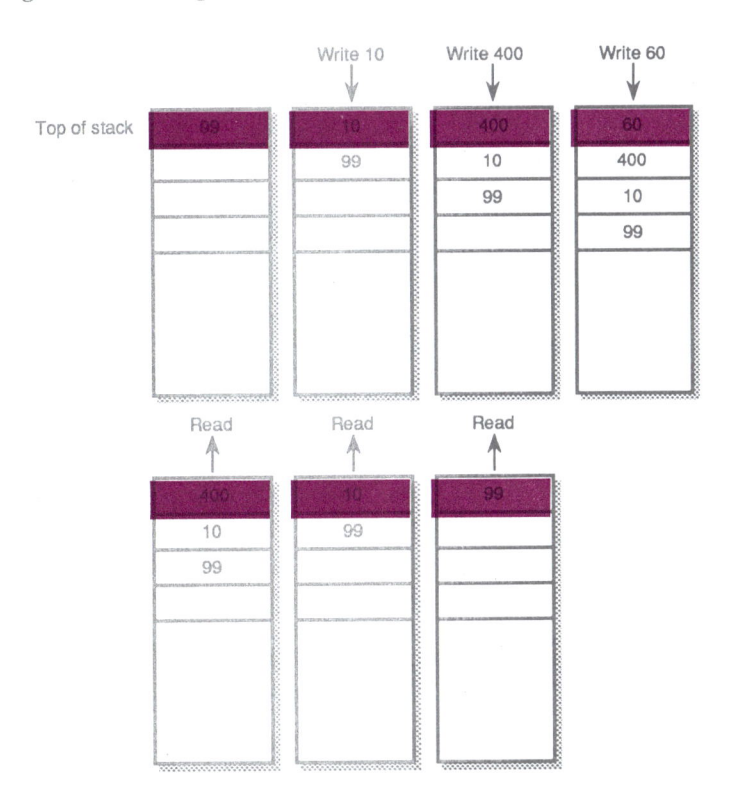

Figure 7.1 Typical stack operations.

In summation, subroutine use in GW-BASIC is extremely flexible. Subroutines can call other subroutines. They can be located anywhere in the program but should be preceded by STOP, END, or GOTO statements to prevent accidental execution. Subroutines can contain multiple RETURN statements if necessary; whichever

RETURN statement is encountered first will cause GW-BASIC to transfer execution back to the line that called it.

ON Statements

The ON statement is extremely powerful and can deal with many types of conditions. These statements direct execution to one of multiple lines based on the value of the expression immediately after the ON keyword. For clarity, this section deals only with the ON/GOSUB and ON/GOTO variants, because these are the forms most often used to intentionally control program flow. The generic forms of these statements are:

ON *expression* GOTO *line1[,line2,...]*
ON *expression* GOSUB *line1[,line2,...]*

where *expression* stands for a numeric expression or variable that is evaluated to an integer. The value of the expression must be in the range 0 to 255. All other values result in an Illegal function call error message. The numbers *line1*, *line2*, etc., refer to line numbers where program execution can start, depending on the value of the expression. If the result of the expression is 1, then execution branches to *line1*. If the expression evaluates to a 2, then *line2* is executed next, and so on. Because the action word in the second command is GOSUB, it should not surprise you that the line numbers pointed at by *line1*, *line2*, etc., must be the beginning of subroutines. In the case of the ON/GOSUB statement, GW-BASIC will expect to eventually encounter a RETURN statement to restore execution to the next executable statement after the ON/GOSUB structure. Conversely, the ON/GOTO command will get into serious trouble if you point to the beginning of a subroutine. Thus, you must be careful not to mix subroutine calls and simple GW-BASIC lines when using these two statements. In either case, if the value of the expression is 0 or if it is greater than the number of arguments present after the GOSUB/GOTO keyword, no branch occurs and the program continues at the next executable statement.

These ON statements enable you to implement constructs known as *n-way branching*. They are the equivalent of having a large group of IF statements in a row such as:

```
2000 IF I%=1 GOTO 4000
2100 IF I%=2 GOTO 5013
2200 IF I%=3 GOTO 1270
2300 IF I%=4 GOTO 5013
```

or

```
3000 IF N%=1 GOSUB 2501
2310 IF N%=2 GOSUB 42
3200 IF N%=3 GOSUB 2501
3300 IF N%=4 GOSUB 2501
```

By the way, the line numbers used as targets in ON statements do not need to be unique; the preceding examples illustrate that several values of expression can transfer execution to the same line number. The ON equivalents for the preceding statements would be:

```
2000 ON I% GOTO 4000,5013,1270,5013
```

and

```
3000 ON N% GOSUB 2501,42,2501,2501
```

Because program execution depends on the evaluation of the expression, it is strongly recommended that the expression be either a simple integer or a mathematical expression that evaluates into an integer. This will minimize possible rounding errors that can lead to what humans may perceive as erratic program execution.

FOR and NEXT Statements

GW-BASIC provides several methods for performing software loops. One of the most commonly used methods is the FOR/NEXT control structure. These statements are used to execute sections of the program a set number of times. The following is the general form of the structure:

Chapter 7

FOR *loopvar* = *startval* TO *endval*[STEP *increment*]
  .
  .
  .
NEXT [*loopvar*][,*loopvar2*,...]

where *loopvar* represents a variable, *startval* represents the initial value to be assigned to *loopvar*, *endval* represents the final value against which *loopvar* will be compared, and *increment* is the value to be added to *loopvar* each time that the loop is completed. If the optional STEP parameter is omitted, GW-BASIC assumes an increment of 1. If *increment* is positive or omitted, the following occurs: *Loopvar* is assigned the *startval* and is then compared against *endval*. If *loopvar* is less than or equal to *endval*, the statements between the FOR and NEXT statements are executed. If program execution reaches the NEXT statement, *increment* is added to *loopvar* and the comparison is repeated against *endval*. The loop will continue for as long as *loopvar* is less than or equal to *endval*. When *loopvar* finally exceeds *endvar*, the statements in the loop are skipped and execution resumes with the first executable statement after the NEXT statement. If *startval* is greater than *endval* for a positive *increment*, the loop will never be executed.

If a negative *increment* is specified, the sense of the loop test is reversed. The loop starts with *loopvar* being assigned the value *startval* and compared to *endval*. If *loopvar* is greater than or equal to *endval*, the loop is executed and the negative *increment* is added to *loopvar* when the NEXT statement is encountered (to make *loopvar* less positive). As long as *loopvar* is greater than or equal to *endval*, the loop will continue to execute. If *loopvar* becomes less than *endval*, program control will shift to the next executable statement after the NEXT. If *startval* is less than *endval* when a negative *increment* is specified, the entire loop will be skipped and execution will resume with the first executable statement after the NEXT. Now let's look at some examples.

```
1000 FOR I%=1 TO 10
1100 J% = I%*2+7
1200 PRINT J%
1300 NEXT I%
```

This simple example will result in output that looks like:

9
11

13
15
17
19
21
23
25
27

If you now change this example by adding an increment of 3, you get the following program and output:

```
1000 FOR I%=1 TO 10 STEP 3
1100 J% = I%*2+7
1200 PRINT J%
1300 NEXT I%
```

9
15
21
27

A negative increment could result in the following example:

```
2000 FAC%=1
2100 FOR MYVAL%=6 TO 1 STEP -1
2200 FAC% = FAC% * MYVAL%
2300 NEXT
2400 PRINT FAC%
```

This program computes 6 x 5 x 4 x 3 x 2 x 1, which is known to mathematicians as six factorial. Note that in line 2300 the variable name was omitted from the NEXT statement. Whenever the variable is omitted, GW-BASIC matches the NEXT statement with the innermost (most recently invoked) FOR statement.

GW-BASIC allows FOR loops to be *nested*. This means that one or more FOR/NEXT loops can be contained within another FOR/NEXT loop. The only requirement is that the inner loops must be completely contained by the next higher level of loop. Otherwise, the interpreter could get very "confused." Because of the potential for confusion, the NEXT statements of nested loops should provide loop variables to force detection of logic errors. For example:

```
2000 FOR I%=1 TO 10
2100
2200
2500 FOR J%=2 TO 6 STEP 2
2600
2700
2800 NEXT J%
2900
3000 FOR K%=9 TO 5 STEP -2
3100
3200 NEXT K%
3300
3400 NEXT I%
```

is an illustration of a *legal* nested set of loops. Lines 2000 through 3400 comprise the outer loop controlled by the variable I%. An interior loop controlled by J% is defined between lines 2500 and 2800. A second loop controlled by K% is defined between 3000 and 3200. Because both interior loops are completely contained within the larger loop, GW-BASIC has no trouble interpreting this correctly.

Now let's modify the example slightly and move the NEXT associated with J% inside of the K% loop:

```
2000 FOR I%=1 TO 10
2100
2200
2500 FOR J%=2 TO 6 STEP 2
2600
2700
2900
3000 FOR K%=9 TO 5 STEP -2
```

```
3100
3150 NEXT J%
3200 NEXT K%
3300
3400 NEXT I%
```

Because this makes the two loops interlock, this modification violates the rules and results in an error message. This example also illustrates the value of providing loop variables for NEXT statements. If you had not used the variables, GW-BASIC would assume that the NEXT statement on line 3150 belonged to the K% loop and that the NEXT at line 3200 belonged to the J%. This clearly is not what was intended.

For best execution time efficiency and repeatability, FOR loops should use integer counters. Execution speed will increase as a result of the elimination of variable names from the NEXT statements. Variable names should only be removed from NEXT statements when it is certain that the loops are properly defined to prevent overlap.

WHILE and WEND Statements

Another program control structure provided by GW-BASIC is the WHILE/WEND loop. Unlike the FOR/NEXT loop, which executes a specified number of times, the WHILE loop continues to run as long as the loop condition remains TRUE. For example:

```
100 DEFINT I-N:DEFSNG O-Z
200 I=1:CLS
300 WHILE I=1
400 PRINT "Please enter a number for which you want"
500 PRINT "a square root or enter a negative number"
600 PRINT "to quit the program."
700 INPUT VALUE
800 IF VALUE < 0! THEN I=0:ROOT=0!:GOTO 1200
900 ROOT = SQR(VALUE)
1000 PRINT "The square root of",VALUE," is",ROOT
1100 INPUT "Press enter to continue...";J
1200 CLS
```

```
1300 WEND
1400 END
```

    This simple program requests an input value and prints a line that consists of the input and the square root of that value. The only way to get out of the WHILE loop is to enter a negative value. Because the GW-BASIC routine does not allow for the taking of a square root of a negative number, you can test for a negative and use it as a trigger to change the loop variable controlling the WHILE. Line 1100 may seem strange at first glance; you request an input but never use it anywhere! This is done to slow down the machine. If 1100 were not there, the machine would immediately perform the CLS in line 1200 without giving the user a chance to read the answer. Because INPUT allows for a brief message, you don't need an extra PRINT statement to generate the message for continued operation.

    One unnecessary action is taken in line 300. Because of the way GW-BASIC defines TRUE and FALSE, the statement can be simplified to:

```
300 WHILE I
```

and the program will work exactly the same. GW-BASIC always interprets an answer of 0 as FALSE and anything else as TRUE. This is a useful feature, but other BASIC programs may not interpret these answers the same way, so it is usually best to be safe and define the condition fully to avoid portability problems.

Sample Program

Now that you have covered various ways of performing program control and loops, let's return to the mini card index program that was introduced in Chapter 6. You can now expand the functionality of the program by using WHILE and FOR loops to let you view or modify any record at any time.

```
100 'This is the enhanced version of a simple card index
200 'program created to illustrate the use of simple
300 'loop structures.
400 DEFINT I-M
```

```
500 DEFDBL A-H,P-Z
600 DEFSTR N-O
700 INUMCARDS = 10
900 DIM NEWNAME(10),ITEMNUMBER(10),PRICE(10)
1000 CLS
1100 PRINT "Welcome to the Limited Home Inventory Program"
1200 PRINT "This program can now keep ten items in memory."
1300 PRINT "Please enter the name, value, and item number of"
1400 PRINT "each item when requested to do so. The item "
1500 PRINT "number must be in the range -32768 to 32767 and"
1600 PRINT "will be used as an inventory number."
1700 PRINT "The program will first ask you if you wish to"
1800 PRINT "enter a record or view a record. It will then"
1900 PRINT "ask for the record number. You may exit the"
2000 PRINT "program at any time by either entering the Q"
2100 PRINT "option when answering the enter/view question"
2200 PRINT "or by selecting record 0."
2300 PRINT
2400 INPUT "Press the return key to continue";K
2500 FOR I=1 TO INUMCARDS
2600 NEWNAME(I)="**** This is an uninitialized entry ****"
2700 ITEMNUMBER(I)= -32768!:NEXT
2800 '
2900 LOOPSWITCH = 1
3000 WHILE LOOPSWITCH
3100 CLS
3200 INPUT "Which record number";IREC
3300 IF IREC<1 OR IREC>INUMCARDS GOTO 6000
3400 PRINT:INPUT"Enter, View, or Quit (E,V,Q)";N1
3500 IF N1="e" OR N1="E" GOTO 4000
3600 IF N1="v" OR N1="V" GOTO 5000
3700 IF N1="q" OR N1="Q" GOTO 6000
3800 GOTO 3100
3900 '
4000 PRINT "Please provide the item name as a string"
4100 INPUT NEWNAME(IREC)
4200 PRINT "Please provide the item price (i.e., 753.27 )"
4300 INPUT PRICE(IREC)
4400 PRINT "Please provide inventory number as a whole number"
4500 INPUT ITEMNUMBER(IREC)
4600 GOTO 7000
4700 '
5000 PRINT "Here are the contents of record ",IREC
5100 PRINT:PRINT
```

```
5200 PRINT NEWNAME(IREC)
5300 PRINT "$",PRICE(IREC),"ID # ",ITEMNUMBER(IREC)
5400 INPUT "Press the return key to continue";K
5500 GOTO 7000
6000 LOOPSWITCH=0        'This will kill the loop
7000 WEND                'End of the outer loop
7100 '
7200 PRINT:PRINT "* * * * * * * * * * * * * * * * * *"
7300 NETWORTH# = 0#
7400 FOR I=1 TO INUMCARDS
7500 NETWORTH# = NETWORTH#+PRICE(I)
7600 NEXT I
7700 PRINT "Your total net worth is $";NETWORTH#
7800 END
```

There have been substantial changes. The entire active program is enclosed in a WHILE/WEND loop that starts on line 3000 and ends on line 7000. This enables you to enter or view any record as often as you want. The WHILE creates an infinite loop that only terminates when either a record is selected that is out of range or a Q or q is entered as the action selection (Edit, View, or Quit). Lines 3100 through 3800 perform input processing. They test for a valid record number and for a valid action. Notice that the action letter processing software checks for both lowercase and uppercase because the user may expect either to work. If the record selected is a valid number but the action letter is not recognized, the program loops back to line 3100, which will clear the screen and ask the questions again.

The code from lines 4000 to 4700 ask for the various entries in each record. When one record's worth of data has been entered, the program jumps to line 7000 to continue within the WHILE loop. Lines 5000 through 5500 display on the screen the data for a given record and then cause the program to pause. If line 5400 were not present, the program would display the data and then wind up again at line 3100, which clears the screen! Line 6000 simply changes the loop variable to a FALSE state to force a graceful exit.

In the previous discussion, the function of lines 2500 through 2800 was skipped because the program would work perfectly well without them. All they do is initialize some of the record variables to other than null states. GW-BASIC initializes all variables to either 0 or null strings. In Chapter 6's version of this program, if you request to view one of the records before it has been written to, the program displays a blank name field and zeros for both the price and inventory number. In the current program, lines 2500 through 2800 initialize all of the name fields to an error message that immediately informs the viewer that the record has not been written to yet. The program also initializes the inventory number to the largest negative integer to make it stand out.

Because of the loop, you can now dimension the list of items to be as big as you want. You may have noticed that throughout the program a variable, INUMCARDS, was used to control how many records can be processed. You can easily expand the number of records by changing only lines 700 and 900; the rest of the program does not need to change to accommodate more records! This trick is often used in advanced programming: create variables that define the limits for arrays and records. Then, when you need to change the information, you only need to change a few lines rather than having to go through the entire program looking for constants to change.

Reader Challenge

The preceding sample program illustrates several of the concepts introduced in this chapter, but several improvements still can be made to it. Your first challenge is to make a relatively easy improvement. Change the code around line 3300 so that a positive record number greater than INUMCARDS prints a warning message and then loops back to 3100 to restart the loop. It may require several lines of code, but the lines are currently numbered in increments of 100, so you won't have any trouble inserting new lines where you need them (this is why you should number lines by large increments when you develop small programs).

The second challenge is a bit more difficult because it requires reorganizing the program. Can you determine how to change the code for the Enter and View options to make them subroutines? It requires renumbering the lines to move them to someplace convenient. For example, after line 7800. The GOTO 7000 statements also have to be changed to RETURN statements. Finally, GOSUB statements need to be located at lines 4000 and 5000 to transfer execution to your new subroutines. This modification will make the main program quite readable and easy to follow. In fact, you can eliminate lines 4000 and 5000 altogether by locating the GOSUB statements in the IF statements on lines 3500 and 3600. The simplest way to accomplish this is to convert the lines to:

```
3500 IF N1="e" OR N1="E" THEN GOSUB xxxx:GOTO 7000
3600 IF N1="v" OR N1="V" THEN GOSUB yyyy:GOTO 7000
```

where xxxx and yyyy actually contain the beginning line number of the specific subroutines to be called.

Summary

In this chapter, you learned about the various types of program control statements provided by GW-BASIC. These include the various forms of IF statements, ON/GOTO and ON/GOSUB statements, FOR/NEXT and WHILE/WEND loops, and more. You now know enough about the GW-BASIC statements to write fairly complex programs. However, you probably still have a few questions. For example, how can you make your program screens look like the ones created by the expensive commercial programs? To address this question, Chapter 8 first must review the topics covered in Chapters 2 and 3 concerning input and output between the user and the PC.

Quiz

1. What are the two basic forms of IF statements?
2. What statement instructs GW-BASIC to perform an unconditional transfer of control to another part of the program?
3. What two statements are used to temporarily transfer execution to a different part of the program?
4. What statement can be used to perform an "n-way" branch based on the positive value of an integer?

5. What GW-BASIC set of statements will cause a section of program to be repeated a specific number of times?
6. What GW-BASIC set of statements will cause a section of program to be repeated indefinitely until a condition changes?

Chapter 8
Communicating with the User

In This Chapter

Previous chapters took the liberty of using simple input and output statements to make the example programs usable. This chapter will discuss in detail the different ways to exchange information with the user. These techniques include:

▶ Reading several input values at one time
▶ Scanning the keyboard for a pressed key
▶ Inputting data without echoing to screen
▶ Formatting output
▶ Colors, blinking, and reverse video output
▶ Directing data to a printer

Throughout the course of this chapter, you may occasionally want to refer to Chapter 2 to review the operation of the keyboard and display subsystems. First, let's explore how GW-BASIC allows input from the user.

Various Ways to Read Data from the Keyboard

GW-BASIC has three separate commands (INPUT, INKEY$, and READ) to accept input data (excluding data from disk files, which are the subject of the next chapter). As you have seen from the sample programs in previous chapters, the INPUT command is used when a value for a variable is desired. It does not provide the input value(s) to the program until the Enter (⏎) key is pressed. The INKEY$ command is used when the program needs *individual key strokes* pressed by the user. The READ statement is used to get information from special information structures, called DATA statements, which are contained within the program itself. DATA statements are extremely useful when a large amount of information is needed by the program and it is inconvenient or undesirable to ask the user to enter it by hand.

INPUT

You are already fairly familiar with the operation of this statement. The usual form is:

INPUT ["*prompt*";] *variable*[,*variable*[,*variable*...]]

where the items inside the square brackets are optional. The main points to remember about the INPUT statement are that, if a prompt string is used, it must be enclosed in double quotes and the second double quote must be followed by either a semicolon or a comma. If a semicolon is used, a question mark appears immediately after the prompt string. If a comma is used, no question mark appears. This second option can be quite useful when performing user-friendly input such as filling in forms. (Most people don't find filling in forms friendly, but playing twenty questions with a computer is less objectionable if the screen looks "interesting".) For example, the following statements clear the screen and ask the user for the current elevation:

```
100 DEFSNG E
200 CLS
300 INPUT "Current Elevation = ",ELEV
```

If you run the preceding program, you will see the following on the top line of the screen:

```
Current Elevation = _
```

The cursor was moved over by one character due to the blank that was included between the equal sign and the double quotes. Later in this chapter, you will learn how this technique can be used to advantage.

It should be mentioned that multiple variables can be entered at one time using an INPUT statement. A typical application of this might be:

```
100 DEFINT I-N
200 DEFSNG O-Z
300 DEFSTR C
400 CLS
500 LOOP1=1
600 WHILE LOOP1
700 INPUT "Please enter the x and y distance ", X,Y
800 DISTANCE=SQR((X*X)+(Y*Y))
900 ON SGN(X)+2 GOTO 1400,1000,1600
1000 'If X is zero then TrigAngle must be 90 or 270 deg
1100 IF Y<0!GOTO 1300 'If Y negative, angle=270
1200 TRIGANGLE=90!:GOTO 2000
1300 TRIGANGLE=270!:GOTO 2000
1400 TRIGANGLE=(ATN(Y/X)*180!/3.14159)+180!
1500 GOTO 2000
1600 TRIGANGLE=ATN(Y/X)*180!/3.14159
1700 'At this point we have an angle from -90 to +270
1800 'measured counterclockwise from the right. We need
1900 'an angle measured clockwise from straight up.
2000 BEARING=90!-TRIGANGLE
2100 IF TRIGANGLE>90! THEN BEARING=BEARING+360
2200 PRINT DISTANCE,BEARING
2300 INPUT "Type in any numerical digit to stop ",K
2400 IF K<>0 THEN LOOP1 = 0
2500 CLS:WEND
```

In this example, the program requests an *X* and *Y* displacement (where positive *X* is assumed to the right and positive *Y* is assumed up, as illustrated in Figure 8.1).

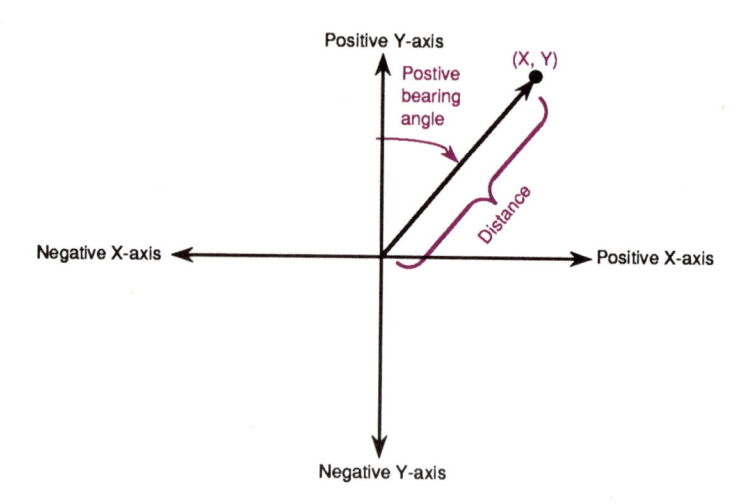

Figure 8.1 Distance and bearing coordinate system.

The program then calculates the distance from (0,0) to the point and the bearing to the object, measured as a clockwise angle from the positive y-axis. At first, this may seem a strange way to measure things, but it's actually the way surveying is done, as well as aircraft and ship navigation. If you type this program and execute it, line 700 demands two inputs, X and Y (in that order). GW-BASIC expects both parameters to be entered on the same line with a comma separating them. If the user simply presses the carriage return without entering any data, a ?Redo from start message appears on the screen and the prompt is printed again on the next line. The screen would look like this:

```
Please enter the x and y distance
?Redo from start
Please enter the x and y distance _
```

The screen will not be cleared again. The information is simply reprinted on the next two lines. In fact, if you keep pressing the carriage return, the entire screen eventually fills with the alternating lines.

It is also possible to enter strings using the multiple variable feature. However, it is generally a good idea to enclose the string inputs within double quotes to avoid "confusing" GW-BASIC. Therefore, the user can respond to the following:

```
1000 INPUT "Enter full name, age ",FULNAME$,AGE%
1100 PRINT FULNAME$,AGE%
```

as either:

`Enter full name, age` **Chuck Jones,40**

or

`Enter full name, age` **"Chuck Jones",40**

Both responses place the same information in the two variables. On the other hand, if you want the FULNAME$ variable to contain the last name, a comma, and then the first name, the only option is to enter the entire field within double quotes (to prevent GW-BASIC from "confusing" the comma separating the last and first names with a data separator between variables). Therefore:

```
1000 INPUT "Last name, first name, age ",FULNAME$,AGE%
1100 PRINT FULNAME$,AGE%
```

requires a response of:

`Last name, first name, age` **"Jones, Chuck",40**

because omitting the quotes makes GW-BASIC try to assign the string "Chuck" to the variable AGE%, resulting in the following on the screen:

```
Last name, first name, age Jones, Chuck,40
?Redo from start
Last name, first name, age _
```

When GW-BASIC detects a type mismatch between the input list and the user response, the `?Redo` message appears. For this reason, it is often a good idea to limit input variable lists to only two or three variables and to place them in separate INPUT statements if they are of different types. Another advantage to using the double quotes for strings is that they indicate explicitly which characters are to be included in the string. For example:

```
Enter full name, age Chuck Jones,40
```

and

```
Enter full name, age " Chuck Jones",40
```

assign different strings to the variable FULNAME$. In the first example, FULNAME$ contains a string of length 11 that begins with an uppercase *C* and ends with a lowercase *s*. The second response generates a string of length 12 that begins with a space and ends with a lowercase *s*. The same thing could have been done with trailing blanks. When the double quotes are not used, GW-BASIC scans for the first nonblank character to start the string and ends on the last nonblank character before the comma or carriage return.

Now look at line 2300 in the sample program that displays distance and bearing. This line is used to prevent the display from being erased until the reader has had a chance to read the results. It also lets the user exit the loop by entering any nonzero number. If the user simply presses the carriage return when the prompt from line 2300 appears, GW-BASIC will assign a value of 0% to *K* and continue the loop. If *K* had been a floating-point variable, it would have been assigned a value of 0.0. If *K* had been a string variable, it would have been assigned a *null* string (empty) value. GW-BASIC will use these defaults when only one variable is associated with the particular INPUT statement. Otherwise, the `?Redo` statement appears. The single variable default is handy in cases such as line 2300, but there is an even friendlier way of doing this: the INKEY$ command.

INKEY$

As was explained previously, the INPUT command takes no action until the Enter (⏎) key is pressed. Therefore, a user must press the Enter key before anything else happens (excluding, of course, a coincidental power glitch that wipes out the disk). The INKEY$ command executes as soon as it is invoked. It always returns a string of length 0, 1, or 2. If the returned value is of length 0, then no key has been pressed. A length of 1 indicates that one of the normal keys has been pressed and the content of the string is a code that represents the actual key pressed. A length of 2 indicates that a special key, such as a function key, was pressed. In the case of special keys, the first character in the string will always be 00 hex, and the second character will contain a special code that identifies the key (see Appendix B for the typical values).

Returning to the sample program, you can now replace lines 2300 and 2400 with the following:

```
2300 PRINT "Press any key to continue (Q to quit)"
2400 C=INKEY$:IF C="Q" OR C="q" THEN LOOP1=0
2450 IF C="" GOTO 2400
2500 CLS:WEND
```

At first, replacing two lines with three may not seem like much of an improvement, but the human interface just became much more intuitive. As long as no key is pressed, GW-BASIC continues to loop between lines 2400 and 2450. Once that a key is pressed, the program either falls through line 2450 to continue the WHILE loop or sets the loop variable to 0 if either the lowercase q or uppercase Q is pressed.

The following small program lets you view the ASCII codes returned by all of the keys on your machine.

```
100 DEFINT I-N
200 DEFSTR C
300 CLS
400 LOCATE 10,10
500 PRINT "Press a key to see the codes for it"
600 LOCATE 12,10
700 C1=INKEY$
800 L=LEN(C1)+1:ON L GOTO 700,1000,1200
850 PRINT C1,L
900 PRINT "Error condition":GOTO 2000
1000 PRINT "The single code is ",ASC(C1)
1100 GOTO 2000
1200 PRINT "The codes are ",ASC(LEFT$(C1,1)),ASC(RIGHT$(C1,1))
2000 LOCATE 14,10
2100 PRINT "Press another key when ready or Esc key to stop"
2200 C1=INKEY$:IF C1="" GOTO 2200
2300 LOCATE 12,10: IF ASC(C1)=27 GOTO 2500
2400 L=LEN(C1)+1:ON L GOTO 2200,1000,1200
2500 CLS:LOCATE 23,1:PRINT "Returning to GW-BASIC":END
```

There are a couple of new tricks introduced in this program. First, it uses the LOCATE statement to place the cursor on the

Chapter 8

screen. Even though this command won't be covered until later in the chapter, it seems appropriate to use it here because the screen output appears bland otherwise. Another surprise is the use of several string functions: LEN, ASC, LEFT$, and RIGHT$. The LEN function simply returns the length of the entire string. This is useful because the INKEY$ function returns a null string (length 0) when no key has been pressed. You also know from previous work that the ON/GOTO statement processes values starting with 1. Because the answer from the LEN function should always be either 0, 1, or 2, simply add 1 to the answer to make the contents of L go from 1 to 3. This lets you use the ON/GOTO statement in line 800 to either infinitely loop to 700 or to branch out to single- or double-character areas.

The ASC function simply returns an integer value corresponding to the ASCII code contained in the first character of the string. The LEFT$ and RIGHT$ statements let you select the leftmost or rightmost "n" characters in the input string. They are used in line 1200 to select the first and second characters of the string C1 (you know that the string only has length 2 from the ON/GOTO statement). Notice that in lines 2200 and 2300 things had to be done a bit differently. The program needed to pause for user input before returning to the print section. It also needed to search for a specific key code (27) which is the value returned by the Esc key; this is how you get out of the program (if you get really desperate you can also try Ctrl-Break).

A funny thing happens the first time that you run this program. If you happen to press the F1 through F10 keys, you will see the screen go through a bunch of numbers. This occurs because the function keys have been predefined by GW-BASIC to stand for things like RUN and LOAD". When you've tried this with the keys in their normal states, do the following experiment. While in GW-BASIC command mode (the Ok displayed), type in the line **KEY 1,""**↲. Notice that the information in the lower left corner of the screen associated with F1 disappears. Use the cursor to go up to the previous command and change the number to 2, 3, etc., until you wipe out the definitions of all 10 function keys. Now type the command **KEY OFF**↲ to turn off the display on the bottom line. Rerun the program and press the function codes to observe the natural values created by these keys. The predefined function keys can also be undone by inserting the following lines at the beginning of the program:

```
50 KEY 1,"":KEY 2,"":KEY 3,"":KEY 4,"":KEY 5,""
60 KEY 6,"":KEY 7,"":KEY 8,"":KEY 9,"":KEY 10,""
```

The KEY statement can also be used to redefine the operation of the function keys. (See Chapter 12 for more details.)

INKEY$ does not echo the keystrokes onto the screen, which can be very useful if you want to perform operations such as entering a password. For example:

```
100 DEFINT I-N
200 DEFSTR C
300 CLS:CSTR="":KEY OFF
400 LOCATE 12,20:PRINT "Please enter the secret password :";
500 C1=INKEY$:IF C1="" GOTO 500
600 J=ASC(C1):IF J=13 GOTO 900
700 IF J>96 AND J<123 THEN J=J-32 'Convert to uppercase
800 CSTR=CSTR+CHR$(J):PRINT "?";:GOTO 500
900 IF CSTR="PLUGH" GOTO 1300
1000 LOCATE 22,20:BEEP
1100 PRINT "Wrong password. System will self-destruct..."
1200 GOTO 1500
1300 LOCATE 22,20
1400 PRINT "Your short-term memory works..."
1500 KEY ON:END
```

This small program clears the screen and requests a password. If the password PLUGH is entered, the message on line 1400 is printed, otherwise the machine beeps before printing line 1100. Several new tricks were also employed in this program. For example, KEY OFF and KEY ON commands were used to black out the bottom line while the program is running (makes for a nicer appearance). Line 600 tests for a carriage return because this is the trigger to perform the comparison. CSTR is a string variable used to accumulate the various key presses so that the program can test them against a specific password later. Line 700 tests for lowercase letters and converts them to uppercase before appending them to the rear of CSTR. The built-in function CHR$ accepts an integer as input and returns a one-character string.

Chapter 8

You may have noticed an unusual statement in line 800:

```
800 ... :PRINT "?";: ...
```

Normally, this print statement would not be present in a password program because you end up displaying on the screen the number of characters in the successful *login*. The strange feature here is the "extra" semicolon. A dangling semicolon is also present at the end of line 400. These semicolons tell GW-BASIC *not* to insert an automatic carriage return and linefeed at the end of the individual PRINT statement. This means that the next PRINT statement begins where the previous one left off. If you remove the semicolon from either place, the cursor will immediately jump to column 1 of the next line each time that the PRINT statement is executed (try modifying the sample program by removing the semicolons to familiarize yourself with this feature).

READ and DATA Statements

The third major method for getting information into a program without accessing storage devices is via the READ/DATA statements. This form of data storage dates back to the early days of computers. Back then, it was customary for the input data to follow the program deck of computer punch cards. GW-BASIC's DATA statement performs the same function by attaching the data stream to the program source. This can be very useful when the programmer wants to provide the program with certain constant information, but does not want to bother with a disk file. Imagine that you want to write a professional-grade program, including the now-obligatory *welcome screen*. One way to generate the welcome screen might be to use something like the following:

```
100 DEFINT I-N
200 DEFSTR C
300 CLS
400 READ N
500 FOR I=1 TO N
600 READ J,K,C
700 LOCATE J,K:PRINT C
800 NEXT I
900 READ J,K,BUCKS
```

```
1000 LOCATE J,K:PRINT "Current software price is $",BUCKS
1100 LOCATE 23,1:END
50000 DATA 8
50100 DATA 5,25,"Welcome to Engulf & Devour's"
50200 DATA 6,25,"Data Processing Extravaganza"
50300 DATA 16,5,"Warning: This program is provided under license to"
50400 DATA 17,5,"Engulf & Devour. Unauthorized use of this software is"
50500 DATA 18,5,"strictly prohibited and is punishable by a sentence of no"
50600 DATA 19,5,"less than 5 years. For further information, please contact:"
50700 DATA 21,30,"Dewey, Cheatom, & Howe, Attorneys,"
50800 DATA 22,30,"Show Low, Arizona."
50900 DATA 11,20,827.32
```

In this program, line 400 retrieves an integer from the first data statement (line 50000) and uses it as a loop limit for lines 500 to 800. Here, the contents of subsequent data statements are read as triplets consisting of line number, column number, and string to be placed on the screen. This allows for a fairly flexible screen display system. Note that you can even get fancy and display the lines out of order for effect. As you can see, line 900 reads a floating-point number called BUCKS and prints it as part of a message in the middle of the screen. This program illustrates how integer, real, and string data can be retrieved from DATA statements. It should be mentioned that READ operations are subject to the same restrictions as "live" input; if the type of data does not agree with the variable type being read, a syntax error occurs. This can happen very easily if the data gets out of sync with the program. For example, imagine that due to a typo, the column number in one of the data statements was dropped so that you have:

```
50800 DATA 22,"Show Low, Arizona."
```

When the program reads this line, it will encounter a string, rather than an integer, as input to the integer *K*. Because this is clearly an unacceptable situation, the program will stop execution with:

```
Syntax error in 50800
Ok
50800 DATA 22,"Show Low, Arizona."
```

at the bottom of the screen and the blinking cursor immediately under the first double quote to indicate where in the line the problem occurred.

Chapter 8

One thing that hasn't been mentioned so far is that the contents of data statements can be thought of as one long stream of information. This means that it is perfectly reasonable for one READ statement to read information from several lines of DATA statements. If a READ statement only uses part of the information in one DATA statement, the next READ statement will pick up on the next field of that particular DATA line. For example, you could have combined lines 50000 and 50100 in the above program into one line:

```
50000 DATA 8,5,25,"Welcome to Engulf & Devour's"
```

If you had done this, everything would continue as before because the READ statement on line 400 would consume the first parameter (an 8) and the remainder of the line would be used when line 600 was executed the first time.

There is one last trick remaining concerning the READ/DATA combination. As you continue to execute READ statements, parameters are taken from the DATA statements until all of them are used. GW-BASIC has a RESTORE command that allows the pointer associated with DATA statements to return to point to the first DATA statement or to the beginning of any other DATA statement. If you want to start reading information from the very beginning, the command is simply:

```
1100 RESTORE
```

If you want to specify the line number of a specific data statement, you may do so with a statement such as:

```
1100 RESTORE 50700
```

Again consider the welcome screen program fragment, and imagine that you want to print the name and address of the firm for a second time at the top left corner of the screen. You could "back-up" the data pointer by inserting the following code in place of line 1100:

```
1100 RESTORE 50700
1200 READ J,K,C
1300 LOCATE 1,4:PRINT C
1400 READ J,K,C
1500 LOCATE 2,8:PRINT C
1600 LOCATE 23,1:END
```

This code will force the DATA pointer to the beginning of line 50700, will re-READ the information, and will then display it in the upper left corner of the screen. Please note that the program ignored the *J* and *K* information this time, it only included the variables in the READ statement to maintain data alignment. By the way, DATA statements do not have to be at the end of a program. However, it does seem to work out better if they are set up in a line range that is high enough so they are out of the way. Another advantage to having DATA statements in a specific range is that you can then merge in a different set of lines to alter the operation of the program. For example, imagine that your company sells granular products (in large industrial drums) to both U.S. and foreign customers. In order to minimize shipping costs, you have written a program for calculating the weight of the various drums in both English and metric units. In order to provide flexibility and minimize the programming, you have decided to store all of the drum sizes and materials density information as DATA statements. All that the user needs to do to run the program successfully is to first load the program itself, then load the appropriate file containing either metric or English data, and then run the program.

Character Output to the Screen

So far, this chapter has dealt, for the most part, with input techniques. It has, however, introduced a few simple output features such as the LOCATE command and placing semicolons after PRINT statements to concatenate output. You will now learn about some of the output features that let the user fabricate professional-looking displays. Some of these features may not be available on your PC, depending on your display card/monitor combination. For the purpose of discussion, assume that you have a display card that is capable of either monochrome or color graphics. If you are using a monochrome display with a CGA card, you may notice that text written in certain colors appears as a barely legible blur on the screen. This is perfectly normal and has to do with the electrical properties of the composite video signal. Certain third-party manufacturers make cards that will automatically display the individual colors as different shades of gray, thus alleviating the problem.

Chapter 8

Placing the Cursor and Drawing Borders

You have already been introduced to the LOCATE command, so you should have an intuitive feel for how it works. If your program needs to use the 25th line on the screen for output, use the KEY OFF command to free it up. If you intend to use the function keys for your own purposes, then you must use the KEY n," " to null them out.

Assume that you want to draw a border around a certain part of the screen. Most of the IBM-compatible display cards contain special characters that let you perform limited forms of graphics when operating in text mode. The following program clears the screen and draws a box around the upper part of the screen:

```
100 DEFINT I-N:DEFSTR S
200 KEY OFF:CLS
300 INPUT "Please enter starting line of box ",M
400 INPUT "Please enter number of blank lines in box ";N
500 IF M+N>23 THEN PRINT "Screen lines exceeded":GOTO 300
600 INPUT "Please enter number of blank spaces in box ";NW
700 IF NW>78 THEN PRINT "Width is too large":GOTO 600
800 CLS:LOCATE M,1
900 S1$=CHR$(201)+STRING$(NW,205)+CHR$(187)
1000 S2$=CHR$(186)+STRING$(NW,32)+CHR$(186)
1100 S3$=CHR$(200)+STRING$(NW,205)+CHR$(188)
1200 PRINT S1;
1300 FOR I=M+1 TO N+M
1400 LOCATE I,1:PRINT S2;
1500 NEXT I
1600 LOCATE N+M+1,1:PRINT S3;
1700 LOCATE 23,1:KEY ON:END
```

This program uses three strings (S1, S2, and S3) to help build the box. STRING$ is a built-in GW-BASIC function that the programmer can use to create a string of identical characters in a specified width. There are two forms of this function:

STRING$(*width, inputstring*)

and

STRING$(*width, asciinumber*)

where *width* indicates how many times the second argument is to be repeated. If the first form is used, only the first letter of the input string is repeated:

```
PRINT STRING$(10,..Hello..)
```

results in:

```
HHHHHHHHHH
```

It should be noted that *width* and *inputstring* are both valid only in the range 0 to 255. If you wonder where the magic constants used in the STRING$ and CHR$ statements came from, see Appendix B. If you have display card hardware that is reasonably compatible with the original CGA design, this program should enable you to draw boxes of various sizes. Of course, a serious program may have several boxes on the screen and may even use color, so this is the next topic to be covered.

How to Change Colors and Set Blinking

As was explained in Chapter 2, there are several types of color video display cards, the main ones being CGA, EGA, and VGA. Fortunately, the EGA and VGA cards tend to default to the standard CGA color capability. For the purposes of this chapter, color and blink control explanations will refer only to the basic CGA mode. Chapter 10 contains tables and additional explanations for those of you who have the higher-capability hardware and want to tackle something more ambitious. When operating in CGA-compatible mode, you can control the foreground color, the background color, and the border color. You can also determine whether or not the foreground color blinks. These color changes are accomplished through parameters passed to the COLOR statement which is of the following form:

```
COLOR [foreground] [,background] [,border]
```

Foreground and *border* must be numbers or integer variables in the range 0 to 15. The *background* parameter must be in the range 0 to 7. On a standard CGA card, the colors are defined as shown in Table 8.1.:

Table 8.1 CGA Standard Colors

0 - Black	8 - Gray
1 - Blue	9 - Bright Blue
2 - Green	10 - Bright Green
3 - Cyan	11 - Bright Cyan
4 - Red	12 - Bright Red
5 - Magenta	13 - Bright Magenta
6 - Brown	14 - Bright Yellow
7 - Dim White	15 - Bright White

Add 16 to the foreground color for blinking

As you can see from Table 8.1, the colors in the right column generally correspond to the ones in the left column, except for the fact that they are high-intensity (brighter). Because of hardware limitations in the original CGA hardware, the background color is limited to one of those in the left column (if you assign a number greater than 7, the program will use the residue from an integer division of the specified number divided by eight). If the number passed as the foreground parameter is greater than 15, the foreground characters will begin to blink. To demonstrate this, a few minor modifications must be made to the previous box-drawing program. If you modify or create the lines:

```
750 INPUT "Frgnd/Bkgnd ";I,J:COLOR I,J
1700 LOCATE 23,1:COLOR 7,0:KEY ON:END
```

you have enough flexibility to experiment with the color settings. After you answer the questions to define the size of the box, the cryptic message Frgnd/Bkgnd reminds you to enter the desired foreground and background colors (ignore the border color for now to minimize confusion). When the COLOR command in line 750 is executed, all future output is created using this coloring scheme. This is why you also need to add a statement to line 1700. The COLOR 7,0 statement forces GW-BASIC to redefine the screen defaults to the "normal" settings. If you only insert line 750 and do not make the change to 1700, everything that is sent to the screen from that point on will come out with the new color settings. If you ever find yourself in this predicament you can quickly recover by simply entering

```
COLOR 7,0↵
CLS↵
```

to force things back to normal. Remember that you can omit any parameter you want to omit when you're dealing with the COLOR statement. For example, imagine that you are performing some screen processing and you want to make the background color cyan, but you can not easily predict the foreground color (it might need to be entered by the user or it might be based on some other program parameter). You can change *only* the background color by using the statement:

```
1200 COLOR ,3
```

You can even change the background *and* the border without affecting the foreground color with the statement:

```
1200 COLOR ,3,8
```

which makes the background cyan and the border gray. If you want to change the foreground and the border but not the background, use:

```
1200 COLOR 13, ,1
```

to make the foreground bright magenta and the border blue and leave the background color as whatever it was already defined as. There are only three pitfalls to watch out for when tinkering with the screen colors. The first is that if you turn on blinking and forget to turn it off later in your program, everything written after that point (including GW-BASIC and sometimes even DOS commands) will also come out blinking (this can be corrected by entering the recovery commands discussed earlier). The second problem is that your user will get very bored if you define the foreground and background colors to be the same (black on black is the toughest to deal with because you can't tell if your program is doing anything at all). The third problem is garish color combinations (just because a specific permutation of foreground and background colors is possible doesn't mean that it won't make the user nauseous).

Retrieval of Screen Information

Have you ever wondered how the fancy TSR (Terminate and Stay Resident) programs can pop up in the middle of any program, put up a small window that allows the user to communicate with it, and finally disappear without leaving a trace of disturbance on the screen? These programs take advantage of the fact that the display card memory can be read from, as well as written to. GW-BASIC lets you read the contents of this memory block by using the SCREEN function. First, it is important to differentiate between the SCREEN *function* and the SCREEN *statement*. The function is used to retrieve the contents of one character position on the screen. The SCREEN statement is used to set the hardware mode of the display card, which is beyond the scope of this chapter. The SCREEN function consists of:

integervalue = SCREEN(*row,column*[*,requestcolor*])

where *row* and *column* mean integers in the range 1 to 25 and 1 to 80, respectively. If the *requestcolor* parameter is not included or if it is set to 0, the value returned by this function is the ASCII code for the character at the specified location. If the optional third parameter is included and is a nonzero value (which stands for TRUE), the value returned by this function is an eight-bit number that represents the color attributes for that particular location on the screen. The following program shows how the information can first be retrieved into an array and then later reconstructed:

```
100 DEFINT I-N:DEFSTR S,T:DIM MCOLOR(10,10),MASCII(10,10)
200 KEY OFF:CLS
250 COLOR 11,7
300 PRINT "This is a test of the screen capture ability"
350 COLOR 6,0
400 PRINT "of GW-BASIC. We will print this"
450 COLOR 12,6
500 PRINT "material at a known area of the screen and"
550 COLOR 14,1
600 PRINT "will then ask the program to go back and"
650 COLOR 10,7
700 PRINT "retrieve some of this information and print it"
750 COLOR 1,5
800 PRINT "out at the bottom of the screen in the right"
```

```
850 COLOR 0,2
900 PRINT "colors."
950 COLOR 10,6
1000 FOR I=1 TO 5
1100 FOR J=1 TO 6
1200 IROW=I+1:ICOL=J+9 'Scan rows 2-6 & cols 10-15
1300 MASCII(I,J)=SCREEN(IROW,ICOL)
1400 MCOLOR(I,J)=SCREEN(IROW,ICOL,1)
1500 NEXT J
1600 NEXT I
1700 ' Now we will reconstruct the slice starting at
1800 ' location 10,20
1900 FOR K=1 TO 6
2000 FOR L=1 TO 5
2100 NEWROW=L+9:NEWCOL=K+19
2200 LOCATE NEWROW,NEWCOL
2300 COLOR (MCOLOR(L,K) MOD 16),((MCOLOR(L,K)\16) MOD 8)
2400 PRINT CHR$(MASCII(L,K));
2500 NEXT L
2600 NEXT K
2700 COLOR 7,0:KEY ON:END
```

The first part of the program (through line 900) generates a wildly colored message on the screen that will be the target for the retrieval program. Line 950 actually does nothing useful, it is simply there to force yet a different color scheme should the bottom loop fail to generate the proper color scheme (this is a useful trick for debugging color changes). The double FOR loops between lines 1000 and 1600 retrieve the ASCII code and color information from the hardware and store them into the two arrays. The remainder of the program goes through the reverse process to reconstruct the screen slice lower and to the left on the screen. A couple of tricks were employed to get the data for the COLOR statement. The foreground color was straightforward because it only needed to perform a MOD 16 operation to obtain the number in the four least significant bits (the four digits farthest to the right). The background color was a bit trickier because it was stuffed into the upper half of the 8-bit number (see Figure 8.2).

If you run this program, you will be able to match the chunk that was copied with the text above it. One trick you may not have noticed when looking at the program is that the display hardware was scanned from left to right across the screen and then dropped to the next line. The screen-writes went down each column and then right to the next column. There was no technical reason for doing this, it just shows that the data does not have to be retrieved in exactly the same way that it was saved (the material could even have been written from the bottom to the top and right to left).

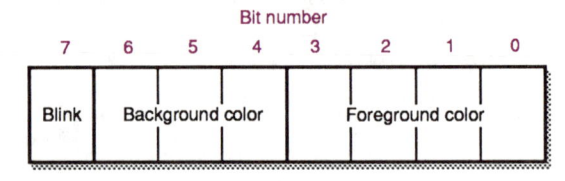

Figure 8.2   Structure of screen color number.

Formatting Output Data to Make It Readable

Until now GW-BASIC has performed all output formatting using internal rules. In the program that displayed the keycodes, this resulted in unnecessarily wide spacing between numbers when the two numbers associated with the F1 key were displayed:

```
The codes are       0              59
```

To reformat the screen, you need to tell GW-BASIC to allocate 2 digits per number. GW-BASIC lets you allocate spacing by using the PRINT USING statement. This statement consists of:

PRINT USING *formatstring*;*item1*[,*item2*,...]

The *formatstring* specifies how wide the various fields to be printed will be. If you look back at the keycodes program, you will note that the output statement that you want to change is:

```
1200 PRINT "The codes are ",ASC(LEFT$(C1,1)),ASC(RIGHT$(C1,1))
```

To obtain the desired numeric spacing, split the print statement into separate statements for the string and for the numbers. You must also define a format string that will consist of "###" which inserts a space before each number and reserves three digits for each integer. The result of these changes is the following code fragment:

```
1200 I1=ASC(LEFT$(C1,1)):I2=ASC(RIGHT$(C1,1))
1300 C3="###":PRINT "The codes are ";
1400 PRINT USING C3;I1,I2
```

The I1 and I2 variables are simply aesthetic conveniences to keep the PRINT statements from getting too cluttered. Because a previous LOCATE command has already placed the cursor at the desired location, the execution of the PRINT statement in line 1300 has the same effect as in the original example. By placing a semicolon after this PRINT statement, you can print the numbers immediately after the string on the screen. The real change in technique is in line 1400. This line invokes a PRINT USING statement that refers to C3 to provide the formatting information to be used in printing I1 and I2. If these three lines are substituted for the original line 1200, the following output shows up when the F1 key is pressed:

```
The codes are   0  59
```

which is what you wanted in the first place. You may wonder why lines 1300 and 1400 couldn't have been:

```
1300 C3="###"
1400 PRINT USING C3;"The codes are ",I1,I2
```

If you had tried to execute those lines, GW-BASIC would have halted with an error on line 1400. When PRINT USING tries to format the output, it wants to format ALL of the output (including the string constant). Because the ### fields are only valid for numbers, GW-BASIC will be very "unhappy" when it attempts to apply a numeric format on a string. You can combine them together by adding more material to the C3 string:

```
300 C3="\              \### ###":CLS
1000 PRINT USING C3;"The code is ",ASC(C1);
1100 PRINT "    ":GOTO 2000
1200 I1=ASC(LEFT$(C1,1)):I2=ASC(RIGHT$(C1,1))
1400 PRINT USING C3;"The codes are",I1,I2
```

As you can see, by appending two backslashes enclosing 14 spaces at the beginning of C3, you allocate enough spaces for the messages to be printed. A second ### set was added to define the position of the second number (if needed). When GW-BASIC begins to use C3 as a format template, it will expect to find a string because the backslashes with spaces are only used to format string output. It will reserve a total of 16 spaces for the string (14 blanks plus the spaces taken by the backslashes). If the string is longer than 16 characters, only the first 16 characters will be printed. If the string is less than 16 characters, it will be left-justified within the 16 space field and will be padded on the right with blanks. GW-BASIC will then find the ### group and reserve a total of three places for the first integer. The blank between the sets of ### groups tells GW-BASIC that you want a space between the first integer and the second one. If you had placed three spaces between the ### groups, there would have been at least three spaces between the two numbers on the screen. Notice that it was also necessary to modify the PRINT section for the single-number case to make them both have the same format and to clear out the area of the second number (in case there was something on the screen).

At this point you are probably wondering what the different control symbols are for PRINT USING statements. Table 8.2 shows each with a brief explanation.

Table 8.2   Special Print Codes

##	Used to indicate the size of a numeric field. Numbers are right-justified in the field. Only whole numbers will be printed.
##.#	Indicates that a real number will be printed with up to two digits before the decimal point and one digit after the decimal point. Add additional # symbols to increase the whole number or decimal part as desired.
+##	A plus before or after a numeric definition field tells GW-BASIC to always display the sign of the number before or after it (respectively).
##−	A minus sign following a numeric definition field indicates that negative numbers should be printed with a trailing minus sign.
**##	Double asterisks before a numeric definition field indicate that leading blanks in the number field should be filled with asterisks.
$$##	Double dollar signs before a numeric definition field instruct GW-BASIC to insert a dollar sign

Continued

Table 8.2 Continued

	and a blank to the left of the field. This increases the entire field width by 2. This option cannot be used with the exponential format. It will not work with negative numbers unless the minus sign is printed to the right (see above).
**$##	This combines the two options described earlier so that a dollar sign is printed and then leading blanks are filled with asterisks.
##,.##	A comma instructs GW-BASIC to insert a comma between the 100 and 1000 digits, etc. This option does not work with the exponent option
##^^^^	Four carets after the digit's place tell GW-BASIC to print the number using the exponential format (also known as scientific notation).
_	An underscore tells GW-BASIC to literally print the next character on the screen. Thus _! prints a vertical bar at that location. This can be handy when printing tables or spreadsheets.
&	Specifies a variable length field. This means that the entire string will be printed.
!	Indicates that only the first character of a string is to be printed.
\n blanks\	This reserves a field of length n+2 for a string. If the string is shorter than the field, it will be left justified and padded with blanks. If the string is bigger than the field, the first n+2 characters of the string will be printed. Note that this command uses the backslash character as the delimiter.

There are a few additional details that do not appear in the table. If a number is bigger than the specified field, GW-BASIC will print a % symbol in front of the number and will then go ahead and print the entire number. If you specify more than 24 digits for a number, execution will stop at that print statement and an illegal function call message will appear. Use two underlines in a row if you want to use the underline option to print out an underline. Now for some examples:

```
100 DEFINT I-M:DEFSTR S,C
200 FPNEG=-327.125
300 FPPOS1=1234.5678#:FPPOS2=65535.27
```

```
400 INTNEG = -1066
500 INTPOS = 2001
600 S1="Civili, ci vilirum, runvi lirun"
700 CLS:KEY OFF
800 CF1="####  #####.##"
900 CF2="\                    \ ####.####    !"
1000 CF3="######,.#   #####.####-  $$####.##-   **$#####.##-"
1100 CF4="##.######^^^^    #.#######^^^^    .#######^^^^"
1200 CF5="######  #####  ####  ###"
1300 CF6="##### _@ $$####.##"
1400 CF7="##### _@ _$#####.##"
1500 CF8="The price is $ ####.##"
2000 PRINT USING CF1;INTPOS,FPNEG
2100 PRINT USING CF2;S1,FPPOS1,S1
2200 PRINT USING CF3;FPPOS2,FPNEG,FPNEG,FPNEG
2300 PRINT USING CF4;FPPOS2,FPPOS2,FPPOS2
2400 PRINT USING CF4;FPNEG,FPNEG,FPNEG
2500 PRINT USING CF5;INTNEG,INTNEG,INTNEG,INTNEG
2600 PRINT USING CF5;INTPOS,INTPOS,INTPOS,INTPOS,INTPOS
2700 PRINT USING CF6;INTPOS,FPPOS1
2800 PRINT USING CF7;INTPOS,FPPOS1
2900 PRINT USING CF8;FPPOS1
```

If you run this program, you will see a screen that looks like:

```
                                                       display
                                                       line number
2001  -327.13                              1
Civili, ci vilirum, 1234.5680   C                      2
 65,535.3   327.1250-    $327.13-  ****$327.13-        3
6.553527E+04   0.6553527E+05   .65535270E+05           4
-3.271250E+02  0.3271250E+03   .32712500E+03           5
-1066  -1066  %-1066  %-1066                           6
 2001   2001   2001  %2001  2001                       7
 2001 @ $1234.57                                       8
 2001 @ $1234.57                                       9
The price is $ 1234.57                                10
```

To clarify the subsequent discussion, line numbers have been appended on the far right of the screen image (these numbers don't really appear on the screen). Display lines 1 and 2 are what could be regarded as typical formatted output. Notice that the ! command in program line 900 resulted in the single uppercase C following the floating-point number. Display line 3 illustrates various options for displaying floating-point numbers, including dollar signs and trailing minus signs. Display lines 4 and 5 were both generated with the same format string (CF4). They illustrate the effect of reduced field size in exponential format. In line 5, the number ends up losing the minus sign because enough digits were not allocated in front of the decimal point. In general, you should use at least two # symbols in front of the decimal point when formatting exponential fields. Display lines 6 and 7 illustrate what happens when you attempt to display positive and negative integers with insufficient field width. Line 7 demonstrates what happens when more parameters are specified than formats (it requested that five numbers be displayed but had only specified four #-groups in CF5). When this happens, GW-BASIC returns to the beginning of the format string and re-uses it to display the additional data. Keep this feature in mind when you are using format strings because adding an extra parameter to a print list can lead to errors if you forget to modify the format string. GW-BASIC is perfectly "happy" with the converse: specifying more fields than there are variables (which can come in handy when you attempt to use a format string for more than one print statement). Display lines 8 and 9 show how you may want to use the underline command to include special symbols in your output. The 10th line illustrates something that has not yet been mentioned: display strings can also be embedded within format strings. The string "The price is" was defined as part of the CF8 definition. The main disadvantage to inserting string fragments within the format strings is that these fragments cannot use any of the special control symbols (because they may "confuse" GW-BASIC).

Interaction between Input and Output Commands

Now that you have a reasonable mastery of basic input and output, you can consider how to merge the techniques covered in this chapter to create professional looking displays. For example, you can use color attributes and special features such as LOCATE and INKEY$ statements to help guide the user.

The following short program draws a magenta box on the screen and then identifies several fields: Name, Address, Phone, etc. As the cursor appears in a specific field, the entire field is highlighted in dim white to indicate the size of the field. Data can be entered, then erased using the backspace key (usually just above the Enter key). Each field is completed by either pressing Enter or by filling the entire field. At that point, the highlighting is cleared and the next string is highlighted.

```
100 DEFINT I-N:DEFSTR S,C
200 C1=CHR$(201)+STRING$(51,CHR$(205))+CHR$(187)
300 C2=CHR$(186)+STRING$(51," ")+CHR$(186)
400 C3=CHR$(200)+STRING$(51,CHR$(205))+CHR$(188)
500 CLS:COLOR 5,0
600 LOCATE 5,10:PRINT C1
700 FOR I=6 TO 11
800 LOCATE I,10:PRINT C2
900 NEXT I
1000 LOCATE 12,10:PRINT C3
1300 COLOR 7,0
1400 LOCATE 7,15:PRINT "Name:"
1500 LOCATE 8,12:PRINT "Address:"
1600 LOCATE 9,15:PRINT "City:"+STRING$(20," ")+"State:    ZIP:"
1700 LOCATE 10,14:PRINT "Phone:(   )   -"
3000 COLOR 11,7:ISTARTX=21:ISTARTY=7:IFIELDW=30
3100 GOSUB 35000
3200 SNAME=SGEN
4000 COLOR 11,7:ISTARTX=21:ISTARTY=8:IFIELDW=30
4100 GOSUB 35000
4200 SADDR=SGEN
5000 COLOR 11,7:ISTARTX=21:ISTARTY=9:IFIELDW=18
5100 GOSUB 35000
5200 SCITY=SGEN
6000 COLOR 11,7:ISTARTX=47:ISTARTY=9:IFIELDW=2
6100 GOSUB 35000
6200 STATE=SGEN
7000 COLOR 11,7:ISTARTX=55:ISTARTY=9:IFIELDW=5
7100 GOSUB 35000
7200 SZIP=SGEN
8000 COLOR 11,7:ISTARTX=21:ISTARTY=10:IFIELDW=3
8100 GOSUB 35000
8200 SACODE=SGEN
9000 COLOR 11,7:ISTARTX=25:ISTARTY=10:IFIELDW=3
9100 GOSUB 35000
9200 SEXCH=SGEN
9300 COLOR 11,7:ISTARTX=29:ISTARTY=10:IFIELDW=4
```

```
9400 GOSUB 35000
9500 SNUMBR=SGEN
20000 LOCATE 23,1:COLOR 7,0
20100 END
35000 SGEN=" "     'This subroutine does screen work and
35010 ' expects the cursor position in ISTARTX and ISTARTY.
35020 ' The field width is also expected in IFIELDW.
35040 LOCATE ISTARTY,ISTARTX:PRINT STRING$(IFIELDW," ")
35050 LOCATE ISTARTY,ISTARTX,1
35100 S=INKEY$:IF S="" GOTO 35100
35200 L=LEN(S):IF L=2 THEN BEEP:GOTO 35100
35300 IF ASC(S)=13 GOTO 36000
35400 IF ASC(S)<>8 GOTO 35800
35500 L=LEN(SGEN):IF L<=0 THEN SGEN=" ":GOTO 35100
35550 SGEN=LEFT$(SGEN,L-1)
35560 IX=POS(0)
35570 IY=CSRLIN
35600 LOCATE IY,IX-1:PRINT " ";
35700 LOCATE IY,IX-1,1:GOTO 35100
35800 SGEN=SGEN+S:PRINT S;
35900 IF LEN(SGEN)<FIELDW GOTO 35100
36000 COLOR 7,0:LOCATE ISTARTY,ISTARTX:PRINT STRING$(IFIELDW," ")
36100 LOCATE ISTARTY,ISTARTX:PRINT SGEN;
36200 RETURN
```

Note that the vast majority of the work is done by an I/O routine that starts at 35000. It requires three parameters: the starting position of the string (*X* and *Y*) and the width of the field. You may want to experiment with this subroutine to gain further insight into the interaction between keyboard input and screen output.

Reader Challenge

The preceding sample program provides an opportunity for further experimentation. For example, You might consider how you would modify the I/O routine in lines 35000-36200 to restart the entire process when the F1 key is used.

Also, what would happen on the screen if lines 36000 and 36100 were deleted and line 36200 renamed as 36000? Would old data be visible if this change were made? After you've made these changes, you may want to try your own modifications.

Chapter 8

Character Output to the Printer

There's one more "friendly" output device that hasn't been discussed yet: the printer. GW-BASIC treats output to the printer the same way it treats output to the screen. The only differences are that formatting and field placement tricks are pretty much limited to what can be done with format strings in LPRINT USING statements.

The first consideration that must be dealt with is the output *width*. GW-BASIC assumes a *default width* of 80 characters (which means that after 80 printable characters, it inserts a carriage return and linefeed to force the print head to the leftmost position on the next line on the sheet of paper). This setting can be changed using the WIDTH statement. The general form of the statement is:

WIDTH *size*

or

WIDTH *device,size*

where dev*ice* can be SCRN:, LPT1:, LPT2:, LPT3:, COM1:, or COM2: and *size* can be a number between 1 and 255. The printer is usually connected to LPT1:. A typical form for setting the printer width to 132 characters would be:

WIDTH "LPT1:",132

Selecting a width of 255 disables the insertion of carriage returns and linefeed into the data stream. (You wouldn't normally want to do this for a printer, but you will for a communications port such as COM1 or 2.)

A powerful technique available for controlling printer output is the use of *control codes*. Most modern printers respond to certain sequences of special characters by changing character spacing, changing line spacing, and even moving the paper up and down by amounts that are not multiples of normal line spacing (this is handy when printing superscripts and subscripts in mathematical formulas). Because printers differ in their capabilities and in the codes they respond to, no specific examples will be provided here but general techniques will be discussed for using control codes.

Imagine that you have a dot-matrix printer capable of printing in condensed mode. Many of these printers need to be fed a code 15 at the beginning of each line to set the character font to condensed mode. The simplest way to do this is to precede each LPRINT command with the statement:

```
LPRINT CHR$(15);
```

Another way to do this would be to insert CHR$(15) at the beginning of each list to be printed. Of course, this could get a bit complicated if you are employing an LPRINT USING statement, but we've already discussed how the string would be set up to print a leading string. To change the printer back to normal mode you may need to send something like:

```
LPRINT CHR$(18);
```

All of the printer codes available for your unit should be listed in the owner's manual. In some cases, printers may require two control numbers to set a mode. If, for example, your printer wants an <esc> E sequence (27 and 69) to start underlining, you could handle the sequence with a statement:

```
LPRINT CHR$(27)+"E";
```

or

```
LPRINT CHR$(27)+CHR$(69);
```

You will need to do some reading and experimenting to discover what your particular printer needs for different options, and whether you must send the control codes at the beginning of each line or only once at the beginning of the document.

Summary

In this chapter, you were exposed to a large amount of material regarding Input/Output interaction with the user. You learned how to move the cursor around the screen, how to control display colors and blinking, and how to draw simple objects (like boxes)

Chapter 8

using character graphics built into the display card. You also received a brief introduction to programming a display to make it friendly and intuitive to the user by using INKEY$ and keystroke decoding. Finally, there was a brief discussion regarding how to use LPRINT and LPRINT USING statements, rather than PRINT and PRINT USING statements, to direct output to the printer.

Because printers tend to treat control codes differently, you may want to create a small program that asks the user for information unique to his machine and saves it in a disk file that your main program can access each time that the program is run. This saves the user the aggravation of answering the same printer questions at the beginning of each run. To do this, you must understand how to read and write disk files, so this topic will be covered in the next chapter.

Quiz

1. Which GW-BASIC function returns a value from the keyboard without displaying it on the screen?
2. What statement accesses information that has been stored in the program itself? What statement holds the data?
3. How can you locate the cursor at line 23 and column 10?
4. What would the command look like to set the foreground color to bright cyan?
5. How would you find out the ASCII value of the character at row 10 and column 12 on the screen in text mode?

Chapter 9

Disk Files

In This Chapter

In the previous eight chapters, you learned how to create GW-BASIC programs and you were exposed to the various I/O mechanisms for transferring data between the PC and the user. The only drawback has been that your programs have been unable to store or retrieve data from disk files. This chapter explains the fundamentals of disk storage and introduces the various GW-BASIC commands available. It explains the philosophy used to implement the disk I/O commands and introduces various ways to write data to a file. The last section of this chapter introduces several statements that are not directly connected with disk I/O and are usually associated with disk management.

Disk Operation: The Man behind the Curtain

Disk operations on a PC often remind people of the Wizard of Oz—"Pay no attention to the man behind the curtain...." Many technical details are handled out of the user's sight. As you may recall from Chapter 2, disk files are stored on spinning magnetic media. A disk controller card inside the PC provides the electronic communications path between the microprocessor and the actual disk drives. Because of complex technical trade-offs, the data transfers between the microprocessor and the disk drives are typically done in blocks of 512 bytes each. DOS software makes this block available to programs like GW-BASIC. DOS acts like a diplomatic courier in a spy thriller—it conveys information from point A to point B but doesn't look at the data; the contents are someone else's problem. GW-BASIC receives the block from DOS and subdivides it into smaller chunks called data records (which will be discussed shortly). If a data record overlaps the end of a disk block, GW-BASIC knows how to request the next block from DOS to retrieve the rest of the needed information. GW-BASIC also handles the ugly details when you write a file record to the disk.

These hidden activities are explained at the beginning of this chapter because you may notice some strange things happening when you run the sample programs. For example, your program may perform several disk-read operations, but the disk-read light may only come on once. This happens because the first read forces a data transfer from the disk via DOS, but the second and third read operations may still be dealing with information in the first block of data, so GW-BASIC does not ask DOS to get more blocks (DOS turns on the disk-access light when it begins to communicate with a particular drive). The same sort of thing can happen when you perform disk writes. Your program may open a file and write some information to it but GW-BASIC won't give the block to DOS until the block is filled, so the disk light won't come on right away.

Fortunately, GW-BASIC and DOS handle most I/O details, so you can concentrate on the task at hand.

Disk Operation: A GW-BASIC User's Perspective

Disk files are like food-storage bags. You have to open them carefully before you can get to the contents. The contents can then be altered (removed, added to, replaced), and the bag must be closed if you want to keep what's inside. Thanks to DOS, there is no need to differentiate between files on floppy disks and files on hard disks: they are treated identically.

GW-BASIC allows several disk files to be open at the same time, so it must have a way to identify each individual file. This is accomplished with a *file number*. This number is used with almost all disk-related statements and is usually preceded by a # sign. Let's begin by introducing how to instruct GW-BASIC to find a file.

How to Open and Close Disk Files

There are two fundamental statements for disk operations: the OPEN and CLOSE statements. For reasons that are probably now lost in the sands of time, four distinct forms of the OPEN statement are supported by GW-BASIC. They are:

OPEN *smode*,[#]*filenum*,*path*[,*reclength*]
OPEN *smode*,[#]*filenum*,*filename*[,*reclength*]
OPEN *path* [FOR *mode*] AS[#]*filenum* [LEN=*reclength*]
OPEN *filename* [FOR *mode*] AS[#]*filenum* [LEN=*reclength*]

Because the first two forms are less verbose and are generally favored today, this book will always use those forms. The parameters are:

smode This is a single capital letter enclosed in double quotes. An *I* indicates that the file is to be used only for input. An *O* indicates that the file is intended only for output. An *R* indicates random access input/output. An *A* indicates that you want to append data to the end of the current file.

filenum This is the file number referred to by other GW-BASIC statements. GW-BASIC defaults to a maximum of three files that can be open at the same time. If you want to increase this number, you must specify the /i and /f:*maxfilenum* when invoking GW-BASIC.

filename This is the full name of the file, such as TEMP.DAT, and it must adhere to the DOS standard of eight character maximum for the name and three character maximum for the extension.

reclength   This optional parameter defines the amount of data moved by a specific GET or PUT statement. The default value is 128. If you want to increase this value above 128, you must specify the desired length using the /s:*reclength* option when invoking GW-BASIC.

path   This is an alternate to the *name* field, and it can be as simple as B:TEST.DAT, or it can include all of the path information using the backslashes. This parameter is limited to 63 characters maximum.

mode   This works the same way as the *smode* parameter discussed above, but it must consist of one of the following keywords: INPUT, OUTPUT, RANDOM, or APPEND. The keywords must not be surrounded by quotation marks, and they must appear in capital letters to avoid possible problems.

When writing new programs that use disk I/O, you should keep the files that you want to open in the active (current) directory. You can always change the file specification later, when everything is working correctly. In this book, files will always be accessed from the current directory to avoid confusion.

Closing a file is much easier than opening it. The closing statement is:

CLOSE #*filenum*

where *filenum* is the same number specified in the OPEN statement. If you want to close several files at once, you can specify them in one CLOSE statement or use several close statements at the same time:

CLOSE #2,#3

or

CLOSE #2
CLOSE #3

A rather useless (but legal) program could be:

```
100 OPEN "O",#1,"TEST.DAT"
200 CLS:PRINT "Made it through the OPEN"
300 CLOSE #1
400 PRINT "Made it through the CLOSE"
500 END
```

In this particular case, a new file for output called TEST.DAT was created and then closed without being written to (you don't know how to do file I/O yet). The file had to be specified for output because GW-BASIC will "complain" if it tries to open a nonexistent file for input. Run this brief program, exit to DOS and type in a **DIR *.DAT** command. You will find a new file, called TEST.DAT, in your current directory. Now, let's see what else you have to do to write to the file.

Simple File Output

The simplest (and least efficient) way to write data to a file is to use PRINT # or PRINT # USING statements. For example, you can modify the previous do-nothing program by inserting four lines:

```
100 OPEN "O",#1,"TEST.DAT"
200 CLS:PRINT "Made it through the OPEN"
230 F!=.125
240 I%=1
250 PRINT #1,I%,F!
260 PRINT #1,I%;F!
300 CLOSE #1
400 PRINT "Made it through the CLOSE"
500 END
```

Lines 230 and 240 simply create some variables (F! and I%) that can be written to the file. Lines 250 and 260 actually move data to the file. If you run this modified program, exit to DOS, and then execute the following command:

>TYPE TEST.DAT

You will see the following on your screen:

```
1            .125
1  .125
```

The first line in the file was created by line 250 in the program and looks the way that you would expect to see it on the screen. The second line in the file was created by line 260 and illustrates the effect of using semicolons as *argument separators* (symbols that GW-BASIC needs to identify the start of a new variable name in a list) rather than commas. The problem with both of these PRINT statements is that you cannot later read the information using an INPUT # statement because the INPUT # statement expects to see delimiter commas between the data items. This can be corrected by using the PRINT # USING statement:

```
100 OPEN "O",#1,"TEST.DAT"
200 CLS:PRINT "Made it through the OPEN #1"
230 F!=.125
240 I%=1
250 PRINT #1,USING "# , ##.###";I%,F!
260 PRINT #1,I%,F!
300 CLOSE #1
400 PRINT "Made it through the CLOSE #1"
500 OPEN "I",#3,"TEST.DAT"
600 INPUT #3,M%,X!
700 PRINT:PRINT M%,X!
800 CLOSE #3
900 PRINT:PRINT "All done now..."
1000 END
```

In this example, a PRINT # USING statement created a specific format for the output of the first line in the file. The simple PRINT # in line 260 remains so that you can compare the outputs of the two statements easily. Run this program, exit to DOS, and execute another TYPE TEST.DAT command. Notice that this time the first line contains a comma between data items. Because there is now a delimiter between the data items on the first line, it seems appropriate to illustrate the INPUT # statement. Notice that once that the file was written, it was closed for output at line 300. Once that a file is closed, GW-BASIC forgets completely about it, allowing you to immediately reopen it for input as #3. You could have reopened the file as #1 again, but this illustrates that there is absolutely no connection between the previous file operations and the input operation that is about to be performed. Line 600 reads two entirely different variables from the file (again, to show no connection to the previous operations) and prints out the new variables on the screen.

The same techniques employed in the previous programs for integer and single-precision data can also be used with double-precision and string data. The only caution that should be observed is that string data should always be bracketed by double quotes to guarantee that an INPUT # statement will later be able to read it. For example, a string could be printed using one of the following statements:

```
1200 PRINT #1,CHR$(34)+"This is a test"+CHR$(34)
```

or

```
1100 A$="This is a test"
1200 PRINT #1,CHR$(34),A$,CHR(34)
```

Another way to accomplish the same thing is to use the WRITE # statement rather than PRINT #. The WRITE # is of the form:

```
100 WRITE #filenum, var1, var2, ...
```

The useful feature of the WRITE # statement is that it automatically inserts commas between variables and delimits strings with double quotes. It also inserts a carriage return and a linefeed after the last parameter in the WRITE statement.

There is one drawback to the disk I/O commands discussed so far: they can consume a great deal of disk space because all output is performed with ASCII characters (which is not very efficient). For example, imagine that you want to store large quantities of integer data in the form of one place for a sign, five digits, and a trailing comma to separate the numbers (the following illustrates the format):

-12345,

This will use a total of seven characters (which means seven bytes of storage for each item in the file). As you may recall from Chapter 6, an integer requires only two bytes of memory in the machine. Thus, by using this representation, you are taking more than three times the storage actually needed.

A more efficient way to store the information is directly as a binary pattern on the disk (the way that it is represented in the computer's memory), but this requires some trickery on your part because GW-BASIC does not directly support binary output. Before you can accomplish this, you need to learn about the FIELD statement.

The FIELD Statement

You may recall that the OPEN statement has an optional parameter called *reclength* that has been ignored up to now. The problem is that there is usually no reasonable way to predict the length of a message created by a PRINT # statement, so there isn't much point in trying to optimize disk storage by specifying a record length. The FIELD statement changes this because it identifies the length of each data record to be contained in the file and the variables that are to be loaded with the information. The format is:

FIELD [#]*filenum, length1* AS *var1*[,*length2* AS *var2*,...]

Where *filenum* is the number assigned in the OPEN statement, *varx* represents the name of each string variable, and *lengthx* indicates how many characters (bytes) of data will be placed in the particular variable when a GET statement is executed (relax, the GET statement will be covered next). When a record is retrieved from the file, the data is automatically transferred into these variables in the order they appear in the FIELD statement. For example:

FIELD #1, 32 AS A$, 14 AS B$, 5 AS Z$

instructs GW-BASIC to transfer the first 32 bytes of each record in file #1 to A$, then to transfer the subsequent 14 bytes in the record to B$, etc. The important thing to remember here is that the FIELD statement operates on *each record*. In the example above, you retrieved a total of:

32 + 14 + 5 = 51 bytes

If you allow the OPEN statement for file #1 to use the default of 128 bytes, you will be wasting the back 77 bytes (128-51) of the record! For maximum efficiency, the OPEN statement for this example should define a *reclength* of 51 so all of the storage is used. Please do not confuse the *logical record length* (the number of bytes transferred by a GET or PUT statement) of the OPEN statement with the actual *physical block length* used to move the data between the physical hard disk and the computer memory. (The physical block length is the number of bytes that DOS sends or receives at one time when it communicates with the disk controller card.) The operating system and GW-BASIC are smart enough to take care of those headaches for you automatically, so the typical user rarely has to know that they are different. All you need to do is add the individual byte lengths of the variables and make the record length that size.

Returning to record length, the sum of all of the string lengths in a FIELD statement must be less than or equal to the record length in the OPEN statement (or 128 if the default was used). Otherwise, GW-BASIC will generate a Field overflow error message. Figure 9.1 illustrates the desired relationship between the sum of lengths in a field statement and the record length in an OPEN statement.

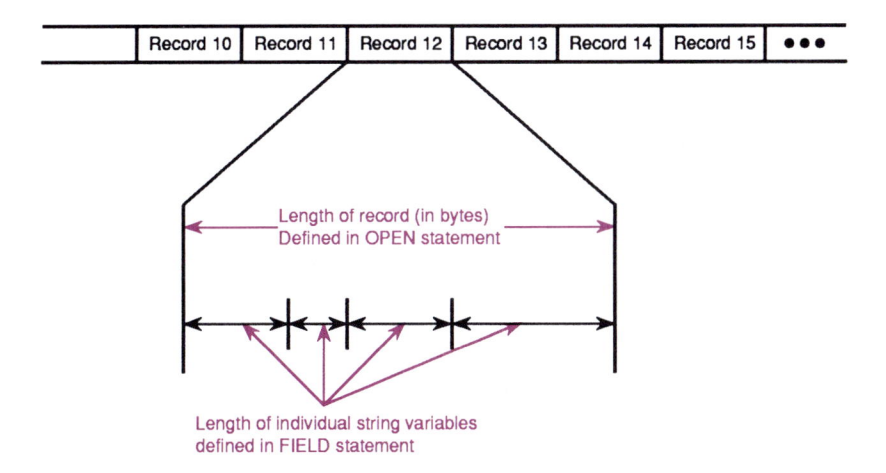

Figure 9.1 Desired relationship between FIELD items and record size

One of the more unusual features of GW-BASIC disk I/O is that the user can execute more than one FIELD statement on a single file. This lets the user retrieve data from the file in more than one format. Because all of the data is retrieved as strings, there really isn't much of an advantage to using this technique and there are definite disadvantages in terms of confusion and program complexity. To avoid unnecessary confusion, avoid multiple FIELD statements for one file until you become very experienced with disk I/O.

The FIELD statement does for disk I/O what a format string does for a PRINT USING statement; it tells GW-BASIC how the data is to be formatted. The commands to read or write a particular record are controlled by two other commands called GET and PUT which will now be explained.

The GET and PUT Statements

This is it, the last piece of the puzzle! The GET and PUT statements are the commands that actually initiate data transfers to and from the disk. The statements are of the form:

GET [#]*filenum* [,*recnum*]

and

PUT [#]*filenum* [,*recnum*]

where *filenum* is the file number defined in the OPEN statement and used in the FIELD statement. If the optional *recnum* parameter is specified, the data associated with that particular record will be retrieved from or written to the disk. If *recnum* is not specified, GW-BASIC will default to the next record in the file (if the file has just been opened, it will default to record number 1). The *recnum* parameter can only be specified when the file has been opened for either RANDOM or "R" operation.

When GW-BASIC executes a GET statement, it goes to a file buffer area to see if that particular part of the disk file is already in memory. This happens because file transfers handled by DOS are usually done in 512-byte groups (DOS does not know and does not care about the record length parameter used by GW-BASIC, it deals strictly with the realities of disk hardware). Because your record will typically be much smaller than the block of data brought in by DOS, there is a good chance that a particular GW-BASIC data record may already be in memory. If the entire record is already in memory, GW-BASIC copies the data from the buffer to the variables specified in the appropriate FIELD statement. When control is returned to your BASIC program, all of the information contained in the record is available through the string variables identified in the FIELD statement. You can now easily copy the information from these FIELD variables to other normal variables within your program. You can think of the GET statement as a sort of READ or INPUT command that transfers the data from the disk to your FIELD variables. If the particular record is not in the disk buffer, GW-BASIC makes the necessary arrangements with DOS to get the information from the disk to you. The following program creates a simple file with records of fixed length and then allows you to read any of the individual records:

```
100 DEFINT I-N:DEFSTR S
200 OPEN "O",#1,"TEST.DAT"
300 CLS:PRINT "Made it through the OPEN #1"
400 FOR I=1 TO 30
500 PRINT #1, USING "Hello, this is record number ##";I
600 NEXT I
700 CLOSE #1
800 PRINT "Made it through the CLOSE #1"
900 'Here start the disk read portion of the program
1000 OPEN "R",#1,"TEST.DAT",33
1100 FIELD #1, 33 AS S
1200 CLS:INPUT "Please enter record number (1-30) ",I
1300 IF I<1 OR I>30 THEN BEEP:GOTO 1200
1400 GET #1,I
1500 PRINT:PRINT S
1600 PRINT:INPUT "Would you like to quit (Y or N)",SQUIT
1700 IF SQUIT="N" OR SQUIT="n" GOTO 1200
1800 CLS:LOCATE 22,10:PRINT "Returning to GW-BASIC..."
1900 CLOSE $
```

This small program creates a file containing thirty entries of identical length. Each entry consists of the string within quotes in the PRINT # USING statement in line 500, which includes two spaces for an integer number. If you run this program, you will be asked for a number between 1 and 30. GW-BASIC will then employ the GET statement in line 1400 to retrieve that particular record so it can be displayed on the screen. The record size specified in the OPEN and FIELD statements (lines 1000 and 1100) might baffle you. If you count the characters between quotes in the PRINT # USING statement, you can account for only 31 (including the # signs for the two digit integer). The discrepancy is because GW-BASIC inserted a carriage return (⏎) and a linefeed (<lf>) character at the end of each record. This is why the TEST.DAT file looks perfectly normal and neat when you send it to the screen using the DOS command TYPE TEST.DAT (try it). Because you really don't want these two extra characters in there, you can modify three lines of the program to correct the problem:

```
500 PRINT #1, USING "Hello, this is record number ##";I;
1000 OPEN "R",#1,"TEST.DAT",31
1100 FIELD #1, 31 AS S
```

The added semicolon at the end of line 500 suppresses the insertion of the carriage return and linefeed at the end of every write operation. You also changed the record length and field length to 31 to compensate for the shorter record. If you now run the modified program, exit to DOS, and then TYPE **TEST.DAT**, you will see that the data comes out in a jumble of characters rather than the organized form of the previous program.

You probably wonder why you didn't use the PUT statement to generate the data in the previous example. The PUT statement was avoided because there is another detail that needs to be explained. GW-BASIC creates the variables in FIELD statements differently from the usual string variables that have been used until now. Because of this, it is possible to receive data from those variables; however, you cannot directly place data in them. This happens because the normal disk write statements (such as PRINT #) also need to be able to place data in the FIELD variable so that it can be sent to the file. For example, the previous sample programs defined a string variable *S* in the FIELD statement. It is perfectly legal to insert the following statement in the sample programs:

```
1450 A$=LEFT$(S,5)
```

Here, GW-BASIC will find *S* and copy the first five letters (Hello) into the normal string A$. If you use the same FIELD statement with a PUT statement, you need to move the information into the FIELD variable. Unfortunately, the statement:

```
3000 S="First"
```

will not accomplish this because GW-BASIC will create a new, normal, string variable called *S* and assign the letters "First" to it. The only way to move data into the FIELD variable *S* is to use either LSET or RSET. These instructions can move one string to another. If the source string is less than the destination string, the destination string will left- or right-justify (respectively) and pad with blanks. For example, the previous program defined *S* to be of length 31. If you execute the following statement:

```
3000 LSET S = "Short string"
```

the FIELD variable *S* will be filled with the 12 characters of the string constant, followed by 19 blanks (because you told it to left-justify). If the statement:

```
3000 RSET S = "Short string"
```

is executed, the FIELD variable *S* will consist of 19 blanks followed by the characters for "Short string" because you told it to right-justify.

Another complication concerns the number at the end of the string. In order to mimic the operation of the PRINT # USING statement, you first need to convert the value held in integer I to a string. This conversion can be accomplished using the STR$ function because it converts any number into a string. The STR$ is of the form:

```
1100 A$ = STR$(number)
```

where *number* is a valid numeric constant or variable. The string typically contains the ASCII characters that would be sent to the screen if a PRINT *number* command were executed. If the number is positive, a leading blank is inserted. A negative number always begins with a minus sign followed by the first digit of the number. Because you can guarantee that the value of I is positive, you only need to worry about removing the leading blank when you have a double-digit number (you actually want the leading blank for single digits because you need to pad out to two places so that the statement is the same length). The removal of the leading space is accomplished using the MID$ function. The MID$ function is of the form:

```
1100 B$ = MID$(string, startchar[, length])
```

Chapter 9

where *string* is either a string constant (contained in double-quotes) or the name of a string variable. The *startchar* parameter tells how far to the right from the beginning of *string* to go to select the first character of the new string, and the optional *length* parameter specifies how many characters to copy from *string* to the new string. This function copies a section of one string into another.

If you use a PUT rather than the PRINT # USING statement, several additional changes are required. First, you need to specify the record length in the OPEN statement at the beginning of the program. You also must add a FIELD statement to define the FIELD variable that will be used to convey the data into the file buffer. When the dust settles, you end up with the following program:

```
100 DEFINT I-N:DEFSTR S
200 OPEN "R",#1,"TEST.DAT",31
250 FIELD #1, 31 AS S
300 CLS:PRINT "Made it through the OPEN #1"
400 FOR I=1 TO 30
410 A$=STR$(I)
420 IF LEN(A$)>2 THEN A$=MID$(A$,2,2)
430 LSET S="Hello, this is record number "+A$
500 PUT #1
600 NEXT I
700 CLOSE #1
800 PRINT "Made it through the CLOSE #1"
900 'Here start the disk read portion of the program
1000 OPEN "R",#1,"TEST.DAT",31
1100 FIELD #1, 31 AS S
1200 CLS:INPUT "Please enter record number (1-30) ",I
1300 IF I<1 OR I>30 THEN BEEP:GOTO 1200
1400 GET #1,I
1500 PRINT:PRINT S
1600 PRINT:INPUT "Would you like to quit (Y or N)",SQUIT
1700 IF SQUIT="N" OR SQUIT="n" GOTO 1200
1800 CLS:LOCATE 22,10:PRINT "Returning to GW-BASIC..."
1900 CLOSE $
```

Statements 200, 250, 410, 420, 430 and 500 were either modified or newly created to deal with the requirements of the PUT statement. One other change needs to be explained. GW-BASIC files must be opened for random access ("R") whenever PUT or GET statements are used. This is usually not a problem because random access is the most flexible of the file modes, allowing both read and write operations. Please compare the modified lines with those in the previous sample programs to make certain that you understand what the changes were and why they were made.

You are probably asking yourself why you should bother with PUT and GET statements when PRINT # and INPUT # appear to be so much easier to use. Imagine that you want to read a file that is not made up of normal ASCII characters. Trying to read an ASCII file into strings by using INPUT # can cause all sorts of strange things to happen. On the other hand, the FIELD and OPEN statements work together nicely to limit the data to a manageable unit. Fortunately, GW-BASIC doesn't try to analyze the information brought in through a GET statement; all values between 0 and 255 are legal. The following program is designed to read *any* file that can be accessed by DOS, as long as the file is less than approximately eight megabytes in size. This limitation exists because file record numbers are restricted by GW-BASIC to be in the range of 1 to 32767. Because the OPEN statement defines a record to be 256 bytes long, the longest possible file must be:

```
256 x 32,767 = 8,388,352 bytes
```

There is one small catch that you must know about before running this program; it concerns the GW-BASIC record size switch. As was mentioned earlier, GW-BASIC will default to a record length of 128 if no value is provided in the OPEN statement. What you weren't told is that you must define the maximum file record length when you invoke GW-BASIC if the record length is to be greater than 128 bytes. This is accomplished via the /S: switch. For example, the following program needs a record length of 256 bytes, so you need to invoke GW-BASIC using the following DOS command:

```
>GWBASIC/S:256
```

By adding the "/S:256" to the back of the familiar GWBASIC invocation, you tell GW-BASIC that you want the largest record to be 256 bytes in size. If you do not do this when a record larger than 128 bytes is requested, GW-BASIC will stop execution with an error #5 (illegal function call).

```
100 DEFINT A-N:DEFSTR S:DIM K$(10)
200 '*************************************************************
300 '* The following loop turns off all automatic keys
400 '* defined by GW-BASIC
500 '*************************************************************
600 KEY OFF:FOR I=1 TO 10:KEY I,"":NEXT
700 '*************************************************************
800 '* If error occurs, jump to line 23300
900 '*************************************************************
1000 ON ERROR GOTO 23300
1100 '*************************************************************
1200 '* Draw a set of boxes for professional-looking display
1300 '*************************************************************
1400 GOSUB 40300
1500 ' define function keys for this display
1600 GOSUB 21300
1700 K$(1)="Select FIle":K$(10)="Quit"
1800 GOSUB 20200 ' Clear dialog box
1900 GOSUB 21400
2000 ON K GOTO 2200,2100,2100,2100,2100,2100,2100,2100,2100,7600
2100 BEEP:GOSUB 20200:PRINT"Illegal function key!":GOTO 1900
2200 '*************************************************************
2300 '* This section selects a file
2400 '*************************************************************
2500 GOSUB 40000:COLOR 7,0:GOSUB 20900:GOSUB 20200
2600 INPUT "Please enter file name (i.e., TEST.JNK) ";DF$
2700 GOSUB 20200
2800 GOSUB 22600:IREC=1 'Open the file and set to record #1
2900 J=LEN(DF$):COLOR 3,0:LOCATE 20,72-J:PRINT DF$;
3000 GET #1,IREC:COLOR 7,0:LOCATE 20,6
3100 PRINT USING "###";IREC
3200 GOSUB 20200:PRINT "Please stand by..."
3300 '*************************************************************
3400 '* This double loop converts the data in the two FIELD
3500 '* strings SF1 and SF2 to hexadecimal form and to a
3600 '* printable character if possible (otherwise a period)
3700 '*************************************************************
3800 FOR I1=1 TO 8:CRY=I1+1
3900 FOR I2=1 TO 16:I=I2+(16*(I1-1))
4000 CRX1=7+(2*I2):CRX2=51+I2
4100 SO=MID$(SF1,I,1):J=ASC(SO):K=J\16 AND 15:L=J AND 15
4200 IF K<10 THEN S1=CHR$(48+K) ELSE S1=CHR$(55+K)
4300 IF L<10 THEN S2=CHR$(48+L) ELSE S2=CHR$(55+L)
4400 LOCATE CRY,CRX1:PRINT S1+S2;
```

```
4500 IF J<32 OR J>122 THEN SO="."
4600 LOCATE CRY,CRX2:PRINT SO;
4700 SO=MID$(SF2,I,1):J=ASC(SO):K=J\16 AND 15:L=J AND 15
4800 IF K<10 THEN S1=CHR$(48+K) ELSE S1=CHR$(55+K)
4900 IF L<10 THEN S2=CHR$(48+L) ELSE S2=CHR$(55+L)
5000 LOCATE CRY+9,CRX1:PRINT S1+S2;
5100 IF J<32 OR J>122 THEN SO="."
5200 LOCATE CRY+9,CRX2:PRINT SO;
5300 NEXT I2:NEXT I1
5400 '*********************************************************
5500 '* This is the end of the character conversion loops
5600 '*********************************************************
5700 GOSUB 20200
5800 '*********************************************************
5900 '* Print out file maneuvering function key operations
6000 '*********************************************************
6100 K$(1)="Previous record":K$(2)="Next record"
6200 K$(3)="Sel. record #":K$(5)="Return to menu"
6300 GOSUB 21400:ON K GOTO 6600,6500,7100,6400,1500
6400 BEEP:GOSUB 20200:PRINT "Illegal key":GOTO 6300
6500 IREC=IREC+1:GOTO 3000 'Next record requested
6600 IF IREC>1 THEN IREC=IREC-1 'Previous record requested
6700 GOTO 3000
6800 '*********************************************************
6900 '* This section jumps to a specific record
7000 '*********************************************************
7100 GOSUB 20200:INPUT "Record number ";E
7200 IF E>0 THEN IREC=E
7300 GOSUB 20200:GOTO 3000
7400 '*********************************************************
7500 '*  This section exits the program
7600 '*********************************************************
7700 CLOSE #1:RESET:COLOR 7,0:CLS:END
20000 '*********************************************************
20100 '* This section clears the action box
20200 '*********************************************************
20300 FOR CRY=22 TO 23:GOSUB 20800:NEXT:CRY=22:LOCATE CRY,6:RETURN
20400 CRY=22:GOSUB 20800:LOCATE CRY,6:RETURN
20500 CRY=23:GOSUB 20800:LOCATE CRY,6:RETURN
20600 ' Clear the function key command line
20700 CRY=25:LOCATE CRY,1:PRINT SPACE$(78);:RETURN
20800 LOCATE CRY,6:PRINT SPACE$(66);:RETURN
20900 '*********************************************************
21000 '* Clear out entire K$ array used to define  function
```

```
21100 '* keys and erase the command line
21200 '***********************************************************
21300 FOR I=1 TO 10:K$(I)="":NEXT:GOSUB 20700:RETURN
21400 '***********************************************************
21500 '* This section prints function key legends and
21600 '* returns a code number between 1 and 10
21700 '***********************************************************
21800 GOSUB 20700:J=1:FOR I=1 TO 10
21900 IF K$(I)="" THEN J=J+2:GOTO 22100
22000 COLOR 15,0:LOCATE 25,J:PRINT I;:COLOR 0,7:PRINT K$(I);:J=J+3+LEN(K$(I))
22100 NEXT:COLOR 15,0
22200 A$=INKEY$:IF A$="" GOTO 22200
22300 IF LEFT$(A$,1)<>CHR$(0)GOTO 22200
22400 K=ASC(RIGHT$(A$,1))-58:RETURN
22500 BEEP:GOTO 22200
22600 '***********************************************************
22700 '* This section opens the selected file for random
22800 '* access and a record length of 256 bytes
22900 '***********************************************************
23000 RESET:OPEN "R",#1,DF$,256
23100 FIELD #1,128 AS SF1,128 AS SF2
23200 RETURN
23300 '***********************************************************
23400 '* This section deals with run-time errors by printing
23500 '* the line and error number before returning to BASIC
23600 '***********************************************************
23700 BEEP:GOSUB 20200
23800 RESET
23900 PRINT"error number "ERR" in line number="ERL;
24000 GOSUB 20500
24100 PRINT"All files are closed. Returning to GW-BASIC";
24200 LOCATE 23,79:COLOR 7,0:END
40000 '***********************************************************
40100 '* This routine builds the boxes for the display
40200 '***********************************************************
40300 KEY OFF:CLS
40400 M=1:N=18:NW=66
40500 COLOR 2,0
40600 CLS:LOCATE M,5
40700 S1=CHR$(201)+STRING$(NW,205)+CHR$(187)
40800 S2=CHR$(186)+STRING$(NW,32)+CHR$(186)
40900 S3=CHR$(200)+STRING$(NW,205)+CHR$(188)
41000 PRINT S1;
41100 FOR I=M+1 TO N+M
```

```
41200 LOCATE I,5:PRINT S2;
41300 NEXT I
41400 LOCATE N+M+1,5:PRINT S3;
41500 LOCATE N+M+2,5:PRINT S1;
41600 FOR I=N+M+3 TO N+M+4
41700 LOCATE I,5:PRINT S2;
41800 NEXT I
41900 LOCATE N+M+5,5:PRINT S3;
42000 RETURN
```

As you can see, this program is divided into three general sections. Lines 100 through 7700 can be considered the main body of the program (the parts that are relatively unique). Lines 20000 to 24200 are basically concerned with display management and disk control (for the most part, these routines are utilities that make screen manipulation easier). The last routine starts at line 40000 and should look quite familiar; it is the box-drawing program from Chapter 8. These routines are in different number ranges to keep them as separate utilities files that the GW-BASIC MERGE command can bring together when you are ready to start testing. The idea here is reusable code. When you have debugged a utility, you should never need to tinker with it again (if you are careful).

This program converts the data in strings SF1 and SF2 into a screen display in *hexadecimal data format*. Table 9.1 illustrates the conversion between decimal numbers, hexadecimal numbers (called hex for short), and binary numbers (the 1s and 0s actually stored in the computer):

Table 9.1 Equivalence between Decimal, Hex, and Binary

Decimal Number	Hexadecimal Number	Binary Number
0	0	0000
1	1	0001
2	2	0010
3	3	0011
4	4	0100
5	5	0101
6	6	0110
7	7	0111

Table 9.1 *(continued)*

Decimal Number	Hexadecimal Number	Binary Number
8	8	1000
9	9	1001
10	A	1010
11	B	1011
12	C	1100
13	D	1101
14	E	1110
15	F	1111

If you look carefully at the program between lines 4100 and 5200, you will notice a certain amount of repetition. In this section, the individual characters in SF1 and SF2 are split into upper eight bits and lower eight bits before being converted into hex digits to be displayed.

Before leaving the section on GETs and PUTs, you should examine a simple data encryption program that illustrates how all of the pieces can work together. This sample program takes a file and alters its contents in a predictable way so that it is unusable. The program can also take the scrambled file and convert it back to its original form (more or less). The scrambling is controlled by a unique phrase that only you know, preventing unauthorized persons from using your files. This can be useful if you keep sensitive files on a hard disk and you can't lock the PC at the end of the day.

Because this is only a demonstration program (as opposed to a commercial product) it does not destroy the contents of the original file, it simply creates a different file and writes the data there. It also has flaws that allow the scrambling algorithm to be broken (if you are interested in writing a secure encryption program you should be able to find serious books on the subject at any well-stocked library). It is provided here to illustrate all of the major disk I/O topics covered in this section:

```
100 DEFINT I-N:DEFSTR C,F,S
200 DIM IRAND(256),JRAND(256)
300 DIM JKEY(255)
400 CLS:COLOR 7,0
500 GOSUB 20000 'Load random values into SRAND
```

```
600 LOCATE 20,1
700 PRINT "Please enter the encryption key"
800 INPUT SKEY
900 KLEN=LEN(SKEY)
1000 FOR I=1 TO KLEN
1100 S=MID$(SKEY,I,1)
1200 JKEY(I)=IRAND(ASC(S))
1300 NEXT I
1400 CLS:LOCATE 20,1
1500 INPUT "Do you want to encode or decode (E or D)",S
1600 IF S="E" OR S="e" GOTO 1800
1700 IF S="D" OR S="d" GOTO 4400 ELSE BEEP:GOTO 1400
1800 '***********************************************
1900 '* This section encodes files
2000 '***********************************************
2100 OPEN "R",#1,"TEST.DAT"
2200 OPEN "R",#2,"TEST.CRY"
2300 FIELD #1, 128 AS S1
2400 FIELD #2, 128 AS S2
2500 IREC=1:KINDEX=1
2600 GET #1,IREC:SOUTPUT=""
2700 FOR I=1 TO 128
2800 N=ASC(MID$(S1,I,1))
2900 N=N+JKEY(KINDEX):N=N AND 255
3000 M=IRAND(N)
3100 KINDEX=KINDEX+1
3200 IF KINDEX > KLEN THEN KINDEX=1
3300 SOUTPUT=SOUTPUT+CHR$(M)
3400 NEXT I
3500 LSET S2=SOUTPUT
3600 PUT #2,IREC
3700 IREC=IREC+1:CLS:LOCATE 20,1:PRINT "Record # ";IREC
3800 IF EOF(1) THEN GOTO 4000
3900 GOTO 2600
4000 CLOSE #1,#2
4100 CLS:LOCATE 20,1
4200 PRINT "File encoding completed"
4300 END
4400 '***********************************************
4500 '* This section decodes files
4600 '***********************************************
4700 OPEN "R",#1,"TEST.DEC"
4800 OPEN "R",#2,"TEST.CRY"
4900 FIELD #1, 128 AS S1
```

Chapter 9

```
5000 FIELD #2, 128 AS S2
5100 IREC=1:KINDEX=1
5200 GET #2,IREC:SOUTPUT=""
5300 IF EOF(2) THEN GOTO 6700
5400 FOR I=1 TO 128
5500 N=ASC(MID$(S2,I,1))
5600 M=JKEY(KINDEX)
5700 KINDEX=KINDEX+1
5800 IF KINDEX > KLEN THEN KINDEX=1
5900 J=JRAND(N)-M:J=J AND 255
6000 SOUTPUT=SOUTPUT+CHR$(J)
6100 NEXT I
6200 LSET S1=SOUTPUT
6300 PUT #1,IREC
6400 IREC=IREC+1:CLS:LOCATE 20,1:PRINT "Record # ";IREC
6500 IF EOF(2) THEN GOTO 6700
6600 GOTO 5200
6700 CLOSE #1,#2
6800 CLS:LOCATE 20,1
6900 PRINT "File decoding completed"
7000 END
20000 FOR I=0 TO 255
20100 READ IRAND(I)
20200 IF JRAND(IRAND(I))<>0 THEN BEEP:PRINT I,IRAND(I)
20300 JRAND(IRAND(I))=I
20400 NEXT I
20500 RETURN
20600 DATA 169,202,119,247,65,102,190,118,62,155,101,192,211,156,58,200
20700 DATA 106,234,246,23,17,70,132,9,121,28,61,41,94,215,240,76
20800 DATA 230,142,110,140,97,44,170,124,14,96,63,131,15,189,138,158
20900 DATA 164,196,242,209,69,1,224,85,204,134,84,87,50,22,80,53
21000 DATA 176,146,18,78,123,99,179,64,226,223,195,212,51,21,225,145
21100 DATA 133,201,103,217,49,0,54,27,95,187,38,252,206,137,39,19
21200 DATA 239,40,33,92,167,149,129,250,199,127,46,59,232,248,188,174
21300 DATA 111,37,153,228,122,35,16,113,183,91,227,45,254,159,48,219
21400 DATA 4,175,151,100,251,148,116,10,235,6,42,238,203,117,72,255
21500 DATA 193,221,82,186,71,135,213,79,207,108,136,86,198,157,114,90
21600 DATA 216,144,75,31,163,233,208,177,67,68,60,115,181,52,150,162
21700 DATA 184,229,253,241,172,220,185,93,160,20,55,56,120,112,36,57
21800 DATA 130,147,81,152,166,88,25,245,210,98,11,104,30,126,244,43
21900 DATA 24,47,13,2,194,74,109,237,77,7,89,180,231,168,73,34
22000 DATA 191,83,66,218,125,128,197,5,107,222,182,32,161,26,171,105
22100 DATA 143,12,3,214,178,8,243,173,29,249,236,205,165,141,139,154
```

The central variables of this program are the arrays IRAND, JRAND, and JKEY. The IRAND array is filled with 256 unique random values from the data statements. The array JRAND is a sort of "reverse pointer." Given the value of an element in IRAND, JRAND gives you the initial index in the IRAND array (don't worry about the details for now; just trust that it works). If you are lucky, the PRINT statement in line 20200 will never be executed. It is designed to detect a duplicate value in the DATA statements (everyone makes typing mistakes).

The program section up to line 1700 simply initializes the arrays and then asks whether you want to encode a file (which takes TEST.DAT and creates TEST.CRY) or decode the file (take TEST.CRY and create TEST.DEC). The other two sections of the program are what you really need. Each section opens two separate files and defines FIELD variables for each. In lines 2700 to 3400, an appropriate value from the JKEY array is added to the value of each input character and this summed value is run through the IRAND array to get a random value that represents the sum of the two numbers. This value is then appended to the back of the string that will later be moved to the output file. Line 3800 introduces something you haven't see before: EOF(*filenum*). When the value returned by this function becomes nonzero (TRUE), you have read the last record in the file. When this happens, the program jumps to line 4000 to close both files and terminate execution. The LSET statement in line 3500 transfers the data from the local string array to the FIELD variable S2. The PUT command in line 3600 actually forces the new data contained in the FIELD variable out to the DOS file handler. The program code between lines 4700 and 7000 performs disk operations similar to those in the encode section.

You may have noticed that the IF EOF statement in line 5300 precedes the FOR loop rather than follows it (as in the previous section). This prevents an additional dummy record from being added to the back of the TEST.DEC file. At this point, a word of caution is required. This program has certain deficiencies. For one, it always *pads* files out to a whole number of records. It also may have hidden bugs because it has not been tested thoroughly (it is intended to be a sample program rather than a commercial product). Finally, the algorithm used here is pretty simple (the people at the National Security Agency could break this during their coffee break). The program is good enough to keep your grocery list private, but don't use it for anything important without extensive testing.

One final warning: For this program to work properly, you must enter the key string *exactly* the same way both times. The encryption algorithm is sensitive to case (upper and lower) and even more sensitive to differences in the length of the key. If you type in a key with one extra space, the entire TEST.DEC file will be unreadable except for the first few characters. Have fun!

The CVx and MKx$ Functions

Although these commands do not directly perform disk operations, their discussion here is quite appropriate. Imagine that you want to store true integer data in a file in the most compact form possible. The best way to do it would be to determine a way to place the top and bottom bytes of each integer (remember, integers are two bytes long) into two characters of a string. You could then use normal techniques to "attach" sixty-four of these two-byte strings together into one large string that could then be written and retrieved as a 128-byte record. Because of integer mathematics, this is quite easy to do (you performed the retrieval trick to some extent in the file dump program earlier in this chapter). Unfortunately, it is very difficult to play similar tricks when attempting to manipulate single- and double-precision numbers. This is where the CVx and MKx statements come into play.

The MKI$, MKS$, and MKD$ functions convert integers, single-precision and double-precision variables into two-byte, four-byte, and eight-byte strings (respectively). These strings do not hold ASCII characters and cannot be printed. They hold the actual bit patterns used by the microprocessor to represent the number. For example, the statements:

```
S1 = MKI$(8192%)
S2 = MKS$(14.7!)
S3 = MKD$(6.28E-24#)
```

result in S1 containing two characters, S2 containing four characters, and S3 containing eight characters. (The contents of these characters will make no sense to you unless you are really into computer mathematics.) You can now attach groups of these strings together by statements such as:

```
SOUTPUT=SOUTPUT+S2
```

This technique makes it very easy to build pure binary files (which is the most efficient direct data storage method possible).

As you have probably guessed by now, the CVI, CVS, and CVD functions perform the exact inverse of MKI, MKS, and MKD. One typical way to use the CVx series is:

```
1000 FOR I%=1 to 32
1100 N% = (4*I) - 3
1200 S$ = MID$(SFROMRECORD$,N%,4)
1300 B!(I) = CVS(S$)
1400 NEXT I
```

This takes a 128-byte string, retrieved via a typical GET statement and converts consecutive groups of four bytes into single-precision numbers. Of course, all of the stored variables do not have to be of the same type. For example:

```
1000 FIELD #1, 2 AS A$, 4 AS P$, 8 AS W$
 ...
2500 GET #1
2600 J% = CVI(A$)
2700 O! = CVS(P$)
2800 Z# = CVD(W$)
```

retrieves proper-length strings for direct conversion without needing to pluck out the pieces using string commands. These methods are usually necessary for accessing information from data files created by other languages and by commercial programs, such as databases and spreadsheets..

Miscellaneous

GW-BASIC provides certain disk-oriented commands that are not actually I/O statements, so they are collected here for easy reference. These statements and functions are:

CHDIR	Changes the current (default) directory
CLEAR	Sets all variables to zero and closes all files
FILES	Displays the contents of the current directory on the screen

Chapter 9

KILL file	Deletes the specified file
LOC(f)	Returns the current position in the file
LOF(f)	Returns the length (in bytes) of the file
RMDIR	Deletes a subdirectory

Many of these commands accept wild cards or path data. For example, the FILES command accepts a trailing string, such as:

`FILES"*.DOC"`

so that only document files show up on the screen. The string can also contain disk and path data and will accept both the asterisk and question mark wild card characters (where a question mark is used as a single-place wild card). If you are not familiar with the use of wild card characters when specifying DOS files, please refer to your DOS book for a detailed explanation.

The RMDIR and CHDIR commands need a detailed path specification because they deal specifically with directories. The KILL command also accepts detailed drive and path data—it simply deletes the file from the default (current) directory if the path data is not provided.

The CLEAR command has two optional parameters. The first parameter sets a maximum size for the GW-BASIC area in memory. This can be important if you need to reserve space for machine-language programs (discussed further in Chapter 13). The second parameter defines the amount of stack space allocated by GW-BASIC. This becomes important if you have several layers of nested FOR...NEXT loops or if you have several layers of GOSUBs that call each other. The default stack space is 512 bytes, which is usually adequate. Most users ignore the optional parameters until a problem arises that requires adjustment.

The LOC(#n) function finds out where you are within the specified file (where #n indicates the number defined in the OPEN statement and used in PUT and GET statements). If the file is random-access, LOC returns the value of the current record. If the file is sequential, LOC returns the number of 128-byte records retrieved or written since the file was opened.

Finally, the LOF(#n) function returns the size of the file in bytes. If you have this value and you know the size of each record, you can calculate the last record number by dividing the result of the LOF function by the record length and rounding. This can be very useful when adding new records to random-access files.

Summary

This chapter covered a great deal of material on disk operations. It began by introducing the concepts behind GW-BASIC disk file operations and then went on to introduce the OPEN, CLOSE, and FILES statements. It also covered the various ways to transfer data to and from a disk file and ended with a brief explanation of several miscellaneous commands used in conjunction with disk I/O.

Quiz

1. Which statement defines the length of each file record?
2. What is the relationship between the length of the file record and the length in bytes of the FIELD variables?
3. Explain two separate methods to transfer data to a file.
4. What function converts strings to variables?
5. How would you display all .BAS files in the current directory?
6. Can GW-BASIC programs be used to delete files?
7. What GW-BASIC command correlates a file name to a file number?
8. How would you find out which record is currently being processed in file #3?
9. How would you calculate the number of 128-byte records in file #2?
10. What special action do you have to take when invoking GW-BASIC when a file uses a record larger than 128 bytes?

Chapter 10
Introduction to GW-BASIC Graphics

In This Chapter

As you may recall, Chapter 2 briefly discussed the capabilities of the various display adapter cards commonly used in PCs. This chapter describes in greater detail the graphics capabilities of these cards and how GW-BASIC commands operate with each one. First, a brief tutorial on graphics display hardware is required.

Video Hardware

The video display systems of most desktop PCs are comprised of two pieces: the display adapter card, which is installed in a card slot inside the machine, and the video display monitor on which the image appears. Most video displays operate by turning individual dots on and off to "draw" the desired letters or pictures on the screen. These dots are called *pixels* and can be individually set to specific colors when the display cards are in graphics mode.

Different display standards (CGA, EGA, and VGA) have different capabilities for controlling the colors of each pixel. These capabilities are usually restricted by memory limitations in the display cards and by speed limitations in the display monitors. The display cards use memory to remember what colors each

Chapter 10

pixel should be (the more memory, the more colors the card can remember). The speed limitation in the display monitor affects how many dots can be drawn on the screen. This affects the size of each pixel and how many of them can be drawn on the screen. Now, for some specifics. As a general rule, a faster display allows more (smaller) dots to be drawn on a standard-size screen. This results in more pleasant pictures. The faster displays also usually look less blurred.

The CGA Display

The CGA standard is probably the most common combination of adapter card and display in the PC world. The CGA display adapter card installed inside the PC case is capable of driving two separate types of display CRTs: composite video displays and RGB displays. The composite video signal from the CGA card usually conforms to the same national standard as the video signals generated by video cameras and VCRs. Because of the electrical characteristics of this composite signal, the signal tends to produce images on the screen that appear a bit blurred or muddy. The second signal output from a CGA adapter card is called RGB (which refers to the signal lines for Red, Green, and Blue). RGB displays tend to appear a bit crisper than displays that use the composite signal. From a software perspective, both displays behave in exactly the same way because the performance limitations of CGA are mostly in the card rather than in the display.

The CGA adapter card is capable of operating in four separate modes: 40-character text, 80-character text, 320-by-200-color and 640-by-200-monochrome. The 40-character text mode was originally intended for users who were going to connect their PCs to VCRs or color TV sets; this mode is rarely used. Everything that will be said for the 80-character text mode also applies to the 40-character mode.

The 80-character (by 25 line) color text mode is the default mode of the CGA card. It can display letters, numbers, and other characters in up to 15 colors (and black) at the same time.

The 320-by-200-color graphics mode lets the user select a color for each pixel in a pattern that is 320 pixels wide and 200 pixels tall. Because of memory limitations within the card, the user can only select one background color (in the range 0 to 15). This color is selected from those defined for text mode (see Chapter 8). The remaining three colors come from one of two palettes, as illustrated in Table 10.1, and are assigned to specific numbers.

Table 10.1 Color palettes available in CGA color graphics mode

Color number	Palette 0	Palette 1
0	Black	Black
1	Green	Cyan
2	Red	Magenta
3	Brown	White

A color palette is selected by using the command:

1100 COLOR [*bkcolor*][,*palette*]

where *bkcolor* identifies a background color in the range 0 to 15 and *palette* is either a 1 or a 0. This command, however, should not be executed until the display card is first placed in color graphics mode. To select color graphics mode for a CGA card, the following command must be executed:

1000 SCREEN 1

This command tells the CGA card to switch electronically into mode 1, which is the 320-by-200-color graphics mode. The allowed modes for the SCREEN command for a CGA card are

Mode Number	Mode Description
0	Text mode (either 40- or 80-character mode).
1	320-by-200-color graphics mode.
2	640-by-200-monochrome graphics mode.

Once the screen mode has been set, various commands can be used to control the pixels on the screen. The most fundamental commands are PSET and PRESET. They are of the form

Chapter 10

PSET(*xpixel,ypixel*)[,*pcolor*]

and

PRESET(*xpixel,ypixel*)[,*pcolor*]

where the PSET command is used to set the pixel at coordinates (*xpixel,ypixel*) to the color identified by *pcolor* (the values represented by *pcolor* are defined by palette 0 and palette 1). If the *pcolor* parameter is omitted from the PSET command, it defaults to color number 1 in the current palette. If the *pcolor* parameter is provided for the PRESET command, it operates identically to the PSET command. If the *pcolor* parameter is omitted from the PRESET command, the specified pixel is set to the background color (as defined by the last COLOR command).

The following program provides a simple vehicle to test the 320-by-200-graphics mode. Note that the loops start on zero and end on the maximum number minus 1. This happens because GW-BASIC always defines the pixel at the top left corner of the screen as (0,0). Positive x-values go to the right and positive y-values move down the screen (negative coordinates are not allowed).

```
90 KEY OFF
100 CLS:SCREEN 1
150 COLOR 0,1
200 FOR I%=0 TO 199
250 FOR J%=0 TO 319
300 PSET(J%,I%),((J%+I%) MOD 4)
400 NEXT J%
450 NEXT I%
500 IF INKEY$="" GOTO 500
800 END
```

Notice that the SCREEN statement was used in line 100 to select the card mode and that the color palette was selected in line 150. The strange algorithm at the end of line 300 is intended to make the color parameter go from 0 to 3 and then back to 0 again. By adding I% to the algorithm, the color pattern appears to move slowly to the left as you go down the screen. This helps to illustrate more clearly the size of the pixels. You may wish to play around with the loop limits of this program.

The previous program can also be modified to demonstrate the 640-by-200-monochrome mode:

```
90 KEY OFF
100 CLS:SCREEN 2
200 FOR I%=0 TO 199 STEP 2
250 FOR J%=0 TO 639 STEP 4
300 PSET(J%,I%)
400 NEXT J%
450 NEXT I%
500 IF INKEY$="" GOTO 500
800 END
```

In this program, the hardware mode was set to 2, and the COLOR command (line 150) was completely removed. The STEP increments in the FOR loops are used to obtain a fine checkerboard pattern on the screen. Notice that the color parameter was removed to illustrate that the color defaults to 1 (white) in monochrome mode.

The EGA and VGA Displays

EGA and VGA displays are capable of much higher pixel densities than CGA. Unfortunately, the version of GW-BASIC shipping with MS-DOS 4.01 (version 3.23) does not differentiate between EGA and VGA cards. In addition to the modes 0, 1, and 2 supported by CGA cards, EGA and VGA cards can operate in three additional modes:

Mode Number	Mode Description
0	Text mode (either 40- or 80-character mode).
1	320-by-200-graphics mode with 3 colors.
2	640-by-200-monochrome graphics mode.
7	640-by-200-graphics mode with 16 colors and 40-by-25 text.
8	640-by-200-graphics mode with 16 colors and 80-by-25 text.
9	640-by-350-graphics mode with either 64 or 16 colors and 80-by-25 text.

The following program illustrates the highest resolution mode available from an EGA card. It generates a fine diagonal pattern that looks like corduroy.

```
90 KEY OFF
100 CLS:SCREEN 9
200 FOR I%=0 TO 349
250 FOR J%=0 TO 639
300 PSET(J%,I%),((I%+J%)MOD 16)
400 NEXT J%
450 NEXT I%
500 IF INKEY$="" GOTO 500
700 END
```

If lines 200, 250, and 300 are changed as follows, the program produces 16 color bars across the screen.

```
200 FOR I%=0 TO 49
250 FOR J%=0 TO 639
300 PSET(J%,I%),(J%\40)
```

The Line Command

GW-BASIC provides certain commands for performing operations such as drawing lines, circles, and ellipses. These commands also allow the user to draw circular and elliptical arcs by drawing only parts of the circle or ellipse. The first of these commands to be described is the LINE command, which is of the form:

1100 LINE [(x1,y1)]-(x2,y2)[,[lcolor],B[F][,dash]

where the beginning point is specified by the coordinates (x1,y1), and the end point is defined by (x2,y2). The *lcolor* parameter is subject to the same mode restrictions as is the PSET command. The capital letter B "tells" GW-BASIC that you want to draw a box with points (x1,y1) and (x2,y2) at opposite corners. If you specify BF rather than B, the box interior is filled with the color specified by the parameter *lcolor*. The *dash* parameter is used to control line dashing. The algorithm looks at the number of 1s in the *dash* number in order to decide which pixels to set to *lcolor* and which to skip. For example, a *dash* value of 32767 contains a 0 in the most significant bit and 1s in the remaining 15 bits (you may wish to review Chapter 6 if you have forgotten about the internal representation of integers). This value generates a dashed line that is mostly line with only small blank spots. A *dash* value of 255 has the top eight bits set to zero and the bottom eight bits set to 1, so the dashed line appears to be half line and half blanks. If the *dash* value is set to 1, all that you see are dots that are spaced widely apart.

The following program illustrates some of the capabilities of the LINE command when used with an EGA or VGA card. If you have a CGA card, set the mode to either 1 or 2 and limit the color selections that are valid for the selected mode.

```
100 KEY OFF
200 CLS:SCREEN 9
300 LINE (10,10)-(400,100),13
400 LINE -(400,150),12
500 LINE -(550,25)
600 LINE (0,30)-(200,100),9,B
700 LINE (250,110)-(450,210),6,B,16383
800 LINE (0,230)-(639,300),2,BF
10000 IF INKEY$="" GOTO 10000
10100 LIST:END
```

Notice that lines 400 and 500 did not specify a beginning point; this tells GW-BASIC that you want to draw the next line from the end of the previous line. Line 500 also neglected to specify a color, so GW-BASIC defaulted to bright white. Line 700 illustrates how to draw a dashed box, and line 800 draws a short, wide, color-filled box near the bottom of the screen.

Notice that line 10100 seems a bit strange. To make it easier to "tinker" with the various parameters, a LIST command was inserted to force an automatic listing of the current program. This trick keeps you from repeatedly typing the word **LIST** ↵ or pressing the function key and the carriage return to request the listing.

Chapter 10

The Circle Command

The CIRCLE command operates similarly to the LINE command except that filling is not an option. The general form is

1100 CIRCLE
(x1,y1),r[,[ccolor][,[start],[end][,eccen]f]]

where (x1,y1) specifies the center of the circle, r specifies the radius of the circle in pixels, and the optional *ccolor* specifies the color of the circle. If the *eccen* parameter (which stands for eccentricity) is provided and is less than 1.0, GW-BASIC draws an ellipse that is wider than it is tall with an x-axis of the specified r value and the y-axis equal to r * *eccen* in height. If the *eccen* value is greater than 1, an ellipse is drawn that is taller than it is wide and the y-axis height is the value specified by r, but the x-axis is reduced to a value of r/*eccen*. The *start* and *end* parameters are used to specify the starting and ending points for circular and elliptical arcs. A value of 0 corresponds to a line drawn to the right from the center of the circle. Increasing positive angles run in a counter-clockwise direction to a maximum value of 2 * pi (which is approximately 6.2832). If either parameter is defined as a negative value, GW-BASIC takes the absolute value of the number to determine the angle and draws a line from that point to the center of the circle or ellipse. Thus, you can draw pie charts by determining the positive beginning and end angles and then negating them to force GW-BASIC to draw lines from the endpoints to the center. The following program illustrates several possible options of the CIRCLE command:

```
100 KEY OFF
200 CLS:SCREEN 9
300 CIRCLE (100,100),40,13
400 CIRCLE (200,200),100,11,,,,.5
450 CIRCLE (200,200),100,14,,,,.75
460 CIRCLE (200,200),100,10,,,,.25
500 CIRCLE (300,150),100,15,,,2.5
600 CIRCLE (450,100),80,12,0!,2.1
700 CIRCLE (450,200),80,2,0!,-5!,2.5
10000 IF INKEY$="" GOTO 10000
10100 LIST:END
```

You are strongly encouraged to experiment with the various options provided by the LINE and CIRCLE commands by modifying these sample programs.

Summary

In this chapter, you learned how to use the PSET, PRESET, LINE, and CIRCLE commands to generate picture elements on the screen. To successfully perform these operations, you also learned about the capabilities of the various display adapter cards and how to select the operating modes and default palettes for these cards. The information provided in this chapter should allow you to create extremely interesting graphics output for your programs.

Now you know how to read and write files, how to read data from the keyboard, and how to send it to a printer. With the graphics information in this chapter, you can even create programs to draw pictures and diagrams. However, the only noises that have emerged from your PC are disk-drive noises and the whirring of the cooling fan. The next chapter introduces you to the PC's limited music capability.

Quiz

1. What is the resolution of the two graphics modes available on a CGA card?
2. Which GW-BASIC statement is used to select the various graphics modes of a display card?
3. Which GW-BASIC statements are used to set a pixel to a set color?
4. What must the user do to draw several connected lines in a row using the LINE statement?
5. Which statement would you use to draw an eliptical arc?

Chapter 11
Sound from the Box

In This Chapter

There is one last interface that hasn't been covered: the tone generator. Although the PC's tone generator isn't as sophisticated as some competitor's equipment, it is capable of providing a certain amount of fun. In this chapter you will learn:

- ▶ How the tone generator works
- ▶ How to control it to play music
- ▶ How to tell when a music buffer is getting low

The Tone Generator

The tone generator in most PCs is a simple circuit that generates a *square-wave*. Most natural sounds are *sine-waves*, which explains why the tones from PCs sound a bit harsh (like a screeching violin). Figure 11.1 illustrates several typical waveforms used in making music. Another limitation of PC sound generators is that they cannot control the *amplitude* (or loudness) of the sound; this is why music from PCs tends to sound very even. The two things that you can control are the *pitch* (or tone) and the *duration* (time of play) of the note.

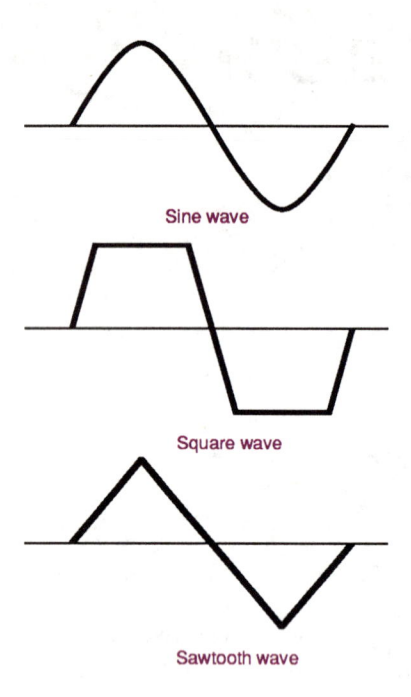

Figure 11.1 Different waveforms used in music synthesis

The SOUND Statement

GW-BASIC provides two commands for controlling the tone generator: SOUND and PLAY. The SOUND statement is of the form:

SOUND *frequency,clockticks*

where *frequency* is a number, or expression, between 37 and 32767 cycles per second (known as Hertz). The second argument, *clockticks*, is a number in the range 0 to 65535 which refers to how long the note should play. There are 18.2

clockticks per second (1,092 clockticks per minute). For example, the following command sets the generator to middle C for one-half second:

SOUND 523,9

(See Figure 11.2 for a depiction of notes on a keyboard and their corresponding frequencies.) If you want to set a period of silence (called a rest), set the frequency to 20000 and then set the clockticks to the desired value of delay. A clockticks value of 0 always turns off the current sound output.

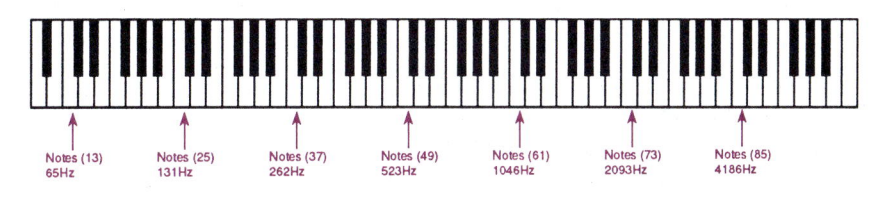

Figure 11.2 Relationship between keyboard notes and frequencies

The following program initializes an array to the value of the various notes on a standard keyboard and then plays a tune:

```
100 DEFINT A-N
200 DIM NOTES(108)
300 ON ERROR GOTO 1000
400 GOSUB 20000
500 READ FREQ,CLOCKS
600 SOUND NOTES(FREQ),CLOCKS
700 GOTO 500
1000 PRINT "I.m done..."
1100 END
20000 NOTES(97)=8392     'C
20100 NOTES(98)=8870     'C#
20200 NOTES(99)=9397     'D
20300 NOTES(100)=9956    'D#
20400 NOTES(101)=10548   'E
20500 NOTES(102)=11175   'F
20600 NOTES(103)=11840   'F#
20700 NOTES(104)=12544   'G
20800 NOTES(105)=13290   'G#
20900 NOTES(106)=14080   'A
21000 NOTES(107)=14917   'A#
```

```
21100 NOTES(108)=15804 'B
21200 FOR I=97 TO 108
21300 L=2
21400 FOR J=1 TO 8
21500 K=I-(J*12)
21600 NOTES(K)=NOTES(I)\L
21700 IF NOTES(K)<37 THEN NOTES(K)=32767
21800 L=L*2
21900 NEXT J
22000 NEXT I
22050 NOTES(0)=20000
22100 RETURN
35000 DATA 56,4,59,4,62,4,66,4,64,10
35100 DATA 62,4,52,4,56,4,59,4,64,8,0,2
35200 DATA 56,4,57,4,59,4,60,4,61,8,0,1
35300 DATA 60,4,61,8,0,1,60,4,61,26,0,4
35400 DATA 52,8,0,1,53,4,54,6,0,1,50,16
35500 DATA 0,4,53,4,54,6,0,1,50,20,0,4
35600 DATA 53,4,54,8,0,1,56,4,54,4
35700 DATA 49,4,52,4,57,4,61,32,0,4
35800 DATA 56,4,59,4,62,4,66,4,64,10
35900 DATA 62,4,52,4,56,4,59,4,64,8,0,2
36000 DATA 56,4,57,4,59,4,60,4,61,8,0,1
36100 DATA 61,7,0,1,56,4,0,1,61,5,0,2
36200 DATA 61,8,0,2,61,4,54,4,57,4,61,6
```

The subroutine starting at line 20000 first initializes the top octave of the array (elements 97 to 108). The notes are arranged as indicated by the comments. The other octaves are easy to generate because each lower octave is one-half the frequency of the higher one. Thus, the frequency of A in the top octave is 14080, the values in lower octaves are 7040, 3520, 1760, 880, 440, 220, 110, and 55 hertz. The other notes have the same relationship to each other (see Figure 11.2). It also initializes element 0 of the NOTES array to a value of 20000 hertz (which is ultrasonic) to make it easy to play spaces between notes. Notice that by placing short spaces between notes you get a *staccato* (choppy) feel to the note.

Lines 500 through 700 actually perform the work by retrieving two integers at a time from the DATA statements and using the FREQ value as an index into the NOTES array to get the proper frequency. One of the fun things about organizing the input data in this way is that you can shift the entire tune down by one octave by inserting the line:

```
550 IF FREQ>12 THEN FREQ=FREQ-12
```

This line shifts everything down by exactly one octave (and protects against negative values of FREQ). Line 300 breaks the infinite loop. When you attempt to read past the last line in the DATA statements, an error condition occurs and execution jumps to statement 1000.

Using this program, you may want to enter your own tunes by replacing the DATA statements starting at line 35000. The main thing to remember is that the NOTES array starts with a low-C in NOTES(1); the other C notes are located in elements NOTES(13), NOTES(25), NOTES(37), NOTES(49), NOTES(61), NOTES(73), NOTES(85), and NOTES(97).

The PLAY Statement

GW-BASIC offers a second way to produce music via the PLAY statement. This statement is extremely simple:

PLAY *string*

but the string contents can become very complex. The main advantage that the PLAY statement has over SOUND is that it can operate in a background mode that allows the PC to perform other tasks while the music is playing. Notes are specified using the capital letters A through G. A # or + sign after the letter means a sharp, and a - sign (hyphen) after the letter means a flat. GW-BASIC only understands sharps and flats that correlate to the black keys on a keyboard; a C- is not a valid note. The default octave starts at the C at 1046 hertz and can be varied using the O command (see Table 11.1 for an explanation of the various commands). The note duration can be selected from a whole note (L1) to a sixty-fourth note (L64), and the tempo can be selected from 32 quarter notes per minute to 255 quarter notes per minute using T32 through T255, respectively (the default is 120 quarter notes per minute, T120). Table 11.1 defines all of the control symbols associated with the PLAY command.

Table 11.1   Control symbols for PLAY statement

A-G	Notes to be played in the default octave (where an octave starts with the C note and goes up to B). The symbols # and + can be used to denote a sharp, and the − symbol can be used to denote a flat.
Ln	Sets default length for notes (where n=1 means whole notes, n=4 means quarter notes, all the way to n=64 which means sixty-fourth notes).
MB	Music Background. Allows up to 32 notes to be placed in a buffer so that the program can do other things while notes are playing.
MF	Music Foreground. This is the default mode. The program plays one note at a time and can do nothing else as long as music is playing.
ML	Music Legato. Each note plays for the full time indicated without "gaps." This makes music sound smooth and flowing.
MN	Music Normal. Each note plays 7/8 of the time indicated. The brief gap makes each note distinct.
MS	Music Staccato. Each note is played for 3/4 of the time indicated. This makes the notes sound a bit "choppy."
Nn	Plays note number "n" at the default length (where n is a number between 0 and 84 that corresponds to the 7 octaves covered by the PLAY statement).
On	Selects the default octave where n is a number from 0 to 6 and the default is 4.
Pn	Pause from 1 to 64.
Tn	Tempo. Defines the number of quarter notes per minute with a default of T120 (120 quarter notes per minute; 30 whole notes per minute). The value n can range from 32 to 255.
.(period)	A period after a note increases the length of that note or pause to 3/2 the default or indicated value.
Xs	Executes (plays) the contents of a string variable named s.
> and <	The symbol > increases the default octave by one, and the < symbol decreases it by one octave.

The following is a brief example of how the PLAY statement works:

```
100 DEFINT A-N:DEFSTR S
200 S1="CDEC5CDEC5"
300 S2="EFG3EFG3"
400 S3="L12GAGFE5C5GAGFE5C5L6C<G>C5.C<G>C5."
500 CLS
600 PLAY "MB O3 L6 XS1;"
700 PLAY "XS2; XS3;"
800 PRINT "This illustrates how the PLAY command"
900 PRINT "works by allowing text to be written"
1000 PRINT "to the screen while the music is playing"
1100 PRINT
1200 PRINT "Isn't this great?"
1300 PRINT
1400 LIST
1500 END
```

Depending on the speed of the processor in your system, you may actually see the entire screen displayed (including the listing of the program) before the tune completes. The main difficulty is that the music will start playing for a while before control is returned to the screen. Still, this isn't bad if you are writing an application in which the screen and the music do not have to be perfectly coordinated. With a bit of work and selective use of pauses, the music can be coordinated with the screen. You may also want to experiment with playing "random" music by using the output of a random number generator to drive the SOUND command.

The PLAY Function

The PLAY(n) function is used to determine the number of notes currently in the PLAY buffer when operating in background (MB) mode. This is useful when you are performing another operation (such as placing information on the screen) and want to check to make certain that the music keeps playing smoothly. The statement is of the form:

1000 J%=PLAY(0)

where the 0 argument is a dummy and J% contains a number between 0 and 32, indicating the number of notes still in the buffer waiting to be played. However, if the music is playing in foreground mode, this function always returns a value of zero.

Summary

In this chapter, you learned how to use GW-BASIC commands to drive the built-in tone generator. The SOUND and PLAY commands, as well as the PLAY function, were introduced. The PLAY command is most useful when a printed musical score is available and when Music Background mode is desired. The SOUND command is more useful when you want to correlate the pitch of the tone to the value of some variable.

Quiz

1. Which two commands can be used to control tones emitted by the built-in tone generator?
2. What are the lowest and highest frequencies allowed by the SOUND command?
3. How many octaves are covered by the PLAY command?
4. What command would you use to speed up or slow down an entire tune?
5. How many clock tics per second are available in the SOUND command?
6. Which command allows multiple strings to be used to play long songs?
7. How can you tell when the play buffer is getting low?

Chapter 12
Built-In Functions and Procedures

In This Chapter

By now you have seen most of the central features of GW-BASIC. This chapter briefly explores functions and commands that provide special services. Many of the special services are mathematical functions such as exponentiation, absolute value, and trigonometric functions. Others provide useful features such as time and date. Some are advanced features that are used for activities beyond the scope of this book.

Trigonometric Functions

GW-BASIC provides four trigonometric functions: SIN, COS, TAN, and ATN (for sine, cosine, tangent, and arctangent, respectively). Typical uses might be:

```
4500 B!=SIN(Q!):C!=COS(Q!)
4600 QNEW!=ATN(B!/C!)
```

All of these functions operate in *radians* (where there are 3.141592653589793 radians in 180 degrees) and they deal only in single-precision numbers unless the /d switch was specified

Chapter 12

when you invoked GW-BASIC. If you need double-precision trig functions, you must invoke GW-BASIC by using the line:

GWBASIC/d

The lines:

1200 PI! = 3.141593!
1300 Z! = SIN(PI/2!)

will assign Z! a value of 1.000 (or something very close) because the sine of 90 degrees (which is what PI/2 means) is, by definition, 1. One way to simplify your life, if you plan to perform many conversions between degrees and radians, is to define conversion constants. For example:

DEGTORAD! = 3.141593!/180!

and

RADTODEG! = 180!/3.141593!

can be defined at the beginning of the program and used each time that a conversion is required. Multiplying a value in degrees by DEGTORAD! will result in a radian value. Multiplying a radian value by RADTODEG! will convert the value to degrees. If you are concerned about the accumulation of error during conversion, define these factors as double-precision numbers (this will slow your computation down a bit but it will guarantee that the result is as accurate as your original value).

One problem you may encounter is that GW-BASIC does not provide an inverse sine function. To overcome this limitation, define your own formula to perform the computation:

ASINE! = ATN(X!/(SQR(1!-X!*X!))

where X! contains a value between −1.0 and 1.0 (which is the normal range for the sine function). These standard trigonometric formulas are available from various sources (especially reference books that have sections on geometry). Please note that a division by zero error may occur if X gets very close to either 1 or −1. Fortunately, we know that the sine goes to 1 when at positive pi/2, and that it goes to −1 at −pi/2. You may, therefore, want to create a small subroutine that tests for the exception cases first and returns limit values if the computation would stop due to a division underflow or division by zero. If the input is a "safe" value, the routine would then use the algorithm to compute the arcsine value. For example:

```
30000 'This routine returns the arcsine of X! in ALPHA!
30100 IF X! > 0.9999999! THEN ALPHA=1.0!:RETURN
30200 IF X! < -0.9999999! THEN ALPHA=-1.0:RETURN
30300 ALPHA!=ATN(X!/(SQR(1!-X!*X!))
30400 RETURN
```

This subroutine declares all values of magnitude greater than 0.9999999 as being too close to 1.0 to be used safely. In the version of GW-BASIC released with DOS 4.01, this critical value appears to be 0.99999997 for single-precision numbers. Your version of GW-BASIC may have a slightly different critical value, so you will have to experiment. Of course, this critical value will also change for double-precision computations.

Mathematical Functions

In addition to trigonometric functions, GW-BASIC provides other important mathematical functions used in scientific and statistical analysis. These include exponentiation and logarithms to base e and pseudo random number generation. Additionally, functions are provided to manipulate the contents of variables.

ABS(x)

The ABS(x) function returns the absolute value (positive magnitude) of the argument x. If the argument is an integer, the result of this function will also be an integer. If the argument is a single- or double-precision number, the output will be single- or double-precision, respectively.

CDBL(x), CINT(x), and CSNG(x)

These three functions allow conversion of one type of numeric variable to another. For example, CDBL(x) will convert any numeric type to a double-precision variable, CSNG(x) will convert numbers to single-precision, and CINT(x) will convert numbers into integers. Typical uses could be:

```
100 A# = CDBL(127.5)
200 B! = CSNG(1.274936D2)
300 I% = CINT(6.7)
```

These functions follow the same conversion rules and restrictions that apply to automatic conversions performed by GW-BASIC (see Chapter 6 for details).

EXP(x)

This is the exponential function and returns the value of the mathematical number *e* (where *e = 2.7182818 and* is the base for natural logarithms) raised to the x power. For example, the following statement yields a value of 22.19795:

```
100 x!=3.10
200 PRINT EXP(x!)
```

This function will overflow for values of x greater than 88.02 because this yields a value of 1.68499E+38.

FIX(x) and INT(x)

These functions accept a floating-point number for x and convert it to an integer. FIX *truncates* it (drops the digits to the right of the decimal point), but INT returns the largest integer that is less than or equal to x. For example:

```
FIX(123.8)   will yield the integer 123
FIX(-123.8)  will yield the integer -123
INT(123.8)   will yield the integer 123
INT(-123.8)  will yield the integer -124
```

LOG(x)

This function returns the natural logarithm of x and is the inverse of the EXP function. For example:

```
12000 Y! = LOG(1.68499E+38)
```

assigns a value of 88.01999 to the variable Y!. The input to the LOG function must be a positive number greater than 3.0E-39 or an `Illegal function call` error will occur.

RND(x) and RANDOMIZE

The RND function generates a random single-precision number in the range 0 to 1. When invoked without the optional argument:

```
1200 W! = RND
```

it will calculate a different value each time statement 1200 is executed. In reality, the random generator function will create a predictable pattern of random numbers (called pseudo-random numbers). To initialize the random-number generator to a known value, you can either provide a negative argument such as RND(-123) or you can invoke the RANDOMIZE statement at some convenient point in the program. The RANDOMIZE statement is followed by a number (integer or floating-point) which is used to initialize the random-number generator. An example of the randomize statement would be:

```
100 RANDOMIZE 27.3
```

SGN(x)

This sign function returns one of three values, depending on the value of the argument x. If x is negative, this function returns a -1 integer. If x is zero it returns a 0, and if x is positive it returns a 1.

SQR(x)

The square root function accepts an argument x and returns the square root of x as a single-precision number. X must be positive and greater than 3.0E-39 in order to obtain a meaningful result.

Special String Functions

The following functions process string information. They either retrieve information from DOS or perform conversions from numbers to strings.

DATE$

This is both a function and a statement. As a function:

`A$ = DATE$`

the A$ will contain a ten character string of the form mm-dd-yyyy (where mm are two numeric digits for the month, the dd stands for two numeric digits for the day, and yyyy stands for four digits for the year). As a statement:

`DATE$ = A$`

can be used to set the date inside DOS (DOS keeps an updated time and date as long as the PC remains on). The string A$ can be any of the following forms:

mm-dd-yy
mm/dd/yy
mm-dd-yyyy
mm/dd/yyyy

HEX$(n) and OCT$(n)

These conversion functions are of the form:

```
13000 A$ = HEX$(n)
13100 B$ = OCT$(n)
```

where n must be an integer value in the range 65535 to −32768 (of course, if you use an integer variable inside the parentheses, GW-BASIC will automatically limit you to the range −32768 to +32767). The HEX function returns a hexadecimal representation of the number n (where each group of 4 bits is converted into one digit in the range 0 to F) and the OCT function returns the octal representation of the number n (where groups of three bits starting from the right are converted into digits in the range 0 to 7).

STR$(x)

The STR$ function accepts a numeric variable or constant as an argument and returns an ASCII string that is equivalent to what GW-BASIC would send to the screen as a result of a PRINT x command. The VAL function is the complement of this function.

TIME$

The TIME$ function and statement are very similar to the DATE$ function and statement and are used in the same general way. When used as a function, TIME$ returns an eight-character string of the form hh:mm:ss (where hh stands for hours in the range 00 to 23, mm stands for minutes, and ss for seconds—both in the range 00 to 59). When used as a statement to update the DOS clock, the string can have one of the following forms:

hh	range 00 to 23; minutes and seconds default to 00
hh:mm	same range as for function; seconds default to 00
hh:mm:ss	same range as for function

Chapter 12

Miscellaneous

The following functions and statements don't fall into any general category; however, they are useful when programming in GW-BASIC.

CHAIN

The CHAIN command allows one GW-BASIC program to call another GW-BASIC program. The general form is:

1000 CHAIN [MERGE] "*filename*"[,[*line*][,[ALL][,DELETE *range*]]]

In its simplest form, this command tells GW-BASIC to delete the current program and replace it with the program in the file *filename*:

25000 CHAIN "TEST2"

where it is implied that the entire file name is TEST2.BAS (if it isn't, write out the entire file name within the double quotes). The argument *line* tells GW-BASIC that you want it to start executing the new program at a particular line number rather than at the very beginning of the program. The ALL parameter indicates that you want all of the variables of the current program to be retained for use by the new program (a nice way to pass information from one program to another). Thus, if you want to chain to another program, want execution to start at line 330, and want to keep all of the variables from the current program, the command might look like this:

23456 CHAIN "OTHERONE.BAS",330,ALL

The MERGE keyword tells GW-BASIC that you want to merge the source code from the target file into the current program rather than replacing the current program with the target program. The DELETE *range* informs GW-BASIC that a range of lines in the current program should be deleted before the new program is merged with it. It is important that the beginning and end line numbers of the range (which are separated by a dash or minus sign) must both exist in the current program. If you specify a beginning or end line that does not exist, GW-BASIC will declare an Illegal function call error.

COMMON

This statement is used with the CHAIN command to transfer information to the next program. The form is:

`23456 COMMON variable[,variable...]`

where the arguments are the variable names that you want to pass to the new program. If you want to pass arrays, simply include the name followed by ( ). You do not need to dimension the array in the new program because GW-BASIC will pass the information to the new program. You may use multiple COMMON statements in one program but you cannot repeat a variable in two COMMON statements in the same program.

CONT

This command simply resumes program execution after a control break has been pressed by the user or after a STOP or END statement. Execution resumes at the point where the break occurred. This command is often used after a STOP command that was used in debugging.

DEF FN

This statement is used to define custom functions. The general form is:

`DEF FNname[(arg1[,arg2...])]= formula`

where *name* identifies the name of the function, *argx* indicates optional arguments enclosed in parentheses, and *formula* indicates how the function will be evaluated. For example, if you want to define a function that calculates the cube of a single-precision number:

`12000 DEF FNCUBE!(A!)=A!*A!*A!`

This can now be used in a normal GW-BASIC statement as if it were a built-in function:

```
13000 P! = 12.25
13100 TOTAL! = X! + CUBE!(P!)
```

Notice that the function type is declared by the *name* in the same way as a variable. If the function type does not match the target variable, GW-BASIC will "complain" about a `Type mismatch` error.

ERASE

This command is used to eliminate arrays from active memory. Imagine that you have a program that uses many arrays, and some of them are not used after the first part of the program. You can use a statement such as:

```
12000 ERASE MYARRAY,YOURSTOO
```

to eliminate these arrays from memory. Of course, if you try to access an array after erasing it, GW-BASIC will generate an error message. This statement is also useful if you want to re-dimension an array. In such cases, you would first ERASE the old array and then dimension it again using the DIM statement with the new limits.

ERR & ERL

These two variables are defined automatically by GW-BASIC to provide your error recovery routine with the error number (ERR) and line in which the error occurred (ERL). The error handler is defined by an ON ERROR *linenumber* statement which transfers execution to *linenumber* whenever GW-BASIC encounters an error condition.

ERROR

This statement lets you simulate a GW-BASIC error condition from within your program. The statement is of the form:

```
13000 ERROR n
```

where n must be a number between 0 and 255. If you have designated an error handler routine using the ON ERROR statement, then ERR should be set to the value n and ERL should be set to 13000 (in this example).

FRE(x)

This function returns the number of free bytes available in memory to GW-BASIC. The variable x is a dummy variable but it does have one use. If you make x a string variable (such as P$), GW-BASIC will first perform some housekeeping (cleanup) before attempting to calculate the amount of free memory. If you pass a numeric dummy variable, GW-BASIC returns the current value of free memory. The cleanup operation is required because string operations in GW-BASIC tend to fragment the free memory area. If you have a program that performs many string operations, you may want to invoke FRE(V$) once in a while to force a memory cleanup. GW-BASIC automatically forces a cleanup when it detects a need for more memory; however, occasional small cleanups are more desirable because they tend to be much faster than one big cleanup.

KEY Statement

In previous chapters, you used the KEY(n) OFF statement to disable the function keys defined by GW-BASIC. A variation of this statement allows you to assign your own values to these keys. The forms of this statement are:

KEY *keynum,string*
KEY ON
KEY OFF
KEY LIST

where *keynum* is a number between 1 and 10, and *string* can be any valid character string up to fifteen characters in length. The KEY OFF and KEY ON commands disable and enable viewing (respectively) the key contents on line 25 of the display. KEY ON and KEY OFF do not enable or disable the operation of the function keys. KEY LIST simply displays the key assignments on the screen.

If you type the following lines in direct mode:

```
KEY 10,"Joe"+CHR$(13)
KEY LIST
```

you will see that the contents of key 10 have been changed to :

F10 Joe ←

Now enter the following small program:

```
100 INPUT A$
200 PRINT "This is a test, ";A$
300 END
```

When you run this program, you will get a question mark prompt. Press the **F10** key. The program will print:

```
This is a test, Joe
```

The program continued to execute after you pressed F10 because we appended a CHR$(13) character (which is the ASCII code for carriage return) to the end of the string "Joe." The GW-BASIC input processor sees four characters: J, O, E, *and* the carriage return. The last character makes the program think that *you* pressed the carriage return key.

LLIST

This command is identical to the LIST command, but it sends the output to the LPT1: port (printer) rather than the screen. It is used when a paper copy of a program is desired. It uses the same optional range commands as the LIST statement.

NEW

This command deletes all of the program lines and variables currently in memory and closes all files. It also turns trace off.

REM

This is the same as using a single quote to indicate the beginning of a REMark on a line of GW-BASIC. It is included to maintain compatibility with some older BASICs, but it is generally out of favor today.

RENUM

This command is of the form:

RENUM [newstart] [,[oldnumber] [,inc]]

where *newstart* indicates the new starting number for the section of program, *oldnumber* identifies the line number currently in memory where renumbering will begin and *inc* indicates the increment to be used to separate the new line numbers. If *oldnumber* is omitted, the entire program will be renumbered. For example:

RENUM 100,,100

instructs GW-BASIC to renumber the entire program, to use 100 for the first line, and to space the line numbers out by 100.

RESET

This command closes all disk files and clears the system buffers. In practice, it operates the same as a CLOSE statement without file numbers. Any program that performs disk I/O should use either a RESET or CLOSE command before the END statement to assure that all files were properly closed.

RESUME

This statement is similar to the CONT command and is used to continue program execution after an error has been encountered. This statement comes in three forms:

```
RESUME
RESUME 0
RESUME NEXT
RESUME linenumber
```

The forms on the first two lines return execution to the line that encountered the error. The RESUME NEXT statement transfers execution to the line *after* the line that encountered the error. RESUME *linenumber* transfers execution to the specified line number. The fourth form is rather hazardous and should not be used without careful consideration to the consequences of uninitialized variables and disrupted program flow.

SHELL

The SHELL command lets the user execute a different program from within GW-BASIC. The program can be anything that can be invoked from the DOS command line (typically these program files end in .COM or .EXE). Once the program completes, execution returns to the GW-BASIC program line immediately after the SHELL command. Notice that the GW-BASIC program in memory is not affected in any way, it simply waits while the other process runs. The form of this command is:

```
13000 SHELL "TEST.EXE"
```

If no string is provided, GW-BASIC transfers execution directly to MS-DOS. Once you are finished performing your DOS operations, you can return to GW-BASIC by entering the DOS command EXIT.

SPC(I)

This command is used in PRINT and LPRINT statements to skip a specified number of spaces (the number in parentheses). The argument must be in the range 0 to 255. A typical use might be:

```
12000 PRINT "Hello" SPC(8) "Over there"
```

which inserts eight blanks between the letter o in Hello and the capital O in Over.

SWAP var1,var2

This statement exchanges the values contained in var1 and var2. Both variables must be of the same type or a Type mismatch error will occur.

TAB n

This function moves the cursor, or print head, to position n on the line before continuing to print information. If the cursor or print head is already past position n on the current line, GW-BASIC will move to position n on the following line. An example of this function would be:

```
13000 PRINT I% TAB(25) J%
```

VAL(S$)

This function returns the numerical value of the string in the parentheses. If the first character of the string is not numeric, a blank, or a plus or minus sign, this function returns a 0. The VAL function is the complement of the STR$ function.

Summary

This chapter exposed you to many diverse GW-BASIC commands and functions that you may want to use in future programs. Some of these commands (such as NEW and RENUM) should be used carefully because they can cause you to lose data. The next chapter is somewhat of a departure from the rest of the book. It discusses the need for methodical program design and introduces concepts that should help you write better GW-BASIC programs.

Quiz

1. What is the default type of the GW-BASIC trigonometric functions (SIN, COS, etc.)?
2. Is it possible to obtain double-precision output from the GW-BASIC trig functions? How?
3. Name the function used to convert a number into a double-precision value.
4. What are the three possible values returned by the SGN(x) function? What do they represent?
5. What is the range of the returned value from the RND function?
6. Which function would you use to convert a number to a string? Which function would you use to convert a string back to a number?

Chapter 13

Programming with Style

In This Chapter

In the preceding chapters, you learned the fundamental concepts of GW-BASIC. By now you should be reasonably proficient at writing programs, and you may have developed favorite ways to do things. This chapter addresses the *philosophy* or *methodology* of programming in GW-BASIC. Methodology is important because programs tend to stay in use much longer than expected and they usually need to be modified or corrected at a later point in time. Frequently, the effort expended in testing and maintaining a program can exceed the initial time and effort to create it. Therefore, it is important to design programs in an organized, methodical manner and to document them well. Documentation is important because it is often difficult to remember how a particular program works when you haven't looked at it for six months.

This chapter is divided into two major sections. The first part introduces you to various software development techniques and philosophies. These techniques can be used with any language. The second section provides you with recommendations that apply more directly to GW-BASIC.

Chapter 13

Software Development Methods

If you were going to build a house, you would probably first create a set of drawings to identify the dimensions of each room and the placement of items such as windows and doors. Careful planning on paper before starting to build would allow you to design a house that would suit your needs and would help you avoid costly mistakes. The same principles apply to writing programs. Before you start writing a program, you should be able to sit down for a few minutes and write a simple description of what the program will do. This lets the people involved (many times the person writing the program is not the person that will actually use it) identify all major features of the program and how these features may interact. Although writing out the requirements may seem to be an obvious step, you would be surprised how often serious misunderstandings about a program occur because the people involved did not bother to write out the program requirements.

There are many different ways to identify program operation requirements. Sometimes program planning consists of several paragraphs of written description, sometimes it is just a few mathematical formulas with a description of how the input data will be obtained. In some cases, the description may contain pictures that depict how information moves within the program. It doesn't matter which method is used; use the one that makes sense to you and appears to do the best job of describing the problem. The following brief descriptions of various methods in use today are not exhaustive because entire books have been written about each method. The intent is to provide just enough information so you can choose the techniques that work best for you. As you will see, each method has its strengths and its weaknesses. There is no ideal method.

Top-Down Design

This is the method currently in vogue at many large corporations and universities. The idea is to first identify all of the requirements of a program. When the various operations have been identified, subroutines are defined to perform the various tasks. The functions of these subroutines are then broken down even further to smaller subroutines and *utilities* (utilities are subroutines or functions that perform fundamental operations which can be used in many different places in one program). Figure 13.1 illustrates a *hierarchy diagram* (which shows the calling relationship between the various levels of subroutines in a program). Hierarchy diagrams usually do not show utilities because they tend to clutter the diagram. Sometimes utilities are shown separately with an explanation of each.

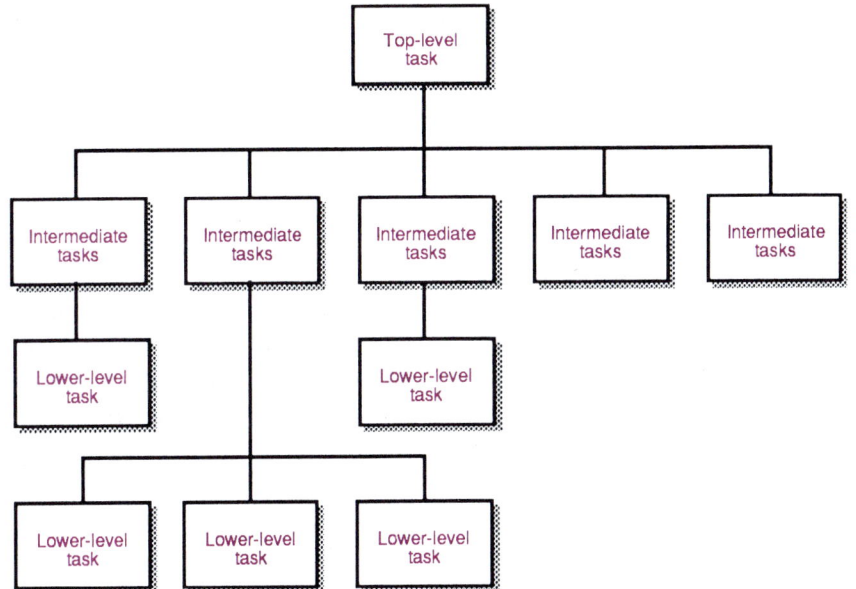

Figure 13.1 Hierarchy chart from top-down design

The main advantage of top-down design is that it forces the designer(s) to identify and explain all of the expected operations of the program at the very beginning. The methodical decomposition of these operations into smaller routines can frequently point out conflicts or oversights in the design. This method also facilitates the partitioning of the program into pieces that can be assigned to separate people or teams. If you need to create a very large program that requires the work of fifty people for a period of nine months, each person or group can be assigned a separate group of routines. One group can work on the human interface (screen, keyboard, mouse, etc.). Another group can work on mathematical utilities, and so on. No *one* person in the project needs to know everything about the entire program.

The main disadvantage of top-down design is that you can expend a great deal of effort before discovering some fundamental flaw with the design. Frequently, flaws do not become apparent until all of the program pieces have been brought together for *system testing* (this is the highest level of testing performed before software is released). Such flaws usually occur because of unforeseen interactions between different parts of the program.

If many people are involved or if the procedures are too formal, top-down design techniques can quickly degenerate into an enormous bureaucratic exercise of daily meetings that generate mounds of paperwork.

Data Flow Analysis

Data flow analysis is normally used when programs that perform many numerical calculations are developed. If you write a program for an automotive engine controller, the program will need information such as: engine speed, engine temperature, air temperature, air pressure (altitude above sea level), exhaust sensor readings, and accelerator pedal position. This information can be fed into complex formulas that eventually output commands to the fuel-injection system (controlling the engine by limiting the amount of fuel being provided). Figure 13.2 illustrates what a data flow diagram might look like for this application.

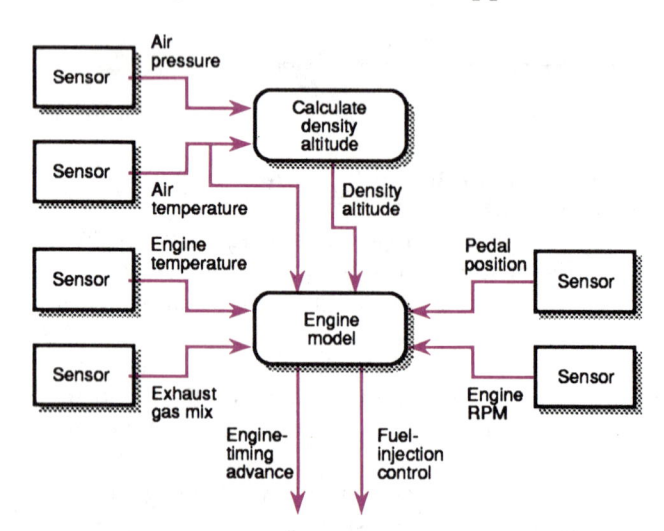

Figure 13.2   Data Flow Diagram for Engine Controller

Data flow analysis is often used with other techniques (such as top-down design) to improve software partitioning.

Flowcharts

When using the flowcharting technique, the programmer attempts to identify each step of a process required to achieve a given result before he begins to actually write the required coding. Diamond-shaped boxes are usually used to identify decisions (If Z is greater than A), and rectangular boxes are normally used to identify processes (add A to B and divide by 42). One of the best-known examples of an ideal flowcharting problem is the IRS 1040 form (this is not a joke). If you look carefully at the various parts of the form, it says things like:

If line 63 is larger than line 55, enter amount overpaid.

or

Multiply $2000 by the total number of exemptions claimed on line 6e.

These are exactly the types of actions that can best be described by flowcharts. Figure 13.3 illustrates a typical flowchart.

When a detailed flowchart has been created, it is usually possible to identify certain operations which appear to go together. These operations are then grouped together as a subroutine. The main advantage of flowcharts is that they can be the optimal representation for certain logic-intensive problems. The main disadvantage is that the flowcharts of large complex programs can become virtually unreadable.

State Diagrams

Another extremely useful tool for designing certain kinds of programs is the state diagram. State diagrams are useful for describing programs that have different modes or states. For example, look at figure 13.4:

This figure illustrates part of a state diagram for a home telephone. The beginning state (when the phone is unused) is illustrated on the left side. If someone tries to call your number, the computer at the central office turns on a special voltage which activates the ringer in your phone. The computer remains in that state until one of two things happens: either you pick up your handset to answer the call, or the person making the call hangs up. Each state is represented by a bubble, and the actions

Chapter 13

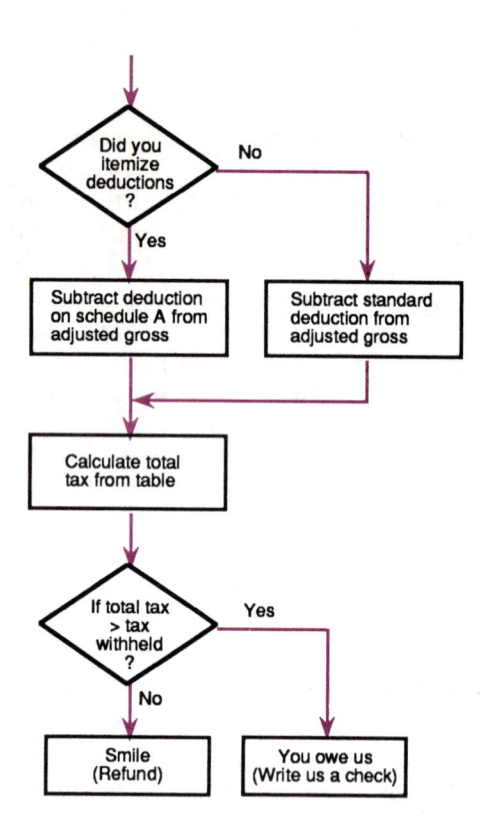

```
                    ▼
            ┌───────────────┐
            │  Did you      │    No
            │  itemize      ├──────────┐
            │  deductions   │          │
            │      ?        │          │
            └───────┬───────┘          │
                    │ Yes              │
                    ▼                  ▼
        ┌─────────────────────┐  ┌─────────────────────┐
        │ Subtract deduction  │  │ Subtract standard   │
        │ on schedule A from  │  │ deduction from      │
        │ adjusted gross      │  │ adjusted gross      │
        └──────────┬──────────┘  └──────────┬──────────┘
                   │                        │
                   ▼◄───────────────────────┘
        ┌─────────────────────┐
        │ Calculate total     │
        │ tax from table      │
        └──────────┬──────────┘
                   ▼
            ┌───────────────┐
            │  If total tax │    Yes
            │    > tax      ├──────────┐
            │   withheld    │          │
            │      ?        │          │
            └───────┬───────┘          │
                    │ No               │
                    ▼                  ▼
        ┌─────────────────────┐  ┌─────────────────────┐
        │      Smile          │  │    You owe us       │
        │    (Refund)         │  │  (Write us a check) │
        └─────────────────────┘  └─────────────────────┘
```

Figure 13.3 Typical flow chart

or events which cause a change in state are represented by the arrows between the bubbles. Notice that the same action can have different consequences, depending on the current state. If the phone is not being used and there are no incoming calls, picking up the handset transitions the computer to the state that turns on the dial tone. If you pick up the handset while a call is coming in, the computer turns off the ringing voltage and connects the call.

State diagrams can be very powerful tools for identifying actions that a program needs to take. They are often used with other software techniques to fully identify a solution. The main disadvantage of state diagram analysis is that it only works for mode-intensive problems. For example, the previously discussed IRS 1040 form would be difficult to analyze using state diagrams because there really aren't states or modes in the problem.

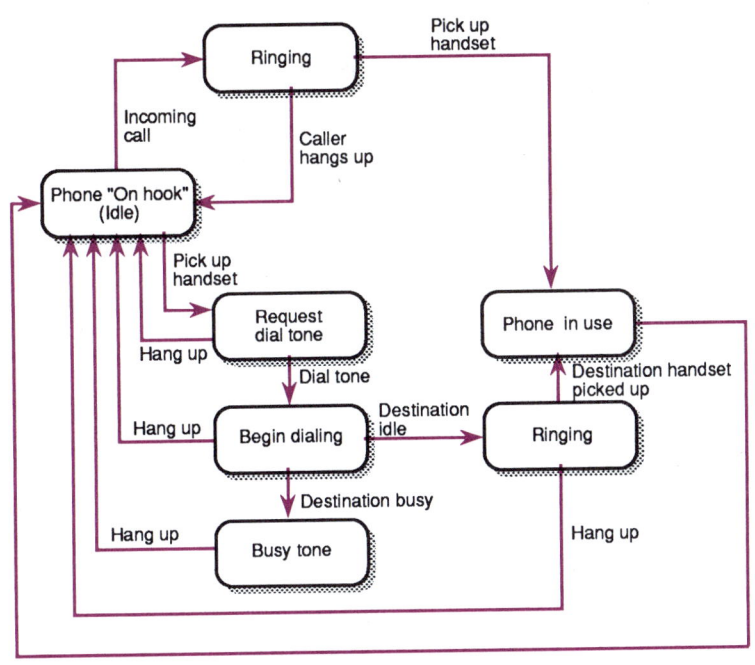

Figure 13.4 State diagram for a telephone

Rapid Prototyping

When you have designed your program using the techniques of the previous section, you still need to sit down and code (actually write) the GW-BASIC statements. There are several ways to do this, the most successful technique is called *rapid prototyping*. Rapid prototyping is based on three simple premises:

- ▶ Paper designs always have hidden flaws
- ▶ The first design may not be what the customer wants
- ▶ Time is money

The first rule is due to the fact that human beings tend to overlook things. Taking the "Two heads are better than one" philosophy to its logical conclusion, many large corporations attempt to compensate for this problem by insisting that software designs be reviewed and approved by many different people in different groups. In theory, the more people who review the design, the better the chances that a design flaw will be caught. In practice, only the people intimately involved in the program's design understand enough of the details to have a chance to find a particular design flaw.

The second rule is even more important because, in many cases, a customer cannot identify in great detail what is needed. There are many instances where all of the formal procedures were followed, voluminous documents generated and reviewed, and the end result was not what the customer actually wanted!

The third rule may be a cliche, but it is especially true in today's highly competitive environment. Imagine that you are responsible for developing internal software tools for a company. The longer you take to write a particular program, the more that particular program costs in terms of your salary, electricity, air-conditioning, computer amortization, etc. There is a much more important cost, however. If you take too long to develop the software tools employees need to do their jobs, you may impact their schedules and delay the introduction of new or improved products into the marketplace. This leads to two additional effects. First, the longer it takes to get the product to market, the more it costs the company in wages, overheads, etc. The second effect is that the longer your products are delayed, the greater the chance that a competitor will develop and market a competing product. If the delay is large enough, your company may not be able to sell enough of the new product to break even! Many companies have employed hundreds of engineers for several years and spent millions of dollars in development without producing a marketable product.

Rapid prototyping attempts to overcome these problems by trying to converge rapidly on a design that is *good enough* to satisfy the customer. Usually, techniques such as top-down design and data-flow analysis are used to come up with an initial architecture. Documentation and review meetings are kept to a minimum. When a group concensus is reached determining that the basic design should work, programmers begin to write the central parts of the software and integrate them into a software prototype. This prototype is then shown to the prospective customer for feedback. The customer is told that the software is only a *proof* of concept and is not intended to demonstrate the entire system.

Customers are usually eager to try these prototypes and express opinions on what they like and dislike. If a serious flaw is found, the design team re-evaluates the design and may generate another prototype. If no major problems are discovered, additional software is added to move the program closer to the eventual goal. By keeping the customer involved during the entire design and development cycle, the likelihood of disappointment is significantly reduced.

When the design appears to be reasonably stable, formal testing begins. The first step is *module testing*, during which each individual subroutine or function is tested and mathematical or logical flaws in the individual software units are identified. If the program is large, the next step is usually *sub-program testing*. Each major collection of subroutines is tested as a group to ensure that they do not conflict with each other. For example, all of the input/output routines (routines that operate with the keyboard, screen, mouse, etc.) might be tested as a group to make certain that they work well together. The final step is *system testing*. The entire package is tested by people who understand how the product is supposed to work (in many cases, these people may have only limited knowledge of the details of the various software packages). Because the rapid prototyping philosophy is to get the customer involved early, some of this testing is actually done by potential customers, marketing representatives, or others interested in the product's success. Because customers and other independent groups perform system testing, the risk of philosophical prejudice in the testing process is avoided. Someone who is extremely familiar with the design may ignore certain cases thinking "no one would ever want to use these options together;" whereas, the customer may actually need that particular mix and crash the program trying to use those options together! The secret to rapid prototyping is that the sooner you know about a problem, the less time and effort it will take to fix it.

Avoiding "Spaghetti Code"

Now that you have read about the various ways to design programs, you probably want concrete examples of how to write good programs in GW-BASIC. The single most important piece of advice is *avoid spaghetti code*. When a program becomes almost impossible to understand because it is extremely disorganized, it is called spaghetti code. Reading spaghetti code can make you feel like the metal ball in a pinball machine, ricocheting around the program in an apparently random fashion! Spaghetti code usually happens because no software methodology was used. The programmers just write code until it "sort of" works. The problem with this type of code is that it is almost impossible to modify or correct. Frequently, a change in one area impacts other parts of the program due to the lack of *modularity* (modular programs use individual subroutines for different operations).

Because GW-BASIC does not support independently compiled subroutines, the temptation to spaghetti code is greater than with other languages. The secret is to use subroutines to perform frequently repeated operations. (Make sure your subroutines are numbered high enough to be out of the way of the rest of the code.) Use a sheet of paper to identify the beginning line number of each subroutine, to identify the variables used and modified by the routine, and briefly explain what the subroutine does. This will help you keep track of the various routines while you are writing the main program.

Comments, Comments, Comments!

Another important attribute of well-written programs is the frequent use of comments. As you have probably concluded, most programs are comprised of groups of lines that perform particular operations. Each of these blocks of lines (as well as each subroutine) should be preceded by a group of comment lines that explain the operation of that group. Additionally, you may want to insert comments at the end of particularly tricky lines. An extremely well-documented program usually does not require a great deal of additional external documentation. The nice thing about comments is that they are always with the source code and, therefore, cannot get lost or misplaced easily.

The Human Interface

Another important part of program design is the human interface. Previous chapters indicated that a program should be professional-looking and should always provide enough information so the user can understand what is happening. A professional interface is not just for the sake of vanity; it is an important advantage to your customers. Have you ever used a program that had an amateurish display that was irritating or hard to use? Have you ever used a program that crashed when you accidentally gave it a wrong file name or an illegal command? Put yourself in your customers place. Will this screen confuse the user? What does the program do when the user accidentally presses the wrong key? Are the commands consistent and intuitive?

If you write programs for sale, this type of questioning is critical to your long-term business success. If you write programs for yourself or for others within a company, they are still important. A brilliant programmer who writes software with mediocre human interfaces will be viewed as a mediocre programmer because the human interface is what his clients see!

Summary

This chapter briefly introduced you to various software development methodologies, including top-down design, data-flow analysis, flowcharting, and state diagrams. It also introduced the concept of rapid prototyping as an efficient philosophy that helps you develop software rapidly and effectively. Finally, certain concrete principles that will help you develop good GW-BASIC programs were provided.

You probably wonder where to go from here. The next chapter introduces certain GW-BASIC features that are too advanced to be covered in depth in an introductory text. It briefly explains each feature and provides examples of where such features might be used.

Quiz

1. What is the philosophy behind top-down design?

2. Is data-flow analysis usually sufficient to describe most problems?
3. What kinds of problems are best described by flowcharts?
4. What are the biggest drawbacks to "spaghetti code?"
5. What are the three fundamental assumptions of rapid prototyping?

Chapter 14

Where Do You Go from Here?

In This Chapter

By this point, you probably wonder what is left to be covered. GW-BASIC has many advanced features that can get a novice programmer into a great deal of trouble. A comprehensive study of these features is beyond the scope of an introductory text, such as *The First Book of GW-BASIC*. However, this chapter will briefly introduce these advanced topics so you are at least aware of them.

Directory Commands

Two commands (MKDIR and NAME) were intentionally omitted from the discussion in Chapter 9. The MKDIR command is of the form:

`MKDIR` *pathname*

where *pathname* can be either a string constant enclosed in double quotation marks or a string variable. In either case, *pathname* should not exceed 63 characters in length and should include a complete path description. An example of this command would be:

```
MKDIR"C:\GWBASIC\MYDATA"
```

which creates a directory below the GW-BASIC directory on drive C and calls it MYDATA. The problem with the MKDIR command is: If your program has a bug, repeated invocations of this command can result in a disk full of useless directories. Always request user verification of the contents of the string before executing this command. The following code illustrates how this might be accomplished:

```
5000 D$="C:\WORD\TEST"
5100 PRINT "Is the following directory name O.K.: ",D$
5300 PRINT "(Y or N)? "
5400 A$=INKEY$:IF A$="" GOTO 5400
5500 IF (A$="Y" OR A$="y") GOTO 6000
5600 PRINT "Please enter new directory path"
5700 INPUT D$
5800 GOTO 5100
6000 MKDIR D$
6100 END
```

This section of code prints out the path data, asks for a **Y** or **N** response, and requests a new string if a negative response is given. When a new string is provided, it goes back to line 5100 and asks for verification again. If the contents of the string are not compatible with DOS path definitions or if the subdirectory already exists, GW-BASIC will stop execution with the following message:

Path/File Access Error

Another disk command that can lead to a great deal of confusion is NAME. This command is similar to the DOS RENAME command and is of the form:

NAME *oldname* AS *newname*

where *oldname* is the present name of the file and *newname* is the name you want it to have after the statement is executed. Both names should be either string variables or string constants enclosed in double-quotes. To avoid ambiguity, the names should include the extension (as in "MYPROG.DAT"). If you specify a *newname* that already exists, GW-BASIC stops execution with the following error message:

`File already exists`

If you specify an *oldname* that does not exist, it will respond with:

`File not found`

Be careful when you use these commands (and the KILL command explained in Chapter 9) because misusing them can cause you to lose files if you are not careful.

Graphics Commands

As you may recall, Chapter 10 discussed simple CGA graphics and briefly introduced the modes for EGA/VGA displays. The following commands are mentioned briefly here so that you will be aware of them. For more information, read the graphics sections in the GW-BASIC reference book or in a book on GW-BASIC graphics.

PAINT

This command is used to "fill in" an object on the screen with a certain color. The general form of the command is:

`PAINT (xs,ys)[,pattr[,battr][,bkattr]]`

where *xs* and *ys* are the beginning coordinates within the object, *pattr* is the attribute color number to be used, and *battr* is the attribute color that defines the border. *Bkattr* defines the background attribute. This command also enables you to perform what is called *tiling* (using a pattern of colors to fill an object). If you look closely at color illustrations in newspapers, you may notice that the pictures are comprised of individual dots of a few colors. Tiling lets you do the same sort of thing with your computer screen.

PALETTE and PALETTE USING

The PALETTE command (valid only for EGA and VGA displays) correlates a particular color attribute number to a specific color. Table 8.1 in Chapter 8 introduced you to the CGA standard color palette. Due to enhanced hardware capability, the user can select the 16 palette colors from a list of 64 possible colors. For example:

```
PALETTE 5,14
```

assigns hardware color 14 to attribute 5. This means that any items drawn on the screen after a COLOR 5,... statement will be drawn as hardware color 14. This command changes the hardware settings, so any pixel on the screen that uses attribute 5 will be drawn with hardware color 14. This happens because EGA and VGA cards use the color attribute to select a mix of red, green, and blue intensities provided by the user program.

If you simply invoke the command PALETTE without any arguments, it will reset the screen to the default palette for that hardware. The PALETTE USING statement is a variant that uses an integer array to define all of the colors in a palette at once. The two constraints are that the array must be at least 16 elements long and each element in the array should hold a number greater than or equal to −1. The −1 value indicates that the color assigned to the particular attribute should not change. This allows the user the flexibility to change some colors in the palette, but not others.

GET and PUT Graphics Statements

The GET graphics statement acts similarly to the SCREEN function introduced in Chapter 8. The statement is of the form:

```
GET (x1,y1)-(x2,y2),array
```

It copies the individual pixels contained in the box defined by the coordinates (x1,y1) and (x2,y2) into the array. The array can be of any type (except string) and must be large enough to hold all the information generated by the GET statement. It is usually simplest to make the array an integer because this enables you to easily inspect the contents of the information retrieved. If the OPTION BASE is set to 0 (the default case), then element 0 will contain the x-dimension and element 1 will contain the y-dimension of the rectangle. The data from each row of pixels is saved starting in element 2. If the amount of data saved is not an even multiple of eight bits, the lower part of that byte will be filled with zeros.

The PUT graphics statements does the converse of the GET statement. It is of the form:

PUT (x1,y1),array[,*action*]

where (x1,y1) is the coordinate of the upper left corner of the rectangle to be filled and array is the same one used in the GET statement. The *action* keyword can assume one of the following values: PSET, PRESET, AND, OR, or XOR. The PSET option inserts the image normally. The PRESET writes the inverse of the image to the screen (pixels that were black in the image captured by the GET statement will end up white on the screen, and vice versa). The AND, OR, and XOR operations retrieve the current state of the pixel on the screen and compare this state with the intended state of the pixel in the captured image. When the AND option is used, the pixel will illuminate only if *both* sources (the current screen and the captured image) specify the pixel is on. The OR option illuminates a particular pixel if *either* source specifies the pixel as active. The XOR option illuminates the pixel only if one source specifies that the pixel is active *and* the other doesn't (if both sources specify the pixel on or if both specify it off, the pixel will remain off).

Obviously, these two commands become much more complicated when used in color modes because four bits are used to represent each pixel (rather than just one bit for monochrome mode).

PCOPY

This command copies the information from one video display page to another. One of the more interesting features of the various video display cards available for PCs is the ability to store more than one image. The availability of this option is generally limited by the current video mode of the card and the total amount of video memory that it contains. This command was

Chapter 14

developed to enable programs to build one video page while displaying another. When the second page is ready, it can be quickly moved to the viewing page to provide what appears to be extremely smooth display operation. The general form of this command is:

100 PCOPY *src,dst*

where *src* is the source page and *dst* is the destination page. Both numbers are integers in the range 0 to n (where n is a function of the particular video card and mode). For more information, read the owner's documentation provided by the manufacturer of your video card and the GW-BASIC reference guide.

POINT

The POINT function is similar to the GET graphics command except that it returns only the value of a specific pixel on the screen. The form of the function is:

POINT(x,y)

where (x,y) represents the coordinate of the pixel. The following program illustrates how the POINT function can be used to retrieve the attributes of pixels on an EGA display:

```
100 KEY OFF
200 CLS:SCREEN 9
300 FOR I%=0 TO 34
400 FOR J%=0 TO 639
500 PSET(J%,I%),((I%+J%)MOD 16)
600 NEXT J%
700 NEXT I%
800 LOCATE  6,1
900 FOR I%=300 TO 316
1000 PRINT POINT(I%,20)
1100 NEXT I%
2600 IF INKEY$="" GOTO 2600
2700 SCREEN 9
2800 LIST
2900 END
```

This program draws a color band along the top of the screen and then prints the attribute numbers associated with different pixels on the screen.

A variant of the POINT function can also be used to retrieve the current position of the current graphics coordinate. The form of this variant is:

POINT(oper)

where the operation performed depends on value of the parameter, as illustrated in Table 14.1.

Table 14.1 *Operation selection for the POINT function*

Operation	Returned Value
0	Returns the physical x-coordinate
1	Returns the physical y-coordinate
2	Returns the physical x-coordinate if WINDOW is not active. If WINDOW is active, returns the x-coordinate relative to the WINDOW origin.
3	Returns the physical y-coordinate if WINDOW is not active. If WINDOW is active, returns the y-coordinate relative to the WINDOW origin.

The WINDOW command allows the user to re-define the coordinate system used by the program. This command will be discussed later in this section.

VIEW

This command is used to define a window within which graphics operations take place. The general form is:

VIEW[[SCREEN][(x1,y1)-(x2,y2)[,[fcolor][,bcolor]]]]

If a CLS statement is used while the VIEW statement is active, only the part of the screen defined by the coordinates (x1,y1) and (x2,y2) are set to the background color; the remainder of the screen is unaffected. The parameter *fcolor* defines the attribute used to fill the entire box, *and bcolor* defines the attribute for the background color. If the SCREEN parameter is omitted, points plotted using subsequent PSET commands will be plotted relative to the window coordinate system. If the SCREEN parameter is present, future PSET commands will plot relative to the physical coordinate system. In either case, points not within the rectangle described by the VIEW statement will not be drawn.

A VIEW command without any parameters resets the graphics attributes to the default values when the machine powers up (the VIEW rectangle is the entire screen).

VIEW PRINT

The VIEW PRINT statement operates similarly to the VIEW command described above. The main difference is that this command identifies a viewport (window) for text output rather than for graphics output. The general form is:

`VIEW PRINT [`*top* `TO` *bottom*`]`

where *top* and *bottom* indicate the top line and bottom line of the text window (both parameters must be in the range 1 to 24, inclusive). A VIEW PRINT command without parameters clears the effects of previous VIEW PRINT commands.

WINDOW

This command enables the user to define a coordinate system that is different from those of the physical screen coordinates. The basic form of the command is:

`WINDOW [[SCREEN](x1,y1)-(x2,y2)]`

where x1, y1, x2, and y2 are single-precision numbers that define the opposite edges of a user-coordinate system. If the SCREEN option is included, the coordinate system is configured so positive y values go down the screen. If the SCREEN option is omitted, the coordinate system is the traditional Cartesian system where positive y values go up the screen.

One way to understand this is to think of WINDOW as defining the portion of Cartesian space that appears in the physical viewport defined by the VIEW command. By making the difference between x2 and x1 smaller, you effectively magnify the screen in the horizontal direction. For example: if you define a WINDOW command in your program so that the difference between x1 and x2 is one-half of what it was and you also make the difference between y1 and y2 one-half of what it was, the viewport will show one-fourth of the area that it showed previously. The center of the viewport will be at location:

((x2-x1)/2, (y2-y1)/2)

As you can see, the interaction between these graphics statements is extremely complex. If you are interested in using these powerful graphics commands, please read the extensive information in the GW-BASIC reference manual and, perhaps, additional information in a book on GW-BASIC graphics.

Commands for Assembly Language Routines

Another powerful GW-BASIC feature is its ability to interact directly with assembly language routines. With very few exceptions, digital computers can understand only their own unique instructions. Products such as GW-BASIC are written in these native instructions and are capable of converting what you type into a form that is understandable by the machine. The material in this section will make no sense to you unless you are familiar with the architecture and addressing capabilities of the 8086 family of products. If you want to learn more about the inner workings of the machine, you may want to read one of the many excellent books on programming in assembly language for the PC.

BLOAD and BSAVE

The BLOAD and BSAVE commands are used to load into memory and save from memory (respectively) binary images usually associated with assembly language routines and data areas. The load command is of the form:

BLOAD *file*[*,segoff*]

where *file* represents the entire file name (which can include device and path information), and *segoff* is an optional parameter that tells GW-BASIC how far (what offset to use) from the beginning of the last defined segment to load the file. If no offset is specified, GW-BASIC uses the offset value (contained in the file) used when the file was created using a BSAVE command. Exercise extreme caution when performing a BLOAD command because it is possible to destroy GW-BASIC program or stack areas.

The BSAVE command is of the general form:

BSAVE *file,segoff,len*

where *file* and *segoff* are the same as for BLOAD, and *len* is a value in the range 0 to 65535 which indicates the number of bytes of memory that should be saved in the file. The first byte to be saved is the location specified by *segoff* and the last defined segment value (see DEF SEG command below).

Because neither command is limited to RAM areas, you can perform certain tricks with these commands. For example, a BSAVE command can be used to capture a copy of the video RAM in the display adapter card so the captured copy can be loaded at a later date using the BLOAD command.

CALL

When you have loaded a machine-language routine into memory using either POKE (which will be covered soon) or BLOAD statements, you can execute them using the CALL statement. This statement is of the form:

CALL *segoff*[(*var1,var2,...*)]

where *segoff* again represents the offset from the current segment, and the optional *varx* parameters within the parentheses represent variables that you may want to pass to the subroutine. You can also use the USR statement (discussed a bit later in this section) to call assembly language routines, but the CALL statement is preferred because it is compatible with more languages and can pass multiple parameters.

When parameters are passed, a two-byte address is placed on the stack for each parameter. The target routine can then reference these values by moving the SP (stack pointer register) into BP (base pointer register) and accessing the individual address as a positive offset from the base pointer register. The target routine will also have to use a RET n instruction to properly align the stack upon returning to GW-BASIC. If a string is a parameter, the passed address will point to a three-byte area called the *string descriptor*. The first byte contains the length of the string. The second and third bytes contain the starting address in string space (string space is the part of RAM where GW-BASIC stores strings). Generally, modifying the length of strings from assembly language routines is dangerous because doing so can "confuse" GW-BASIC if the modification is done improperly.

DEF SEG

This statement defines the default segment for commands such as BLOAD, BSAVE, PEEK, POKE, etc. It consists of the two keywords DEF and SEG separated by one blank. If a number is provided after the keywords, the number will be used with future commands requiring segment data. If no number is provided, the default segment will be defined as the data segment currently being used by GW-BASIC. Segment values should be in the range 0 to 65535; any other values will be rejected with an `Illegal Function Call` error. GW-BASIC does not check to see if this segment points to a valid address range.

DEF USR

This is a much more restrictive way to call assembly language routines. It is of the general form:

`DEF USRx=` *segoff*

where x stands for a digit between 0 and 9 and *segoff* defines the starting address of the routine relative to the current segment. The actual routine invocation is performed using an USRx statement in the program itself. For example:

```
1000 DEF USR3=4096
1100 Y=USR3(42)
```

When the offset from the current segment is defined for a particular function, it can be invoked repeatedly without executing another DEF USRx statement. The disadvantage is that only one argument can be passed and only one value can be returned.

PEEK and POKE

These two functions date back to early versions of BASIC that ran on 6800 and 6502 microprocessors. The standard forms are:

PEEK(*segoff*)
POKE *segoff,val*

where PEEK retrieves a byte from memory at the location defined by *segoff* and the current segment, and POKE assigns the value *val* to the byte location pointed at by *segoff* and the current segment. These functions can form the basis of powerful routines that allow you to inspect and modify any location in memory. Remember, however, that when you start to POKE values into memory, *anything* can happen. You can completely corrupt the contents of a disk or at least wipe out files! PEEK is completely safe because you are only viewing the contents of memory and not changing them.

VARPTR and VARPTR$

These functions are used to obtain the segment offset for variables and file control blocks (FCBs) defined by GW-BASIC. If you want to pass the beginning address of an array to an assembly language routine, you might use:

CALL segoff(VARPTR(Y(0)),...)

The VARPTR$ function returns a three-byte string where the first byte holds a variable descriptor number and the second and third bytes hold the segment offset value. There are certain problems associated with the use of these variables, so serious research in the GW-BASIC reference manual is recommended before you attempt to use either function.

Communications Commands

GW-BASIC supports a group of communications commands that enable your programs to send and receive data directly over PC communications ports. Usually this is unnecessary because MS-DOS provides an excellent group of communications routines. The GW-BASIC communications commands can come in handy when you write programs that interact with a remote system. For example, you could write a program that dials another computer and automatically logs onto that system (including providing a password if necessary). The program could then *download* (transfer) data from the other system to a file on your PC and then log off. Such a program could be valuable if you needed to make long distance calls in the middle of the night (when phone rates are usually low).

COM(n)

This statement enables and disables an interrupt to GW-BASIC from a specific communications port. When the serial communications hardware in the PC receives a message, it attempts to interrupt the microprocessor so that the communications software can move that message to a safe location before the next byte comes in. When the statement:

```
COM(1) ON
```

is executed, GW-BASIC enables the hardware interrupt from serial port number 1. The number inside the parentheses indicates that you want to enable port 1. The allowed values are 1 and 2 because GW-BASIC only recognizes the first two serial communications ports. The

```
COM(1) OFF
```

command instructs GW-BASIC to disable interrupts from port 1. The third variation:

```
COM(1) STOP
```

inhibits the interrupt, but allows incoming characters to be accumulated in the buffer so trapping will occur immediately when a

COM(1) ON command is executed later. To totally enable the port, the command:

`ON COM(1) GOSUB` *linenumber*

must be executed to tell GW-BASIC where in your program it should go when such an interrupt occurs. This way, your program can execute normally until a message is received, at which point GW-BASIC will jump to the line number identified in the ON COM(x) command. You also must allocate a buffer for this data and assign a device number by using the OPEN "COMx statement (explained below).

Data can be retrieved from a communications port through the use of one of the following statements:

```
2000 S$=INPUT$(LOC(1),#1)
2000 INPUT#1,X$
2000 LINE INPUT#1,Z$
```

and can be sent out via a communications port using:

```
3000 PRINT#1, B$
3000 PRINT#1 USING
```

The preferred statements are INPUT$ and PRINT# because they allow all codes to be transferred (which can be important if you are sending control codes to a remote device). There are three other functions that are used in communications routines. The LOC(1) function returns the number of bytes in the input buffer. The LOF(1) returns the number of free bytes remaining in the buffer. The EOF(1) function returns a -1 if the buffer is empty, and returns a 0 if there is any pending data.

INP and OUT

These two commands perform byte-communication with hardware devices that respond as *microprocessor ports*. A microprocessor port is a device that is connected directly to the microprocessor's address and data bus. The address and data busses are ordered wires (or traces on a circuit board) that carry voltages that can be used to represent integer numbers. These busses are used by the microprocessor to communicate with the rest of the hardware in the PC. These are very different from PC I/O ports which communicate to the outside world. The only people likely to use these GW-BASIC commands are those who have built special hardware for their PCs and have chosen to communicate with it via this mechanism. Unless you are extremely familiar with the internal architecture of the 8086 family of microprocessors, these commands will not be very useful to you.

The general forms of the commands are:

```
4000 I%=INP(n)
3700 OUT n,J%
```

where n stands for a microprocessor port number in the range 0 to 65535 and the values in I% and J% must be in the range 0 to 255 because these operations perform byte transfers.

IOCTL and IOCTL$

The IOCTL statement enables the user to send a control string to a device that has been opened via an OPEN "COM statement. The general form is:

IOCTL[#]*filnum,str*

where *filnum* is the file number employed in the OPEN "COM statement and *str* can be a string variable or constant. This command is frequently used to send special control codes to devices, such as printers to set page width, lines per page, font type, etc. The IOCTL$ function performs the converse operation. It is normally used to read back an acknowledgement after an IOCTL command has been sent out. Typical usage of this function is:

A$=IOCTL$(#1)

This statement would read information from device #1.

OPEN"COM(n)

This command allocates buffer space for serial communications ports in the same way that the regular OPEN command allocates buffers for disk I/O. It is of the general form:

OPEN "COM[n]:[*spd*][,*par*][,*dbits*][,*stp*][,RS][,CS[*ms*]]
[,DS[*ms*]][,CD[*ms*]][,LF][,PE]" AS[#]*fnum*[LEN=*lngth*]

The value n indicates that you can select either COM1 or COM2. The *spd* parameter must be one of the following integer constants: 75, 110, 150, 300, 600, 1200, 1800, 2400, 4800, or 9600 (*spd* default value is 300). These numbers indicate the speed of the serial communications port in bits per second. The *par* attribute is a single-character constant whose values are listed in Table 14.2 and which represent the electrical parity signal to be implemented. Even parity means that there are an even number of ones in the transmitted byte. Odd parity indicates that there are an odd number of bits in the byte.

Table 14.2 Valid parity options for the OPEN "COM statement

Option	Meaning
E	**EVEN PARITY.** Data transmitted on this port will indicate even parity. Data received on this port will be expected to have even parity. This is the default parity option.
M	**MARK PARITY.** Parity bit will always be transmitted as a mark (1). Port expects to always receive the parity bit as a mark (1).
N	**NONE.** No transmit parity is asserted; parity is not checked on received data.
O	**ODD PARITY.** Data transmitted on this port will indicate odd parity. Data received on this port will be expected to have odd parity.
S	**SPACE PARITY.** Parity bit will always be transmitted as a space (0). Port expects to always receive the parity bit as a space (0).

The *dbits* parameter is a numeric constant that indicates the number of data bits sent at a time. Accepted values are 4 through 8 (inclusive) with a default of 7 bits.

Stp indicates the number of stop bits between groups of data bits. Valid values for this integer constant are 1 and 2. Usually, 75 and 110 bits per second speeds use 2 stop bits and the higher speeds use only 1.

The *fnum* attribute identifies a file number in the same way as in an OPEN statement for disk I/O. This file number is used by statements such as INPUT$, PRINT#, etc. to identify which port you want to deal with. It is important to remember that GW-BASIC supports two separate PC serial ports. This means that you could be transmitting and receiving data on both of them at the same time. The only way to identify which port you are reading or writing to is via this file number. The *lngth* parameter identifies the record length to be moved by GET and PUT statements.

Think of OPEN "COM as a statement that sets up an environment for serial data that is similar to the environment that is used with disk files (as described in Chapter 9). The only difference between records in a disk file and records from a serial port is that input data from a serial port is not always immediately available and cannot be ignored for long periods of time.

The parameters RS, CS, DS, and CD are special flags used to control the Request to Send (RS), Clear to Send (CS), Data Set ready (DS), and Carrier Detect (CD) control wires that are part of the serial interface electronics. The LF flag is used to insert a line-feed character following each carriage return and the PE flag enables parity checking. The *ms* parameter included with some of these flags indicates the number of milliseconds that the PC should wait for these signals to become valid before declaring a `Device Timeout` error. This option is normally used to inform software when the communications link to the other device has been lost.

It is very difficult for an inexperienced person to become involved with serial communications because of the many options that must be properly selected and the complex interactions of the various hardware signals. Some people make a living as consultants who set up and maintain data communications protocols between computers. If you are really interested in this topic, you should first read the sections in your MS-DOS reference manual that describe the COM ports. Next, find a good book at your local library or bookstore on serial communications. This book should have detailed explanations of the RS-232 electrical communications standard and should also have sections that explain the operation of *modems* (modems are devices that accept information from a PC serial bus and convert the information to tones that can be sent over normal telephone lines). Finally, you will want to read the sections in a GW-BASIC reference guide that explain in detail how GW-BASIC interacts with the serial communications ports.

Miscellaneous Commands

The following GW-BASIC statements don't really fit in any particular category. They are all intended for the advanced programmer who wants to get the most out of the language.

ENVIRON and ENVIRON$

These two functions are used to set and retrieve information from the MS-DOS environment. For example, running the following program from GW-BASIC:

```
100 FOR I%=1 TO 10
200 PRINT I%,ENVIRON$(I%)
300 NEXT I%
400 END
```

will display several lines of information such as:

```
    1           COMSPEC=C:\DOS\COMMAND.COM
    2           APPEND=C:\DOS
    3           PROMPT=$P$G
    4           PATH=C:\DOS;C:\WRDPRC
    .
    .
    .
   10
```

These are keywords that define the MS-DOS environment in which you operate. The ENVIRON function (without the $) is used to set one of these parameters. For example:

```
200 ENVIRON "PATH=C:\DOS"
```

limits the path searching performed by MS-DOS to only the DOS subdirectory. For a list of these parameters, see your MS-DOS reference guide.

ERDEV and ERDEV$

These two variables contain information about the last error encountered by GW-BASIC. ERDEV will contain a number from 0 to 255 which represents the error code encountered by GW-BASIC. ERDEV$ will contain a string of up to eight characters that identifies the device in which that error occurred (for example, LPT1:, COM1:, A:, B:, etc.). These variables can be used to generate error messages to the user.

EXTERR

The function will return extended error information when GW-BASIC is run under DOS 3.0 or later versions. The function is of the form:

    2000 I%=EXTERR(n)

where n modifies the requested information as identified in Table 14.3:

Table 14.3 Options for EXTERR function

Argument "n"	Returned Value
0	DOS Extended Error Code
1	DOS Extended Error Class
2	DOS Extended Error Suggested Action
3	DOS Extended Error Locus

For a detailed explanation of these returned values, please refer to the MS-DOS programmers reference for the particular version of DOS being used.

LOCK and UNLOCK

These statements are used to restrict and enable access to files or file records in a networked environment. The statements are of the form:

Chapter 14

```
100 LOCK[#]n[,[recnum] [TO endrec]]
200 UNLOCK[#]n[,[recnum] [TO endrec]]
```

The #n identifies the file number as defined in the OPEN statement. If *recnum* is omitted, the entire file is either locked or unlocked. If *recnum* is provided, it identifies an initial record that is to be locked/unlocked. If the TO *endrec* parameter is omitted, only the record identified by *recnum* will be locked or unlocked. If TO *endrec* is provided, all records in the range *recnum* and *endrec* (inclusive) will be locked/unlocked.

PEN Statement and Function

The PEN statement enables interaction between GW-BASIC and a light pen. The PEN function can be used to obtain the status and position of a light pen pressed against the screen. Because these devices are fairly rare and only work with specific video display cards, no further discussion will be made here. If you need more information on this topic, please read the appropriate sections in the GW-BASIC reference guide and the IBM Technical Reference manual.

STICK and STRIG

The STICK and STRIG functions obtain status information on joystick position and triggers. These devices are also rare on PCs, so they will not be discussed further. If you need to learn how to use these commands, please investigate further in the GW-BASIC reference guide.

Summary

Congratulations! You have now learned virtually everything needed to write professional-quality programs using GW-BASIC. As mentioned at the beginning of this chapter, the material presented here is provided to give you a taste of GW-BASIC's advanced capabilities. As you become more proficient with the language, you will discover that there are very few things that can be done in other PC languages that can't be done in GW-BASIC. You will also discover that avoiding all of those recompiles when debugging programs actually provides a strong advantage over other languages.

Quiz

1. What GW-BASIC command would you issue to create the following new directory: C:\GWBASIC\TEST?
2. Which GW-BASIC commands would you use to find out the color attribute of a specific point on a graphics screen?
3. Which statement passes multiple arguments to an assembly-language routine: CALL or USR(x)?
4. Which two GW-BASIC commands are needed to inspect the contents of byte anywhere in the microprocessor's memory?
5. Which GW-BASIC command is used to alter the PATH information used by MS-DOS when it searches for files?

Appendix A
GW-BASIC Quick Reference Guide

The following is a brief, alphabetized list of GW-BASIC statements:

ABS	Returns absolute value of a number
ASC	Returns the numeric value of an ASCII string
ATN	ArcTangent function
AUTO	Automatically numbers GW-BASIC statements
BEEP	Generates a short audible beep
BLOAD	Loads a binary image into memory
BSAVE	Saves a binary image from memory
CALL	Used to call machine-language routines
CDBL	Converts number to double-precision
CHAIN	Used to call successive GW-BASIC programs
CHDIR	Changes the default directory

CHR$	Converts an ASCII code to a character
CINT	Rounds numbers to integers
CIRCLE	Draws circles and ellipses on the screen
CLEAR	Sets all variables to zero or null and closes all files
CLOSE	Closes I/O operation to a disk file
CLS	Clears the screen
COLOR	Sets screen colors
COM(n)	Establishes communications with hardware ports
COMMON	Passes variables to CHAINed programs
CONT	Continues program execution after a break
COS	Cosine function
CSNG	Converts a number to single-precision
CSRLIN	Returns the current row of the cursor
CVD	Converts string to double-precision number
CVI	Converts string to an integer
CVS	Converts string to single-precision number
DATA	Used to save numeric and string information within the program
DATE$	Used to read and set system date
DEF FN	Creates a user-defined function
DEFDBL	Declares certain variables as double-precision
DEFINT	Declares certain variables as integers
DEFSNG	Declares certain variables as single-precision
DEFSTR	Declares certain variables as strings

DEF SEG	Defines segment address for PEEK/POKE and other assembly language commands such as BLOAD and BSAVE
DEF USR	Used to access machine-language subroutines
DELETE	Deletes program lines
DIM	Defines arrays
DRAW	Used to draw figures on screen
EDIT	Used for editing specific line
END	Terminates program
ENVIRON	Allows modification of MS-DOS environment definitions
ENVIRON$	Obtains MS-DOS environment definitions
EOF	Used to detect access past end of file
ERASE	Eliminates arrays from program
ERDEV	Returns number associated with device error
ERDEV$	String that holds error device name
ERL	Returns line number containing the error
ERR	Returns error code
ERROR	Used to simulate an error condition
EXP	Returns e to the power x (natural logarithms)
EXTERR	Returns extended error information
FIELD	Allocates space for variables in random file buffer
FILES	Prints the names of files in the specified directory
FIX	Truncates a number into an integer
FOR/NEXT	Program loop control statements
FRE	Returns amount of free memory available to GW-BASIC

GET (files)	Reads specified record from disk file
GET (graphics)	Retrieves graphics information from the screen
GOSUB/RETURN	Used to invoke and return from subroutines
GOTO	Performs a direct jump to a program line
HEX$	Returns string that represents hexadecimal value of argument
IF/GOTO/ELSE	Conditional program control statements
IF/THEN/ELSE	Alternate form of IF statement
INKEY$	Reads single keystroke (does not display it on screen)
INP	Retrieves next byte from specified hardware I/O port
INPUT	Requests data from the user via keyboard
INPUT#	Reads data from disk file
INPUT$	Reads a string from the keyboard or a disk file
INSTR	Searches for first occurrence of one string in another one
INT	Truncates a number into an integer
IOCTL	Allows the program to send control strings to devices
IOCTL$	Allows GW-BASIC programs to receive control strings
KEY	Used to enable, disable, and define strings for function keys
KEY(n)	Used to enable/disable detection of use of special keys
KILL	Used to delete a file from disk
LEFT$	Extracts left part of a string
LEN	Returns number of characters in a string
LINE	Draws lines and boxes on the screen

LINE INPUT	Inputs an entire line from the keyboard
LINE INPUT#	Inputs an entire line from a disk file
LIST	Lists specified line numbers to the screen, printer, or file
LLIST	Lists specified lines to the printer
LOAD	Retrieves a GW-BASIC program from disk storage
LOC	Returns the current position within a disk file
LOCATE	Moves the cursor to the specified location on the screen
LOCK	Locks access to file when operating in a network environment
LOF	Returns length of file in bytes
LOG	Returns natural logarithm of argument
LPOS	Returns current position of line-printer head
LPRINT	Prints data to the line printer
LSET/RSET	Used to align data for disk I/O operations
MERGE	Used to merge a GW-BASIC program on disk with current one
MID$	Extracts center part of a string
MKDIR	Creates a new MS-DOS directory
MKD$	Converts double-precision number to a string
MKI$	Converts integer number to a string
MKS$	Converts single-precision number to a string
NAME	Renames a disk file
NEW	Clears out current GW-BASIC program
OCT$	Converts a number into an octal string

ON COM	Performs GOSUB on detection of I/O port activity
ON KEY	Performs GOSUB on detection of keypress
ON PEN	Performs GOSUB on detection of light-pen actuation
ON PLAY	Performs GOSUB when music buffer gets low
ON STRIG	Performs GOSUB when joystick trigger pressed
ON TIMER	Performs GOSUB when specified time has elapsed
ON ERROR GOTO	Performs GOSUB when error condition is encountered
ON/GOSUB	Performs GOSUB n-way branch
ON/GOTO	Performs GOTO n-way branch
OPEN	Establishes I/O activity with a disk file or hardware port
OPEN COM(n)	Establishes communication with serial port
OPTION BASE	Defines whether all arrays start with element 1 or 0
OUT	Sends a byte to hardware output port
PAINT	Fills in graphic images with specified pattern or color
PALETTE	Defines correlation between color attributes and colors
PCOPY	Used to copy a video screen page to another page
PEEK/POKE	Used to read and write to any location in memory
PEN	Enables use of lightpen
PLAY	Plays music contained as commands in strings
PLAY(n)	Indicates number of notes left in music buffer
PMAP	Graphics function for mapping logical/physical coordinates

POINT	Used to read the color or attribute of a pixel on screen
POS	Returns current column of cursor position
PSET/PRESET	Sets or clears specific pixel on the screen
PRINT	Sends data to the screen
PRINT#	Sends data to a disk file
PUT (files)	Transfers an entire record to the disk
PUT (graphics)	Transfers graphics data to the screen
RANDOMIZE	Initializes the random data generator
READ	Retrieves information from DATA statements
REM	Prefaces a line of remarks
RENUM	Renumbers certain lines in the current program
RESET	Closes all disk files
RESTORE	Adjusts the pointer to DATA statements to allow reread
RESUME	Allows program to recover from error condition
RETURN	Terminates GW-BASIC subroutines
RIGHT$	Extracts right part of a string
RMDIR	Deletes an MS-DOS directory
RND	Returns a random number in the range 0 to 1
RUN	Initiates program execution in GW-BASIC
SAVE	Stores the current program to a disk file
SCREEN	Returns the ASCII code for the character at specified position
SGN	Returns -1 for negative, 0 for zero, and 1 for positive
SHELL	Allows temporary execution of another MS-DOS program

Appendix A

SIN	Sine function
SOUND	Generates tones on PC sound generator
SPACE$	Creates a string of spaces
SPC	Skips a specified number of locations in PRINT or LPRINT
SQR	Square root function
STICK	Returns coordinates of joysticks
STOP	Halts program execution
STR$	Returns a string representing numeric argument
STRIG	Detects status of joystick triggers
STRIG(n)	Enables detection of joystick triggers
STRING$	Returns a string of known length or first character of string
SWAP	Exchanges values between two variables of the same type
SYSTEM	Quits GW-BASIC and returns to MS-DOS
TAB	Moves cursor or print head to position n
TAN	Tangent function
TIME$	Used to set or obtain system four/minutes/seconds
TIMER	Returns the number of elapsed seconds since midnight
TRON/TROFF	Enables/disables system trace
UNLOCK	Unlocks a file in a network environment
USR	Used to call a machine-language routine
VAL	Returns numerical value of a string
VARPTR	Returns memory address of a variable
VARPTR$	Returns string that contains memory address of a variable

VIEW	Defines physical viewport
VIEW PRINT	Defines the boundaries of the screen text window
WAIT	Pauses program execution while waiting for input port
WHILE/WEND	Program loop control statements
WIDTH	Sets character width for printer or screen
WINDOW	Defines logical graphics window
WRITE	Sends data to screen
WRITE#	Sends data to a disk file

Appendix B
PC Character Set

The ASCII Character Set

The following characters are the PC extended form of the standard ASCII character set. Everything above 127 is unique to PCs.

Hex	Dec	Screen	Ctrl	Key	Hex	Dec	Screen	Ctrl	Key
00h	0		NUL	^@	1Ah	26	→	SUB	^Z
01h	1	☺	SOH	^A	1Bh	27	←	ESC	^[
02h	2	●	STX	^B	1Ch	28	∟	FS	^\
03h	3	♥	ETX	^C	1Dh	29	↔	GS	^]
04h	4	♦	EOT	^D	1Eh	30	▲	RS	^^
05h	5	♣	ENQ	^E	1Fh	31	▼	US	^_
06h	6	♠	ACK	^F	20h	32			
07h	7	•	BEL	^G	21h	33	!		
08h	8	▫	BS	^H	22h	34	"		
09h	9	○	HT	^I	23h	35	#		
0Ah	10	◙	LF	^J	24h	36	$		
0Bh	11	♂	VT	^K	25h	37	%		
0Ch	12	♀	FF	^L	26h	38	&		
0Dh	13	♪	CR	^M	27h	39	'		
0Eh	14	♫	SO	^N	28h	40	(		
0Fh	15	☼	SI	^O	29h	41	)		
10h	16	►	DLE	^P	2Ah	42	*		
11h	17	◄	DC1	^Q	2Bh	43	+		
12h	18	↕	DC2	^R	2Ch	44	,		
13h	19	‼	DC3	^S	2Dh	45	-		
14h	20	¶	DC4	^T	2Eh	46	.		
15h	21	§	NAK	^U	2Fh	47	/		
16h	22	▬	SYN	^V	30h	48	0		
17h	23	↕	ETB	^W	31h	49	1		
18h	24	↑	CAN	^X	32h	50	2		
19h	25	↓	EM	^Y	33h	51	3		

Appendix B

Hex	Dec	Screen	Hex	Dec	Screen	Hex	Dec	Screen
34h	52	4	62h	98	b	90h	144	É
35h	53	5	63h	99	c	91h	145	æ
36h	54	6	64h	100	d	92h	146	Æ
37h	55	7	65h	101	e	93h	147	ô
38h	56	8	66h	102	f	94h	148	ö
39h	57	9	67h	103	g	95h	149	ò
3Ah	58	:	68h	104	h	96h	150	û
3Bh	59	;	69h	105	i	97h	151	ù
3Ch	60	<	6Ah	106	j	98h	152	ÿ
3Dh	61	=	6Bh	107	k	99h	153	Ö
3Eh	62	>	6Ch	108	l	9Ah	154	Ü
3Fh	63	?	6Dh	109	m	9Bh	155	¢
40h	64	@	6Eh	110	n	9Ch	156	£
41h	65	A	6Fh	111	o	9Dh	157	¥
42h	66	B	70h	112	p	9Eh	158	₧
43h	67	C	71h	113	q	9Fh	159	ƒ
44h	68	D	72h	114	r	A0h	160	á
45h	69	E	73h	115	s	A1h	161	í
46h	70	F	74h	116	t	A2h	162	ó
47h	71	G	75h	117	u	A3h	163	ú
48h	72	H	76h	118	v	A4h	164	ñ
49h	73	I	77h	119	w	A5h	165	Ñ
4Ah	74	J	78h	120	x	A6h	166	ª
4Bh	75	K	79h	121	y	A7h	167	º
4Ch	76	L	7Ah	122	z	A8h	168	¿
4Dh	77	M	7Bh	123	{	A9h	169	⌐
4Eh	78	N	7Ch	124	|	AAh	170	¬
4Fh	79	O	7Dh	125	}	ABh	171	½
50h	80	P	7Eh	126	~	ACh	172	¼
51h	81	Q	7Fh	127	⌂	ADh	173	¡
52h	82	R	80h	128	Ç	AEh	174	«
53h	83	S	81h	129	ü	AFh	175	»
54h	84	T	82h	130	é	B0h	176	░
55h	85	U	83h	131	â	B1h	177	▒
56h	86	V	84h	132	ä	B2h	178	▓
57h	87	W	85h	133	à	B3h	179	│
58h	88	X	86h	134	å	B4h	180	┤
59h	89	Y	87h	135	ç	B5h	181	╡
5Ah	90	Z	88h	136	ê	B6h	182	╢
5Bh	91	[	89h	137	ë	B7h	183	╖
5Ch	92	\	8Ah	138	è	B8h	184	╕
5Dh	93	]	8Bh	139	ï	B9h	185	╣
5Eh	94	^	8Ch	140	î	BAh	186	║
5Fh	95	_	8Dh	141	ì	BBh	187	╗
60h	96	`	8Eh	142	Ä	BCh	188	╝
61h	97	a	8Fh	143	Å	BDh	189	╜

240

PC Character Set

Hex	Dec	Screen	Hex	Dec	Screen	Hex	Dec	Screen
BEh	190	┘	D4h	212	╘	EAh	234	Ω
BFh	191	┐	D5h	213	╒	EBh	235	δ
C0h	192	└	D6h	214	╓	ECh	236	∞
C1h	193	┴	D7h	215	╫	EDh	237	φ
C2h	194	┬	D8h	216	╪	EEh	238	∈
C3h	195	├	D9h	217	┘	EFh	239	∩
C4h	196	─	DAh	218	┌	F0h	240	≡
C5h	197	┼	DBh	219	█	F1h	241	±
C6h	198	╞	DCh	220	▄	F2h	242	≥
C7h	199	╟	DDh	221	▌	F3h	243	≤
C8h	200	╚	DEh	222	▐	F4h	244	⌠
C9h	201	╔	DFh	223	▀	F5h	245	⌡
CAh	202	╩	E0h	224	α	F6h	246	÷
CBh	203	╦	E1h	225	β	F7h	247	≈
CCh	204	╠	E2h	226	Γ	F8h	248	°
CDh	205	═	E3h	227	π	F9h	249	•
CEh	206	╬	E4h	228	Σ	FAh	250	·
CFh	207	╧	E5h	229	σ	FBh	251	√
D0h	208	╨	E6h	230	μ	FCh	252	ⁿ
D1h	209	╤	E7h	231	τ	FDh	253	²
D2h	210	╥	E8h	232	Φ	FEh	254	■
D3h	211	╙	E9h	233	θ	FFh	255	

241

Extended Codes

The following code numbers are obtained as the second byte from an INKEY$ operation where the first character returned was a 00.

Second Code	Meaning
3	NUL (null character)
15	¦ (shift tab)
16	Alt-Q
17	Alt-W
18	Alt-E
19	Alt-R
20	Alt-T
21	Alt-Y

Appendix B

Second Code	Meaning
22	Alt-U
23	Alt-I
24	Alt-O
25	Alt-P
30	Alt-A
31	Alt-S
32	Alt-D
33	Alt-F
34	Alt-G
35	Alt-H
36	Alt-J
37	Alt-K
38	Alt-L
44	Alt-Z
45	Alt-X
46	Alt-C
47	Alt-V
48	Alt-B
49	Alt-N
50	Alt-M
59	F1
60	F2
61	F3
62	F4
63	F5
64	F6
65	F7
66	F8
67	F9
68	F10
71	Home
72	Cursor Up
73	Page Up

PC Character Set

Second Code	Meaning
75	Cursor Left
77	Cursor Right
79	End
80	Cursor Down
81	Page Down
82	Insert
83	Delete
84-93	F11-F20 (Shft-F1 through Shft-F10)
94-103	F21-F30 (Ctrl-F1 through Ctrl-F10)
104-113	F31-F40 (Alt-F1 through Alt-F10)
114	Ctrl-Print Screen
115	Ctrl-Cursor Left
116	Ctrl-Cursor Right
117	Ctrl-End
118	Ctrl-Page Down
119	Ctrl-Home
120-129	Alt-1 through Alt-9
130	Alt -
131	Alt =
132	Ctrl-Page Up

Appendix C
GW-BASIC Error Code Quick Reference

Error #	Brief Explanation
1	NEXT without FOR (missing FOR or an extra NEXT statement)
2	Syntax Error (line violates rules of GW-BASIC language)
3	RETURN without GOSUB (logic flow error)
4	Out of Data (read past end of DATA statements)
5	Illegal Function Call (parameter out of range)
6	Mathematical Overflow (number is too big)
7	Out of Memory (program is too large)
8	Reference to Undefined Line Number
9	Wrong Number of Subscripts or Subscript Out of Range
10	Duplicate Array Definition or OPTION BASE after DIM
11	Division by Zero or Zero to a Power
12	Illegal Command in Direct Mode
13	Variable Type Mismatch (expected a different variable type)

Appendix C

14	Out of String Space (out of memory)
15	String Too Long (exceeds 255 characters)
16	String Formula Too Long or Too Complex
17	Can't CONTINUE
18	Undefined User Function
19	No RESUME (end of program encountered in error handler)
20	RESUME Statement Encountered with no Error Existing
21	UNDEFINED
22	Missing Operand (no operand after math/logic operator)
23	Line Buffer Overflow (line has too many characters)
24	Device Timeout
25	Device Fault or Error
26	FOR without NEXT (too many FORs or missing NEXT)
27	Printer Out of Paper
28	UNDEFINED
29	WHILE without WEND (too many WHILEs or missing WEND)
30	WEND without WHILE (too many WENDs or missing WHILE)
31–49	UNDEFINED
50	FIELD rec length greater than in OPEN statement
51	Internal Error in GW-BASIC (GW-BASIC file corrupted?)
52	Bad File Number
53	File Not Found
54	Bad File Mode
55	File Already Open
56	UNDEFINED
57	Device I/O Error

58	File Already Exists
59	UNDEFINED
60	UNDEFINED
61	Disk Full
62	INPUT Past End of File
63	Bad Record Number
64	Bad File Name
65	UNDEFINED
66	Statement Without Line Number in File
67	Too Many Files (exceeded directory limit on diskette)
68	Device Unavailable (does not exist)
69	Communications Buffer Overflow
70	Disk Write Protect (floppy drive only)
71	Disk Not Ready
72	Disk System Error (hardware or disk media)
73	Illegal Advanced Feature
74	Rename on Different Disk
75	Path/File Access Error (file not accessible)
76	Path Not Found (tried to use a non-existent path)

Answers to Quizzes

Chapter 1

1. PCs use microprocessors compatible with the Intel 8086 family of products.
2. Floppy disks and hard disks.
3. Microsoft Corporation.
4. Plain text files usually called ASCII files.
5. Yes, if certain precautions are taken.

Chapter 2

1. False. An interpreter executes one line at a time.
2. It uses line numbers to keep program lines in proper sequence.
3. Keywords, variables, constants, and symbols.
4. It stops execution and displays an error message that identifies the type of error and the line number where the error occurred.
5. The video display adapter card and the video monitor (CRT).

6. CGA, EGA, and VGA.
7. Data is usually transferred through serial ports or by taking a floppy disk with the information to a different PC.

Chapter 3

1. Input, processing, and output.
2. (From left to right) A line number, the variable name receiving the assignment, an equal sign, and a numeric expression that creates the value to be assigned.
3. There are several acceptable names: single-precision, double-precision, or floating-point numbers.
4. Multiplication normally has precedence over addition.
5. The simplest GW-BASIC output statement is `PRINT`.

Chapter 4

1. MS-DOS directories are arranged in what is called a tree structure.
2. The > symbol usually ends the MS-DOS prompt.
3. `DIR` or `DIR/W`
4. `LOAD"TEST.BAS"`
5. `SAVE"TESTA.BAS",A`
6. `NEW`

Chapter 5

1. `RUN`
2. You can hold down the <ctrl> and <break> keys down simultaneously. If this doesn't work, you may have to reset your PC by pressing the hardware reset button (if you have one).

3. LPRINT
4. TRON/TROFF
5. The ON ERROR statement transfers execution control to a designated line number which is the beginning of an error handler routine. This routine will usually make an attempt to recover from the error, or it will at least print out the contents of critical variables that may have contributed to the error.

Chapter 6

1. 40 characters maximum.
2. All variable names must start with a letter.
3. -32768 to $+32767$.
4. Seven digits for single-precision; 16 digits for double-precision.
5. OPTION BASE 1.

Chapter 7

1. IF THEN ELSE and IF GOTO ELSE.
2. GOTO statement.
3. GOSUB/RETURN.
4. ON intvar GOTO line1,line2,....
5. FOR/NEXT statements.
6. WHILE/WEND

Chapter 8

1. INKEY$
2. READ and DATA.
3. Using the statement LOCATE 23,10.
4. COLOR 11.
5. I%=SCREEN(10,12).

Chapter 9

1. The OPEN statement.
2. The length of the variables in the FIELD statement should be less than or equal to the record length specified in the OPEN statement.
3. PRINT# and WRITE#.
4. VAL$
5. FILES "*.BAS"
6. Yes, with a KILL statement.
7. The OPEN command.
8. LOC(#3)
9. LOF(#2)\128
10. Must invoke GWBASIC/s=256.

Chapter 10

1. 320 by 200 pixels in limited colors, 640 by 400 pixels in monochrome.
2. The SCREEN command.
3. The PSET and PRESET statements.
4. The first coordinate pair must be omitted. This tells GW BASIC to begin the new line from the end coordinate of the previous LINE statement.

5. To draw an elliptical arc, you must use the CIRCLE statement with the proper eccentricity to define the ellipse. You must also use the start and end parameters that precede the eccentricity factor to define the begin and end points of the arc.

Chapter 11

1. The SOUND and PLAY statements.
2. The allowed range is 37 and 32767 cycles per second (Hz).
3. The PLAY command can cover nine octaves.
4. The Tn (Tempo) control parameter is used to define the number of quarter-notes-per-minute (and thus control the "speed" at which the music is played).
5. Clockticks can range from 0 to 65535.
6. The PLAY "strng1; ..." command can be used to play several long strings one after the other.
7. The PLAY(n) function will return an integer in the range 0 to 32 which indicates the number of notes in the buffer yet to be played.

Chapter 12

1. Single-precision.
2. Yes. By invoking GW-BASIC using the command: GWBASIC/d.
3. The CDBL function.
4. The values are −1, 0, and 1 (for negative numbers, zero, and positive numbers, respectively).
5. RND returns a single-precision value from 0 to 1.
6. STR$ converts a number to a string. VAL$ converts a numeric string to a number.

Chapter 13

1. To methodically decompose a program into successively smaller units that are easier to implement and test.
2. No. Data flow analysis is incapable of describing the algorithms required.
3. Flowcharts are best suited to describing problems that have simple yes-no decisions or that follow methodical algorithms.
4. Spaghetti code is extremely difficult to test and to maintain.
5. Paper designs always have hidden flaws, time is money, and the first design may not be what the customer wants.

Chapter 14

1. `MKDIR"C:\GWBASIC\TEST"`
2. The `POINT` command.
3. The `CALL` statement allows multiple parameters to be passed via the stack.
4. `PEEK` and `POKE`.
5. The `ENVIRON` statement can be used to alter the default path.

INDEX

! (single-precision) declaration character, 27, 76-80
(double-precision) declaration character, 76-80
$ (string) declaration character, 76-77
% (integer) declaration character, 26, 76-80
; (argument separator), 138

A
ABS statement, 229
ABS(x) function, 181
addition (+), 27-31
allocating buffer space for communication ports, 221-223
amplitude, 171
AND graphics option, 211
APPEND keyword, 136
argument separators (;), 138
arithmetic operators, 27-30
array elements, 71-73
arrays, 62, 70
   copying colors into, 210-211
   numeric, 71-73
   one-dimensional, 72
   retrieving pixels from, 211
   string, 74-75, 81
   two-dimensional, 72-73
ASC statement, 110, 229
ASCII (American Standard Code for Information Interchange), 15-16
   codes, 16, 121
      extended character, 239-243
   files, 7-8, 47
   keyboard codes sample program, 109-110
assembly language routines, 215, 218
   executing, 216-217
assigning values to bytes in memory, 218
ATAN function, 179
ATN statement, 229
AUTO statement, 45-46, 229

255

B

background, 117-118
BAS file extension, 44, 46-48
base point register (BP), 217
BASIC, 5
    interpreters, 25
    statements, 25-34
        arithmetic assignments, 25-32
        flow control, 25
        input/output, 25, 32-34
        special operations, 25
        string processing, 25
BEEP statement, 229
binary storage of numeric data, 156-157
bit, 19-20
    patterns, 64-67
bits per second (BPS), 19-20
BLOAD statement, 215-216, 229
borders, 117-118
    drawing, 116-117
BPS *see* bits per second
BSAVE statement, 215-216, 229
buffers, 15
    allocating space for communication ports, 221-223
built-in functions, 179-185
bytes, 19-20
    assigning values in memory, 218
    communcating with hardware devices, 220-221
    retrieving from memory, 218

C

CALL statement, 216-217, 229
cathode ray tube (CRT), 2
CD (DOS) command, 40-41
CDBL statement, 229
CDBL(x) function, 181-182
CGA *see* color graphics adapter
CHAIN statement, 186, 229
character output to printer, 130-131
CHDIR
    DOS command, 40-41
    GW-BASIC statement, 157-158, 229
check password sample program, 111-112
CHR$
    function, 111, 117
    statement, 230
CINT statement, 230
CINT(x) function, 181-182
CIRCLE statement, 168, 230
circles drawing, 168
CLEAR statement, 157-158, 230
clockticks, 172
CLOSE statement, 56, 60, 135-138, 230

CLS statement, 230
COBOL, 5
codes
    ASCII extended character, 239-243
    control, 130
        printer, 131
    error, quick reference, 245-247
    print, 123-127
color
    display, 2-3
    graphics adapter (CGA), 3, 15-17, 117,
        161-167, 209-210
    palettes, 163-166
COLOR statement, 117-119, 164-166, 210,
    230
coloring objects on screen, 209
colors
    changing, 117-119
    selecting, 210
    standard CGA, 118
COM(n) statement, 219-220, 230
commands
    CD (DOS), 40-41
    CHDIR (DOS), 40-41
    DIR (DOS), 41-42
    disk I/O, 133
    GW-BASIC *see* statements
    MKDIR, 40
    PATH (DOS), 42
    TYPE (DOS), 42
comment lines, 35
comments, 204
COMMON statement, 187, 230
communication
    commands, 219-223
    ports
        allocating buffer space, 221-223
        disabling interrupts, 219-220
        enabling interrupts, 219-220
compatability, 12-13
compiled language, 6
compilers, 11-12
    BASIC, 47
computer-controlled execution mode, 43
concatination, 74-75
constants, string, 10
CONT statement, 187, 230
continuing program execution, 187
control
    codes, 130
        printer, 131
    strings
        receiving from I/O devices, 221
        sending to I/O devices, 221

conversion between numeric variable types, 78-80
coordinate system, defining, 214-215
copying
    pixels into arrays, 210-211
    video data from one page to another, 211-212
COS statement, 179, 230
CSGN(x) function, 181-182
CSNG statement, 230
CSRLIN statement, 230
cursor, positioning, 116
custom functions, defining, 187-188
CVD statement, 230
CVD$ function, 157
CVI statement, 230
CVI$ function, 157
CVS statement, 230
CVS$ function, 157
cylinders, 19

D

data
    clocking line, 20
    encryption sample program, 152-156
    flow analysis, 198
    format, hexadecimal, 151-152
DATA statement, 104, 112-115, 174-175, 230
DATE$ statement, 184, 230
debugging programs, 56-60
declaration characters, variable type, 76-80
DEF FN statement, 187-188, 230
DEF SEG statement, 217, 231
DEF USR statement, 217-218, 231
default directory, 41
DEFDBL statement, 230
defining
    graphics coordinate system, 214-215
    custom functions, 187-188
    graphics windows, 213-215
DEFINT statement, 230
DEFSTR statement, 230
DELETE statement, 231
delimiters, 63, 138
DENSNG statement, 230
DIM statement, 231
dimensions of arrays, 81
DIR (DOS) command, 41-42
direct mode, 50
    GW-BASIC editor, 43
directories, 19, 40-42
    creating, 207, 208
    default, 41
    root, 40

Index

disabling interrupts to communications ports, 219-220
disk controller card, 134
disk drives, 134
    floppy, 2, 4-5
    hard, 2, 4-5
disk files, 133-136, 138-157
    manipulating, sample program, 146-151
    output, 137
    printing to, 56
disk I/O commands, 133
disk storage, 18
disks
    floppy, 4-5, 18-19
    hard, 4-5, 18-19
display adapters, 15-16, 161-167
displays, 15-18
    flat panel, 3
    monochrome/color, 2-3
division
    floating point (/), 27-30
    integer (\), 27, 29-31
documentation in programs, 204
DOS (disk operating system), 2, 18, 134-135, 141-144, 147
double-precision
    (#) declaration character, 76-80
    variables, 68-70
DRAW statement, 231
drawing
    borders, sample program, 116-117
    circles, 168
    lines, 166-168
duration, 172

E

EDIT statement, 231
editing program lines, 49
editors
    GW-BASIC, 43
    EDLIN, line editor, 47
EGA *see* enhanced graphics adapter
electronic bulletin board, 13
elements of arrays, 71-73
eliminating arrays from memory, 188
empty string, 74-75
enabling
    access to files, 225-226
    interrupts to communications ports, 219-220
END statement, 55, 89, 231
enhanced graphics adapter (EGA), 3, 7, 16-17, 117, 161, 165-167, 209-210, 212-213
enhancements, 12

entering data via keyboard sample
   program, 105, 109
ENVIRON statement, 224, 231
ENVIRON$ statement, 224, 231
environment, setting, 224
EOF statement, 231
ERASE statement, 188, 231
erasing programs, 50
ERDEV statement, 225, 231
ERDEV$ statement, 225, 231
ERL statement, 188, 231
ERR statement, 188, 231
error
   codes, quick reference, 245-247
   information, 225
ERROR statement, 188-189, 231
errors
   variables, 225
   wraparound, 67-68
even parity, 222
executing
   commands immediately, 50
   machine language routines, 216-217
exiting GW-BASIC, 44
EXP statement, 231
EXP(x) function, 182
expansion slots, 13
exponentiation (^), 27-30
extended
   character codes, ASCII, 239-243
   error codes, 225
EXTERR statement, 225, 231

F

FIELD statement, 140-147, 231
file control blocks (FCB), 218
file extensions, .BAS, 44, 46-48
file number (filenum), 135
filename, 135
files
   ASCII, 7, 8
   disk, 133-157
   enabling access, 225-226
   restricting access, 225-226
FILES statement, 157-158, 231
FIX statement, 231
FIX(x) function, 182
floating-point
   co-processor, 70
   numbers, 27, 67-70
floppy
   disk drives, 2, 4-5
   disks, 4-5, 18-19
flowcharts, 199

FOR/NEXT statement, 92-95, 97-99, 231
    loop, 91-95, 97-99
foreground, 117-118
format, data, 151-157
formatted data entry screen sample
    program, 127-129
formatting output data, 122-131
FORTRAN, 5
FRE statement, 231
FRE(x) function, 189
free memory, 14
frequency, 172
function keys, 2
functions
    ASC, 110
    CHR$, 111, 117
    custom, 187-188
    CVD$, 157
    CVI$, 157
    CVS$, 157
    ENVIRON, 224
    ENVIRON$, 224
    EXTERR, 225
    FRE(x), 189
    LEFT$, 110, 232
    LEN, 110
    mathematical, 181-184
    MID$, 145
    MKD$, 156-157
    MKI$, 156-157
    MKS$, 156-157
    PEN, 226
    PLAY(n), 177-178
    POINT, 212-213
    RIGHT$, 110, 232
    SCREEN, 120-121
    STICK, 226
    STR$, 145
    STRIG, 226
    string, 184-185
    STRING$, 116-117
    TAB n, 193
    trigonometric, 179-181
    VAL(S$), 193
    VARPTR, 218
    VARPTR$, 218

G

generating user error messages, 225
GET statement, 136, 141-143, 146-147,
  210-211, 232
GOSUB statement, 87-89
GOSUB/RETURN statement, 232
GOTO statement, 84-89, 232

graphics adapters
  CGA, 3, 15-17
  EGA, 3, 7, 16-17
  VGA, 3, 7, 16-18
graphics commands, 209-215
graphics options
  AND, 211
  OR, 211
  PRESET, 211
  PSET, 211
  XOR, 211
GW-BASIC, 5
  editor, 43
  exiting, 44
  memory, 6-7
  sample program, 35-36
  statements, 25-34, 87-89
    list of, 229-237
    see also statements, GW-BASIC

H

hard copy, 7
hard
  disk drives, 2, 4-5
  disks, 4-5, 18-19
HEX$ statement, 185, 232
hexadecimal
  data format, 151-152
  representation, 185
hierarchy diagram, 197
human interface, 204-205

I

I/O (input/output)
  ports, 19-21, 24
  devices
    receiving control strings, 221
    sending control strings, 221
IF statements, 83-86, 90-91
IF/GOTO/ELSE statement, 232
IF/THEN/ELSE statement, 83-85, 232
increments, 92
indices, 71-72
indirect mode, GW-BASIC editor, 43
infinite loop, 54
information, error, 225
initialize variables, 35
INKEY$ statement, 104, 108-111, 127, 232
INP statement, 220-221, 232
input, 23-24
INPUT # statements, 138-139, 147, 232
INPUT statement, 32-33, 104-110, 104, 136, 232
INPUT$ statement, 232
INSTR statement, 232

instructions, LSET/RSET, 145
INT statement, 232
INT(x) function, 182
integer (%) declaration character, 26, 64-67, 76-80
Intel 8086 family of microprocessors, 2, 12
interpreters, 6, 9-12, 25
interrupts, disabling/enabling, 219-220
inventory system sample program, 80-81
IOCTL statement, 221, 232
IOCTL$ statement, 221, 232

J
joystick positions/triggers, 226

K
KEY statement, 110-111, 116, 189-190, 232
    LIST command, 189-190
    OFF command, 189
    ON command, 189
KEY(n) statement, 232
keyboard, 2, 15, 24
    reading data, 104-113
keys, function, 2
keywords, 10
    APPEND, 136
    INPUT, 136
    MERGE, 186
    ON, 90, 91
    OUTPUT, 136
    RANDOM, 136
KILL statement, 158, 232
kilobytes (K), 3-4

L
language
    compiler, 11-12
    interpreter, 9-12
Last In/First Out (LIFO), 88-89
LEFT$ statement, 110, 232
LEN statement, 110, 232
LIFO see Last In/First Out
light pen functions, 226
LINE INPUT statement, 233
LINE INPUT # statement, 233
line number, 10
line printer port, 20-21
LINE statement, 166-168, 232
lines, drawing, 166-168
linking GW-BASIC programs, 186
LIST statement, 48-49, 167-168, 190, 233
listing programs, 48-49
LLIST statement, 190, 233
LOAD statement, 44-45, 233

loading, 9
    programs, 44-45
LOC statement, 158, 233
LOCATE statement, 109-110, 115-116, 122, 127, 233
LOCK statement, 225-226, 233
LOF statement, 158, 233
LOG statement, 233
LOG(x) function, 183
logical record length, 141
loops
    FOR/NEXT, 91-95, 97-99
    infinite, 54
    nested, 93-95, 97-99
    WHILE/WEND, 95-99
LPOS statement, 233
LPRINT statement, 25, 56, 131, 192, 233
LPRINT USING statement, 130
LPT1: port, 190
LSET statement, 145, 233

M

machine language routines
    executing, 216-217
mark parity, 222
mathematical functions, 181-184
    ABS(x), 181
    CDBL(x), 181-182
    CINT(x), 181-182
    CSGN(x), 181-182
    EXP(x), 182
    FIX(x), 182
    INT(x), 182
    LOG(x), 183
    RND(x), 183
    SGN(x), 183
    SQR(x), 184
memory
    assigning values to bytes, 218
    erasing arrays, 188
    free, 14
    GW-BASIC, 6-7
    map, 13-14
    organization, 13-14
    RAM, 3-4, 12, 14
    reserved area, 15
    retrieving bytes, 218
    ROM, 3-4, 12, 14
MERGE statement, 151, 186, 233
messages, error for the user, 225
microprocessors, 2, 12-13, 134
    ports, 220-221
MID$ statement, 145, 233
mini card index sample program, 96-99
MKD$ statement, 156-157, 233

MKDIR
    DOS command, 40
    GW-BASIC statement, 207-208, 233
MKI$ statement, 156-157, 233
MKS$ statement, 156-157, 233
MOD 16 operation, 121
mode, 136
    direct, 43, 50
    indirect, 43
modems, 13, 20, 223
modes
    text, 3
modular programs, 204
modularity, 204
modulo arithmetic (MOD), 27, 29-31
monochrome display, 2-3
MS-DOS, 2, 5, 39-42
    environment, setting, 224
multiplication (*), 27, 30

N

n-way branching, 90-91
NAME statement, 208, 233
names, variable, 62-64
natural logarithm, 183
negation/subtraction (-), 27-28, 30
nested loops, 93-95, 97-99
NEW statement, 50, 190, 233
NEXT statement, 92-95, 97-99
notation, scientific, 68
numbering program lines automatically,
    45-46
numbers, floating-point, 27
numeric arrays, 71-73

O

obtaining segment offset values, 218
OCT$ statement, 185, 233
octal representation, 185
odd parity, 222
ON COM statement, 234
ON ERROR command, 59-60
ON ERROR GOTO statement, 234
ON KEY statement, 234
ON keyword, 90-91
ON PEN statement, 234
ON PLAY statement, 234
ON STRIG statement, 234
ON TIMER statement, 234
ON/GOSUB statement, 90-91, 234
ON/GOTO statement, 90-91, 110, 234
one-dimensional array, 72
OPEN"COM(n) statement, 221-223, 234

OPEN statement, 56, 135-138, 141-142, 144, 146-147, 234
operators, arithmetic, 27-30
option base, 211
OPTION BASE statement, 234
OR graphics option, 211
order of precedence, 30-32
OUT statement, 220-221, 234
output, 23-24, 33
   formatting, 122-131
   to disk file, 56
   width, 130
OUTPUT keyword, 136

P

PAINT statement, 209, 234
PALETTE statement, 210, 234
PALETTE USING command, 210
palettes, color, 163-166
parallel ports, 19-21
parity options, 222
path, 136
PATH (DOS) command, 42
pathname, 207-208
PC DOS, 2
PCOPY statement, 211-212, 234
PEEK command, 217-218, 234
pen, light, 226
PEN statement, 226, 234
peripherals, 12
philosophy of programming, 195-205
physical block length, 141
pitch, 172
pixels, 161, 211
   returning value of specific, 212-213
play a tune sample program, 173-175
PLAY statement, 175, 234
   control symbols, 176
   sample program, 177
PLAY(n) statement, 177-178, 234
PMAP statement, 234
POINT statement, 212-213, 235
POKE command, 217-218, 234
ports
   communication, 219-223
   microprocessor, 220-221
   parallel, 19-21
   serial, 19-20
POS statement, 235
positioning the cursor, 116
precedence, rules of, 30-32
PRESET
   graphics option, 211
   statement, 163-164, 235

PRINT # statement, 56, 137-138, 140,
   144, 147, 235
PRINT # USING statement, 137-138,
   144-146
print codes, special, 123-127
PRINT statement, 25, 34, 56, 112, 122,
   192, 235
PRINT USING statement, 122, 142-143
printers, 7
   character output, 130-131
   control codes, 130-131
printing to disk file, 56
processing, 23-24
program
   documentation, 204
   flow, 23-24
programming methodology, 195-205
programs
   continuing execution, 187
   debugging, 56-60
   editing specific lines, 49
   erasing, 50
   executing immediately, 50
   linking/chaining together, 186
   listing, 48-49
   loading, 44-45
   remarks, 191
   renumbering, 191
   sample *see* sample programs
   saving, 46-47
   stopping GW-BASIC, 54
proof of concept, 202
PSET
   graphics option, 211
   statement, 163-164, 214, 235
PUT statement, 136, 141-142, 144,
   146-147, 211, 235

R

radians, 179
RAM (random-access memory), 3-5, 7, 12,
   14, 217
RANDOM keyword, 136
randomize, 183
RANDOMIZE statement, 235
rapid prototyping, 201-203
READ statement, 104, 112-115, 235
read-only memory *see* ROM
reading data from the keyboard, 104-113
real variable type, 67-70
receiving control strings from I/O devices,
   221
reclength, 136, 140-141
recnum, 142-143
record length, logical/physical, 141

REM statement, 191, 235
remarks in the program, 191
RENUM statement, 191, 235
renumbering the program, 191
reserved words, 64
reserved-memory area, 15
RESET statement, 191, 235
RESTORE statement, 114, 235
restricting access to files, 225-226
RESUME NEXT command, 59-60
RESUME statement, 191-192, 235
retrieving
    bytes from memory, 218
    pixels from arrays, 211
    screen information, 120-122, 124, 126
RETURN statement, 87-90, 235
return value of pixel, 212-213
RGB (red green blue) display, 162
RIGHT$ statement, 110, 235
RMDIR statement, 158, 235
RND statement, 235
RND(x) function, 183
ROM (read-only memory), 3-5, 12, 14
root directory, 40
RPG, 5
RS-232, 19-20
RSET statement, 145, 233
rules of precedence, 30-32
RUN statement, 235

S

sample programs
    ASCII keyboard codes, 109-110
    check password, 111-112
    data encryption, 152-156
    disk file manipulation, 146-151
    drawing borders, 116-117
    entering data via keyboard, 105, 109
    formatted data entry screen, 127-129
    interest rate/five years, 35-36
    inventory system, 80-81
    mini card index, 96-99
    play a tune, 173-175
    retrieving screen information, 121
    using the play statement, 177
    welcome screen, 112-113
SAVE statement, 46-47, 235
saving programs, 46-47, 55
scientific notation, 68
screen
    mode, 163-167
    objects, coloring, 209
    retrieving information, 120-122, 124, 126
SCREEN statement, 120-121, 163-164, 235

Index

segment offset values, obtaining, 218
selecting colors, 210
sending control strings to I/O devices, 221
serial ports, 19-20
setting MS-DOS environment, 224
SGN statement, 235
SGN(x) function, 183
SHELL statement, 192, 235
sign
   argument, 183
   numbers, 66-68
SIN statement, 179, 236
sine-wave sounds, 171
single-dimension arrays, 72
single-precision
   (!) declaration character, 27, 76-80
   variables, 26-27, 68-70
smode, 135
SOUND statement, 172-175, 236
space parity, 222
SPACE$ statement, 236
spagetti code, 203-204
SPC statement, 192, 236
special print codes, 123-127
SQR statement, 236
SQR(x) function, 184
square root function, 184
square-wave sounds, 171
staccato, 174
stack point register (SP), 217
stacks, 88-89
state diagrams, 199-200
statement
   body, 25
   numbers, 25
statements, GW-BASIC, 25-34
   ABS, 229
   ASC, 110, 229
   ATN, 229
   AUTO, 45-46, 229
   BEEP, 229
   BLOAD, 215-216, 229
   BSAVE, 215-216, 229
   CALL, 216-217, 229
   CDBL, 229
   CHAIN, 186, 229
   CHDIR, 157-158, 229
   CHR$, 230
   CINT, 230
   CIRCLE, 168, 230
   CLEAR, 230
   CLOSE, 56, 60, 135-138, 230
   CLS, 230
   COLOR, 117-119, 164-166, 210, 230
   COM(n), 219-220, 230
   COMMON, 187, 230
   CONT, 187, 230

COS, 230
CSNG, 230
CSRLIN, 230
CVD, 230
CVI, 230
CVS, 230
DATA, 104, 112-115, 174-175, 230
DATE$, 184, 230
DEF FN, 187-188, 230
DEF SEG, 217, 231
DEF USR, 217-218, 231
DEFDBL, 230
DEFINT, 230
DEFSTR, 230
DELETE, 231
DENSNG, 230
DIM, 231
DRAW, 231
DRDEV$, 231
EDIT, 231
END, 55, 89, 231
ENVIRON, 231
ENVIRON$, 231
EOF, 231
ERASE, 188, 231
ERDEV, 231
ERL, 231
ERR, 231
ERROR, 189, 231
EXP, 231
EXTERR, 231
FIELD, 140-147, 231
FILES, 157-158, 231
FIX, 231
FOR, 92-95, 97-99
FOR/NEXT, 231
FRE, 231
GET, 136, 141-143, 146-147, 210-211
GOSUB, 87-89
GOSUB/RETURN, 232
GOTO, 84-89, 232
HEX$, 232
IF, 83-86, 90-91
IF/GOTO/ELSE, 232
IF/THEN/ELSE, 83-85, 232
INKEY$, 104, 180-111, 127, 232
INP, 220-221, 232
INPUT, 32-33, 104-110, 232
INPUT #, 138-139, 147, 232
INPUT$, 232
INSTR, 232
INT, 232
IOCTL, 221, 232
IOCTL$, 221, 232
KEY, 110-111, 116, 189-190, 232
KEY(n), 232
KILL, 158, 232

LEFT$, 110, 232
LEN, 232
LINE, 166-168, 232
LINE INPUT, 233
LINE INPUT #, 233
LIST, 48-49, 167-168, 190, 233
LLIST, 190, 233
LOAD, 44-45, 233
LOC, 158, 233
LOCATE, 109-110, 115-116, 127, 233
LOCK, 225-226, 233
LOF, 158, 233
LOG, 233
LPOS, 233
LPRINT, 25, 56, 131, 192, 233
LPRINT USING, 130
LSET, 233
MERGE, 151, 233
MID$, 233
MKD$, 233
MKDIR, 207-208, 233
MKI$, 233
MKS$, 233
NAME, 208, 233
NEW, 50, 190, 233
NEXT, 92-95, 97-99
OCT$, 233
ON COM, 234
ON ERROR GOTO, 59-60, 234
ON KEY, 234
ON PEN, 234
ON PLAY, 234
ON STRIG, 234
ON TIMER, 234
ON/GOSUB, 90-91, 234
ON/GOTO, 90-91, 110, 234
OPEN, 56, 135-138, 141-142, 144, 146-147, 234
OPEN"COM(n), 221-223, 234
OPTION BASE, 234
OUT, 220-221234
PAINT, 209, 234
PALETTE, 210, 234
PCOPY, 211-212, 234
PEEK, 217-218, 234
PEN, 226, 234
PLAY, 175-177, 234
PLAY (n), 234
PMAP, 234
POINT, 235
POKE, 217-218, 234
POS, 235
PRESET, 25, 34, 56, 163-164, 235
PRINT, 112, 122, 192, 235
PRINT #, 56, 137-138, 140, 144, 147, 235

271

PRINT # USING, 137-138, 144-146
PRINT USING, 122, 142-143
PSET, 163-164, 214, 235
PUT, 136, 141-142, 144, 146-147, 211, 235
RANDOMIZE, 235
READ, 104, 112-115, 235
REM, 191, 235
RENUM, 191, 235
RESET, 191, 235
RESTORE, 114, 235
RESUME, 59-60, 191-192, 235
RETURN, 87-90, 235
RIGHT$, 235
RMDIR, 158, 235
RND, 235
RSET, 233
RUN, 235
SAVE, 46-47, 235
SCREEN, 120-121, 163-164, 235
SGN, 235
SHELL, 192, 235
SIN, 236
SOUND, 172-175, 236
SPACE$, 236
SPC, 192, 236
SQR, 236
STICK, 236
STOP, 55, 89, 236
STR$, 236
STRIG, 236
STRIG(n), 236
STRING$, 236
SWAP, 236
SWAP var1,var2, 193
SYSTEM, 44, 236
TAB, 236
TAN, 236
TIME$, 185, 236
TIMER, 236
trace, 57-58
TROFF, 57-58, 236
TRON, 57-58, 236
UNLOCK, 225-226, 236
USR, 216, 236
VAL, 236
VARPTR, 236
VARPTR$, 236
VIEW, 213-215, 237
VIEW PRINT, 214, 237
WAIT, 237
WEND, 95-99, 237
WHILE, 95-99, 237
WHILE/WEND, 237
WIDTH, 237
WINDOW, 213-215, 237

WRITE, 237
WRITE #, 139, 237
STICK statement, 226, 236
STOP statement, 55, 89, 236
stopping GW-BASIC program, 54
STR$ statement, 145, 236
STR$(x) function, 185
STRIG statement, 226, 236
STRIG(n) statement, 236
string, 145-146
   ($) declaration character, 76-77
   array, 74-75, 81
   constants, 10
   descriptor, 217
   functions
      DATE$, 184
      HEX$, 185
      OCT$, 185
      STR$, 185
      TIME$, 185
STRING$ statement, 116-117, 236
strings, 74-75
subroutines, 196, 204
subtraction/negation (-), 27-28, 30
SWAP statement, 193, 236
symbol table, 61-62
symbols, 10
   integer (%), 26
   single precision (!), 27
SYSTEM statement, 44, 236
system testing, 198

T

TAB statement, 193, 236
tables, symbol, 61-62
TAN statement, 179, 236
text mode, 3
tiling, 209
TIME$ statement, 185, 236
TIMER statement, 236
tone generator, 171-178
top-down design, 196-198
trace statements, 57-58
tracks, 19
tree diagram, 40
triggers, joystick, 226
trigonometric functions, 179-181
   ATAN, 179
   COS, 179
   SIN, 179
   TAN, 179
TROFF statement, 57-58, 236
TRON statement, 57-58, 236
truncates, 182
TSR (terminate-and-stay-resident)
  programs, 13, 121

Two's Complement Arithmetic, 66-69
two-dimensional arrays, 72-73
TYPE (DOS) command, 7, 42
type of variables, 64-67, 76-77
    numeric converion, 78-80

U
UNLOCK statement, 225-226, 236
USR statement, 216, 236
utilities, 196-197

V
VAL statement, 236
VAL(S$) function, 193
variable type
    declaration character, 76-77
    integer, 64-67
    numeric converions, 78-80
    real/floating-point, 67-70
variables, 10, 61-62, 65-81
    converting to strings, 156-157
    double-precision, 68-70
    ERDEV, 225
    ERDEV$, 225
    ERL, 188
    ERR, 188
    ERROR, 188
    initializing, 35
    naming, 62-64
    single-precision, 26-27, 68-70
VARPTR statement, 218, 236
VARPTR$ statement, 218, 236
VGA *see* video graphics array
video display terminal (VDT), 15-16, 161
video displays, 15-18
video graphics array (VGA), 3, 7, 16-18,
   117, 161, 165-167,
   209-210
VIEW PRINT statement, 214, 237
VIEW statement, 213-215, 237

W
WAIT statement, 237
welcome screen sample program, 112-113
WHILE/WEND statement, 95-99, 237
    loop, 95-99
width, output, 130
WIDTH statement, 237
WINDOW statement, 213-215, 237
windows, defining graphics, 213-215
wraparound, 66
    error, 67-68
WRITE # statement, 139, 237
WRITE statement, 237

X
XOR graphics option, 211

Reader Feedback Card

Thank you for purchasing this book from Howard W. Sams & Company's FIRST BOOK series. Our intent with this series is to bring you timely, authoritative information that you can reference quickly and easily. You can help us by taking a minute to complete and return this card. We appreciate your comments and will use the information to better serve your needs.

1. Where did you purchase this book?

   ☐ Chain bookstore (Walden, B. Dalton)   ☐ Direct mail
   ☐ Independent bookstore   ☐ Book club
   ☐ Computer/Software store   ☐ School bookstore
   ☐ Other _____

2. Why did you choose this book? (Check as many as apply.)

   ☐ Price   ☐ Appearance of book
   ☐ Author's reputation   ☐ Howard W. Sam's reputation
   ☐ Quick and easy treatment of subject   ☐ Only book available on subject

3. How do you use this book? (Check as many as apply.)

   ☐ As a supplement to the product manual   ☐ As a reference
   ☐ In place of the product manual   ☐ At home
   ☐ For self-instruction   ☐ At work

4. Please rate this book in the categories below. G = Good; N = Needs improvement; U = Category is unimportant.

   ☐ Price   ☐ Appearance
   ☐ Amount of information   ☐ Accuracy
   ☐ Examples   ☐ Quick Steps
   ☐ Inside cover reference   ☐ Second color
   ☐ Table of contents   ☐ Index
   ☐ Tips and cautions   ☐ Illustrations
   ☐ Length of book
   ☐ How can we improve this book? _____

5. How many computer books do you normally buy in a year?

   ☐ 1–5   ☐ 5–10   ☐ More than 10
   ☐ I rarely purchase more than one book on a subject.
   ☐ I may purchase a beginning and an advanced book on the same subject.
   ☐ I may purchase several books on particular subjects.
     (such as _____)

6. Have you purchased other Howard W. Sams or Hayden books in the past year? ____
   If yes, how many? _____

7. Would you purchase another book in the FIRST BOOK series? _____

8. What are your primary areas of interest in business software?
   - ☐ Word processing (particularly _____)
   - ☐ Spreadsheet (particularly _____)
   - ☐ Database (particularly _____)
   - ☐ Graphics (particularly _____)
   - ☐ Personal finance/accounting (particularly _____)
   - ☐ Other (please specify _____)

Other comments on this book or the Howard W. Sams book line: _____
_____

Name _____
Company _____
Address _____
City _____ State _____ Zip _____
Daytime telephone number _____
Title of this book _____

Fold here

BUSINESS REPLY MAIL
FIRST CLASS   PERMIT NO. 336   CARMEL, IN

POSTAGE WILL BE PAID BY ADDRESSEE

HOWARD W. SAMS & COMPANY

11711 N. College Ave.
Suite 141
Carmel, IN 46032-9839

NO POSTAGE
NECESSARY
IF MAILED
IN THE
UNITED STATES